RTI Guide: Making it Work

Strategies = Solutions

Elementary Version (K-6)

by

Concetta Russo, Ed.D.

Ellenmorris Tiegerman, Ph.D.

Christine K. Radziewicz, D.A.

DUDE PUBLISHING
A Division of
National Professional Resources, Inc.
Port Chester, New York

Publisher's Cataloging-in-Publication
(Provided by Quality Books, Inc.)

Russo, Concetta, 1944-
RTI guide : making it work : strategies=solutions /
by Concetta Russo, Ellenmorris Tiegerman, Christine K.
Radziewicz. -- Elementary version (K-6).
p. cm.
Includes bibliographical references.
ISBN-13: 978-1-934032-76-3
ISBN-10: 1-934032-76-X

1. Remedial teaching--Handbooks, manuals, etc.
2. Learning disabled children--Education (Elementary)--
Handbooks, manuals, etc. 3. Individualized instruction
--Handbooks, manuals, etc. I. Tiegerman-Farber,
Ellenmorris. II. Radziewicz, Christine. III. Title.

LB1029.R4R87 2009 371.9'043
QBI09-600014

Production Editor, Cover Design: Andrea Cerone, National Professional Resources, Inc., Port Chester, NY

Dude Publishing: A Division of National Professional Resources, Inc.
25 South Regent Street, Port Chester, New York 10573. Toll free: (800) 453-7461, Phone: (914) 937-8879

Visit our web site: www.NPRinc.com

Printed in the United States of America

ISBN 978-1-934032-76-3

To my son, Freddy, who left me much too early in life.
You have taught me courage, acceptance, humility, compassion, resolve and strength.
Thank you for making my life matter!

Mom (Concetta Russo)

I entered education because I wanted to teach and in the process I was taught by my students.
To my husband and children, I cannot thank you enough for your patience and understanding when I "buried myself" beneath educational journals.

Ellenmorris Tiegerman

To Family with pride and appreciation
Tom, Alisa, Hank, Jule,
Mindy, Ardyn, Lila,
Julius (JouJou)
You are delightful...You are my inspiration.

Christine Radziewicz

Acknowledgement

No one writes alone! The pages of this book reflect countless hours of conversations, lectures and experiences with colleagues, friends and family. But the actual manuscript is based upon quiet yet earnest conversations among the three of us, related to our philosophies about teaching and learning. The result is a truly collaborative work that we hope will be valuable as a simple guide that introduces remediation techniques and activities that are readily and easily provided to struggling students. It is these fledging students and their dedicated teachers whom we honor with this work!

Concetta Russo, Ed.D.
Ellenmorris Tiegerman, Ph.D.
Christine K. Radziewicz, D.A.

Table of Contents

INTRODUCTION

Changes in the educational landscape over the past several years have created challenges to the relationship between general and special education. We, the authors, believe that Response To Intervention (RTI) is a natural outgrowth of new and revised federal legislation, in particular the *Individuals with Disabilities Education Act (IDEA)*. Furthermore, we believe it holds the key to the development of a more unified approach to the education of all students. The purpose of this guide is to provide educators, particularly members of RTI Teams and those who are embracing this model, with organized information and tools (strategies, activities/solutions) to structure the implementation of RTI. It is also hoped that it can simplify a potentially complex process. The materials presented should be used to address the needs of at-risk and struggling learners in an attempt to remediate their weaknesses and eliminate the need for referral to special education. Furthermore, they are presented to facilitate the collaborative decision-making process. In order to enhance this process, critical content information is presented to enable educators to spend their time discussing and resolving student-based issues, rather than searching for educational resources. We believe that the success of RTI hinges on the ability of educators to collaborate with one another, and the capacity of schools to reorganize existing systems. Also of great significance to RTI is the school district's established methodology concerning data management and accountability. It is up to school districts to familiarize themselves with current regulations concerning RTI within their state.

The following terms are used throughout the guide and provide a commonality of language for all readers:

- **Response To Intervention (RTI)** is a multi-tiered, collaborative problem-solving intervention model by which students who fail to master specific general education performance goals are provided with individualized and increasingly intensive interventions to facilitate the development of specific skills;
- **CORE** refers to the primary scientific, research-based instructional program used within a classroom, particularly for reading and math;
- **Interventions** refer to enhanced instruction that may take place within the general education classroom with the general education teacher or specialist, or in a separate setting with a specialist providing targeted and highly individualized instruction. They should be research-based, and supported by assessment measures that document student progress and determine the need for further services;
- **Strategies** involve the instructional methods used by educators to provide effective instruction and individualized support for all students;
- **Solutions** reflect the use of strategies, products and programs that enable students to be successful learners.

Changes in Education Law

Education for All Handicapped Children Act (EAHCA)

Prior to 1975, most children with disabilities were educated in settings other than local public schools. However, with the passage of the *Education for All Handicapped Children Act* (Public Law 94-142) in 1975, after many years of advocacy from parents and service organizations, children with disabilities were guaranteed a Free and Appropriate Public Education (FAPE) to the maximum extent appropriate, in the least restrictive environment (LRE), alongside peers without disabilities. Public Law 94-142 established national procedures and safeguards for parents to ensure that students with disabilities have the same opportunities to an education as students without disabilities.

Since the passage of Public Law 94-142, programs have been developed nationally to provide educational and related therapeutic services to students with disabilities from birth to age 21. This law has been reauthorized several times, changing both the language as well as the emphasis on educational responsibilities to students with disabilities within educational settings. As the law was reauthorized and more students were enrolled in special education programs and services, the cost of special education began to rise markedly. In addition, as parents utilized their due process rights and challenged the decisions made by school districts, the relationship between terms such as appropriate (FAPE) and least restrictive (LRE) also began to change. Eventually, LRE became the general education classroom, and school districts nationwide were required to provide more extensive documentation to substantiate the need for special education services in separate settings. States are now required to submit state improvement plans documenting the percentage of time that students with disabilities receive services in general and special education settings.

In the past several years, educators have attempted to grapple with providing enhanced instructional opportunities to effectively meet the needs of an increasingly diverse population in a general education setting. For students from socially, culturally, linguistically and economically diverse backgrounds, the issue of whether to attribute underachievement and poor assessment scores to diversity differences or disability presented a challenge. Were these students giving rise to issues of over-identification and/or mis-identification in special education? The debate often focused on whether this population actually needed special education services in separate settings. Clearly many of these students required specialized programs and services, but were they being mistakenly placed in special education programs? Based upon these concerns and a desire to help children at earlier ages, a growing interest arose in developing pre-referral instructional methods and assessments which could be employed prior to referring students for special education services.

The Reauthorization of IDEA: 1997

The 1997 reauthorization of the *Individuals with Disabilities Education Act (IDEA)* stated that the education of students with disabilities can be made more effective when schools develop high expectations as well as by the use of the general education curriculum. Additionally, it required that:

- In the referral process, schools give consideration to factors other than disability which may affect a student's performance;
- General education teachers become part of special education evaluation teams;
- The determination to remove a student from general education be justified;
- States establish performance goals for students with disabilities;
- School districts may use special education funds to design, implement and evaluate school-based improvement plans;
- Parents participate in eligibility and placement decisions for their children;
- IDEA funding could be used for personnel preparation to prepare general educators for their role in the education of students with disabilities;
- State funding formulas be placement neutral, meaning that states can no longer utilize funding formulas that encourage more restrictive placement of students with disabilities.

Furthermore, this reauthorization emphasized the need to offer modifications and services throughout a student's school day within the general education classroom. It realigned the relationship between general education and special education, supporting the position that special education should refer to a service for a student with disabilities rather than a place. The supports provided within the general education classroom became critical to the successful development of a whole-school approach. Schools were encouraged to strengthen their total curriculum to serve all students within the general education placement. School districts had to develop indicators to assess students' progress by developing standards, outcomes and performance measures. The emphasis on school accountability was underscored by the fact that assessment and reporting procedures had to be modified to include performance data on students with disabilities.

The Reauthorization of IDEA: 2004

In 2004, when IDEA was reauthorized, it became the *Individuals with Disabilities Improvement Act (IDEIA)*. The revised law focuses on accountability and data, including the requirement that school districts utilize research-based interventions as a way of substantiating student progress and need for services. For struggling students, the IDEIA mandates that school districts rule out general education by carefully documenting student response to increasing levels of specialized intervention. If, after all of these measures, general and special education methodologies fail to positively impact student learning and performance, then a referral may be made to the special education eligibility committee. With this shift in educational decision-making, special education becomes the choice of last resort, not the first. The student must be given every opportunity to remain in general education by adjusting instructional methods, programs and levels of intervention. The accountability of educational decision-making is now scrutinized to a much greater degree. RTI becomes the framework or structure for this to occur.

This reauthorization also eliminates the use of emergency temporary and provisional certification for related services providers while giving states greater authority to establish professional qualifications in public schools. It includes the mandate that state education personnel standards meet the highest requirement for a profession or discipline in that state, and allows each state to set specific qualifications for certification and/or licensing.

IDEIA also instituted several changes regarding the development of Individual Education Plans (IEPs). For example, the law allows parents and school districts to participate in IEP meetings by means of conference calls. In addition, school districts are empowered to amend or modify a child's IEP without having to actually convene an IEP meeting. The reauthorization also provides the option for schools to eliminate the IQ discrepancy requirement, which compares standard ability (IQ) with academic achievement, to qualify for specific learning disability (SLD) eligibility. RTI becomes the favored option, as a process that ensures that referral to special education is only for those students who have not been able to succeed when provided with increasingly targeted, specific interventions.

No Child Left Behind (NCLB)

No Child Left Behind (NCLB), signed into law by President George W. Bush on January 8, 2002, is the latest reauthorization of the *Elementary and Secondary Education Act (Title 1)*. It mandates that all students have fair, equal and significant opportunities to obtain a high-quality education and reach, at a minimum, proficiency on state academic standards and assessments. It also requires annual statewide testing of all students, including those with disabilities, for the purpose of assessing annual yearly progress (AYP), disaggregated by disability, race and nationality. If any one of these groups fails to meet the targeted goals for AYP, then the whole school fails and parents are eligible for options. Schools receiving Title 1 funds are expected to show academic progress in state standardized tests, with the goal of all students scoring at a proficiency level by 2014. Many states have outlined what students need to know and be able to do by specific grade levels. As a result, the school curriculum often focuses on these educational standards. A criticism of this shift in educational programming and philosophy is that many schools now teach to the state assessments. NCLB seeks to close achievement gaps by requiring the use of scientifically-based, data-driven models as well as research-based practices to substantiate academic progress.

In summary, the intent of NCLB is accomplished by:

- Developing high quality academic assessments;
- Establishing accountability systems;
- Providing enhanced teacher preparation;
- Meeting the educational needs of low-achieving students and closing the gap between high and low-performing students;
- Holding schools, local educational agencies and states accountable for student achievement;
- Requiring the use of scientifically-based instructional programs and strategies to substantiate educational accountability;
- Emphasizing the importance of parental participation in the educational process.

Reading First Grant

NCLB established Reading First as a new, high-quality, evidence-based program for American students. This ambitious national initiative seeks to help every young child in every state become a successful reader. As the cornerstone to NCLB, the Reading First Grant provides funding to states and school districts to establish research-based programs for students in kindergarten through third grade so that all students in America will learn to read well by the end of third grade. The grant requires schools to increase teacher professional development to ensure that general and special education teachers have the skills to effectively teach reading. This includes preparing classroom teachers to effectively screen, identify and overcome students' reading barriers. The Reading First Grant relies on rigorous assessments with proven validity and reliability to effectively screen, diagnose and monitor the progress of all students. The Reading First methodology is based on a Tier 1, Tier 2, Tier 3 structure.

Response To Intervention (RTI)

Response To Intervention has developed as an intervention-based approach that provides school districts and child study teams with a formalized and structured mechanism to intervene systematically when early warning signs indicate that a student is struggling and not reaching expected levels of performance. RTI is usually described in terms of a tier methodology, in which increasing levels of intensity in programming are provided before struggling students are recommended for services outside of general education. RTI attempts to ensure that a student who is ultimately placed in special education has a genuine learning disability, rather than one related to poor instruction, environmental issues, or the need for additional time or more intensive interventions. IDEA includes language on the use of RTI in order to identify at-risk students as early as possible. RTI includes the practice of providing high-quality instruction and interventions which are specifically matched to student needs within the general education classroom. Consistent with NCLB, RTI is a data-driven approach which requires schools to monitor progress and make decisions about implementing instruction based on performance data. Within the general educational environment, interventionists or service providers are those same professionals who service the general and special education population, including the general classroom teacher, special education teacher, speech language pathologist, reading specialist, math specialist, occupational therapist, occupational therapy assistant (COTA), psychologist, social worker, guidance counselor and paraprofessionals.

The key components of the RTI process are:

1. Universal Screening which identifies levels of proficiency for each student in essential skills and which should be performed multiple times during a school year;
2. Research-Based Instruction which reflects the accumulation of research on how children learn and teachers need to teach;
3. High Quality Instruction which relates to the training, knowledge and expertise of the teacher and the application of appropriate differentiated instruction by the teacher;
4. Early Intervention which focuses on ensuring that targeted instruction is begun as early as possible and matched to individual student need;
5. Progress Monitoring which includes frequent assessment of student progress to gather information that is used to identify student needs and inform the instructional process.
6. Data-driven decision making that uses data to inform instruction.

Based upon the above, a student's needs are identified and the nature of the problem is determined: is it curriculum-based or student-based, skill-based or performance-based? Next an action plan is developed which includes the measurable problem and documentation of the specific intervention, duration, schedule and interventionist. This is followed by a description of the skill measurement and data-keeping responsibilities, as well as the progress monitoring which will track measurable outcomes at regular, specific intervals, frequently over time. This leads to comparing baseline data and using the results to evaluate for accountability and intervention success.

RTI's multi-tiered intervention model becomes more intense and individualized as students move from tier to tier. The assumption is that the majority of students who are identified as at-risk learners will have their needs met as programming becomes more specialized. A pyramid design highlights the percentage of students within each instructional tier, with the majority of students in Tier 1 and the fewest students at Tier 3. It should be noted that there are a variety of RTI models. The term is descriptive, thus providing latitude for school districts to tailor their own model. For example, in some locales Tier 3 is the entry point to special education whereas in other places special education is outside the pyramid or even referred to as Tier 4.

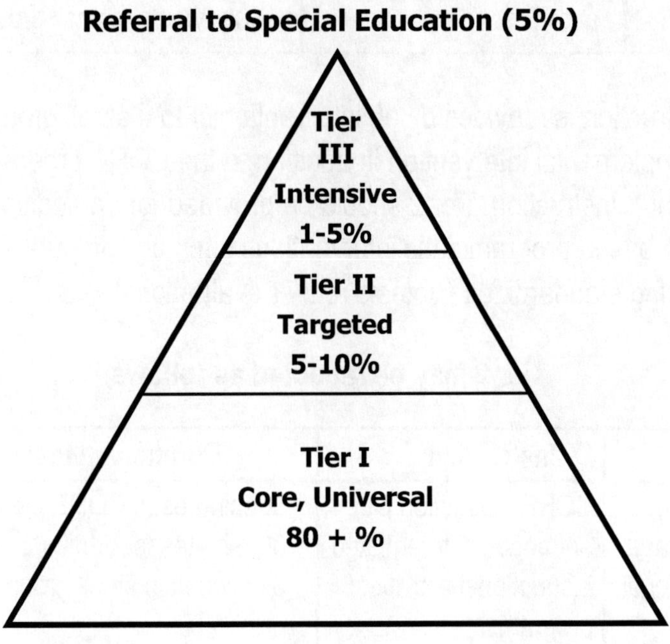

Tier 1 Intervention—Involves enhanced classroom instruction in which the general education teacher provides CORE instruction to all students as well as specialized instruction and activities to students identified as at-risk learners. The definition of at-risk learners should be standardized across the school district. The general education teacher collaborates with a range of interventionists, such as the reading specialist, special education teacher, occupational therapist, occupational therapy assistant (COTA), math specialist, behavior specialist, speech language pathologist, social worker, guidance counselor, and the school psychologist, to develop appropriate differentiated instruction within the classroom. This specialized instruction should be tailored to meet the individual needs of students who may have auditory or visual processing difficulties, phonological deficits and/or other learning difficulties. This requires teaching schedules to be flexible to allow time for collaborative teaming.

Tier 1 may be reflected as follows:

Place	Instructor	Instruction	Duration/Intensity	Assessment
General education classroom	General education teacher	CORE instruction plus enhanced differentiated activities	60 Minutes of CORE plus 10 weeks of 30 minutes supplementary instruction, 2x per week in small groups	Universal Screening and Progress Monitoring

Tier 2 Intervention—More specialized instruction is provided by an interventionist to a small group of students within the classroom for 10-20 weeks. Tier 2 activities are provided as supplemental intervention in addition to the CORE program. It assumes that the general education teacher continues with the differentiated Tier 1 instruction. Tier 2 should be provided for an additional 30 minutes two to three times per week. It may require flexible groups and evidence-based programmatic interventions such as computer-assisted technologies. The RTI team should be prepared to assess student progress using standardized subtests and/or evaluations.

Tier 2 may be reflected as follows:

Place	Instructor	Instruction	Duration/Intensity	Assessment
General education classroom	Interventionists: speech and language therapist, occupational therapist, reading/ math specialist	CORE instruction plus enhanced differentiated instructional activities/ programs	60 minutes of CORE plus 10 weeks of 30 minutes for additional instruction, 2 to 3x a week in small group or individually	Universal Screening and Progress Monitoring

Tier 3 Intervention—Should be provided to the few students who require intensive intervention with extended instructional time, more individualized teaching and modified instructional content. Tier 3 may be most conducive to computer-based instruction that is highly specialized to meet the very special needs of a student who continues to struggle. Tier 3 interventions should be provided for at least 10 weeks by interventionists who monitor specific learning variables and benchmarks. Tier 3 interventions should be provided for approximately 60 minutes daily in a setting outside of the classroom, where distractions can be minimized and direct instruction can be provided by the interventionist. Again, the RTI Team should be prepared to substantiate specific changes in student behavior by a variety of assessment measures, including district and/or state-based assessments.

Tier 3 may be reflected as follows:

Place	Instructor	Instruction	Duration/Intensity	Assessment
Ancillary/separate area from general education classroom	Interventionists: special education teacher, speech and language therapist, occupational therapist, reading or math specialist, psychologist, social worker	CORE instruction plus enhanced differentiated instructional activities/ programs and highly specific interventions	60 minutes of CORE plus 10 weeks of 60 minutes of daily additional instruction in small group or individually	Universal Screening and Progress Monitoring

Educational Collaboration

As indicated previously, RTI emphasizes the need for collaborative interaction amongst professionals at every level of the decision-making process. Collaboration defines how participants interact with each other as equal contributors to generate common or shared goals. This suggests that all school staff involved with the student, as well as the parents, are stakeholders in the decision-making process. In order to be successful, collaborative teams must pay close attention to interactional variables such as communication styles, problem-solving skills and conflict resolution strategies. Research has indicated that these interactive behaviors and communication variables contribute to the effectiveness and the efficiency of the decision-making process. The collaborative process requires a great deal of staff development to change the culture and climate within a public school building. Collaborative teams need to consider some of the following variables:

- Financial costs related to programmatic changes required within the building;
- Hiring of new staff along with the reorganization of existing staff;
- Specific organizational changes required of teachers within the general education classroom;

- Space allocation as additional services are required;
- Necessary classroom resources such as computers, software programs, supplies and materials;
- Fears and concerns of parents, teachers, students and administrators as changes are made in instruction and professional responsibilities.

When implementing a RTI model, the teacher and RTI Team must continually reinforce the need for differentiated instruction and should be very alert to incorporating the appropriate accommodations, modifications and adaptations. Examples of this include:

- **Tier 1: Reinforcing the Activity or Content**

  —Help student with class requirements

  —Pre-teach or re-teach information

  —Develop aids or organizers for class work

  —Add extra practice in the form of "anchoring" activities

  —Develop study guides

  —Develop discipline plans

  —Use alternative academic methods of instruction

- **Tier 2: Adapting/Modifying the Activity or Content**

  —Select appropriate unit outcomes by reducing the quantity of work expected

  —Change mastery or level requirements

  —Slow pace of instruction

  —Use alternative activities in the form of projects

  —Adapt or modify classwork:

    - Highlight text assignment
    - Rewrite worksheets
    - Simplify study guides

- Adapt or modify tests
- Change means of administration
- Change content
- Design alternative assessment activities

- **Tier 3: Developing Parallel Activity or Content**
  —Use appropriate functional educational materials which parallel the regular curriculum
  —Use authentic activities and assessments which mirror the functional value of regular class activities

How To Use This Guide

This guide is a compilation of information about, and suggested strategies and resources for, addressing the major areas of academic performance, including reading, math, spelling and written language through targeting the three areas of processing that underpin academic deficits, including auditory processing, visual processing and language processing. Also included is a section on behavior/social emotional learning. Furthermore, it offers the RTI Team and interventionists suggestions derived from research and the experiences of other professionals in the field for CORE programs (Tier 1), supplemental interventions (Tier 2), and intensive interventions (Tier 3).

When the Response To Intervention Team identifies the skills deficits that a student is experiencing, the Team is able use this guide to identify strategies and activities that address the student's academic/behavior problem, as listed in the Table of Contents. If a student's problem does not improve through Tier 1 strategies or activities, the RTI Team is able to move to the next level of interventions. These interventions are then written on the action plan and given to the classroom teacher or the targeted interventionists. The intention of this RTI Guide is to simplify the complex task of the RTI Team and interventionists.

The authors of this guide are all interventionists and the strategies that are suggested have been implemented to teach and remediate the different areas of processing as well as subject-specific subtopics. At times, we suggest employing the same intervention across two or three of the tiers. This redundancy reaffirms that the strategies offered are the most effective ones for that particular deficit area, as they explicitly address the problem. Thus, the same strategy used at different tiers may be necessary to enable some students to become successful. The differences in these cases are simple. If the classroom teacher is not successful after a period of specific intervention application at Tier 1, then the Tier 2 or Tier 3 interventionists may apply the same strategy. However, the application of the same strategy will be more individualized and directed or/and used with increased frequency and intensity as the student moves up the pyramid.

To add continuity and avoid confusion, the authors elected to use the term "teacher" to include any and all interventionists, and to use it in singular form. They also use the term "student" in singular form, with masculine pronoun and adjectives.

Sample Forms

Eleven sample RTI forms that can be used by RTI teams to document meetings and progress are provided as Appendix A at the back of this book. The focus of these forms is on documentation, which is crucial to RTI because without it, the special education eligibility committee cannot determine whether a student is a responder or non-responder to specific interventions. Even if a state/district/building level administrator determines that the 50% discrepancy rule prevails when determining whether or not a child is eligible for classification as Learning Disabled, the eligibility committee cannot approve this classification when there has been little documentation to support eligibility. Although states and districts are allowed to choose their policy for determining eligibility, IDEA sets parameters for determining eligibility by stating that a child must be offered scientific, research-based intervention. Progress must be monitored and documented in order for a committee to determine whether the child is a responder or non-responder. Therefore, all students should have the opportunity to receive Tier 1, Tier 2 and Tier 3 interventions before they can be considered eligible for special education. The standard for eligibility has been set.

A brief description of each form follows on the next two pages; the actual forms are in Appendix A.

FORMS

Form # 1: Checklist for RTI Teams—to guide RTI Teams through the RTI process.

Form # 2: RTI Team Initial Meeting Minutes for Tier 1— to document activity and action plan.

Form # 3: RTI Strategies Tier 1—to document the number of meetings and number of interventions tried. After this form is completed, the RTI team decides whether the student has made adequate progress or if not, changes the strategies, programs and/or interventionists. It is suggested that the RTI Team meet again 5 weeks after the first meeting in order to hold, modify or change the initial interventions.

Form # 4: RTI Tier 1 Documentation Form: Student Interventions/Strategies—to document all strategies and interventions administered, along with the results, dates and names of the interventionists. If the Tier 1 stage has been completed and there is not significant progress then the student is referred to the Tier 2 level of interventions.

Form # 5: RTI Team Initial Meeting Minutes for Tier 2—to document activity and action plan.

Form # 6: RTI Strategies Tier 2—to document the number of meetings and the number of interventions tried. After this form is completed, the RTI Team decides whether the student has made adequate progress at the Tier 2 level. If the student has made adequate progress, he can be referred back to a Tier 1 status or remain at the Tier 2 status. If the student has not made adequate progress then the Action Plan must reflect changes in the strategies, programs and/or interventionists.

Form # 7: RTI Tier 2 Documentation Form: Student Interventions/Strategies—to document all strategies and interventions administered with results, dates and names of the interventionists. If the Tier 2 stage has been completed and there is not significant progress then the student is referred to the Tier 3 level of interventions. If the Tier 2 stage is completed and the student is making progress, the RTI Team can decide to keep the student at the Tier 2 level. If the student does significantly well, the student can be returned to the Tier 1 level of instruction or the student can be dismissed.

Form # 8: RTI Team Initial Meeting Minutes Form for Tier 3—to document activity and action plan.

Form # 9: RTI Strategies Tier 3—to document the number of meetings and number of interventions tried. After this form is completed, the Team decides whether the student has made adequate progress at the Tier 3 level or if not, changes the strategies, programs or interventionists.

Form # 10: RTI Tier 3 Documentation Form: Student Interventions/Strategies—to document all strategies and interventions administered, with the results, dates and names of the different interventionists. If the Tier 3 stage has been completed and there is not significant progress, then the student may be referred to the special education eligibility team. If the Tier 3 stage is completed and the student has made progress, the RTI Team can decide to keep the child at the Tier 3 level, indefinitely. If the student does significantly well, the student can be returned to the Tier 1 or Tier 2 level of instruction or the student can be dismissed.

Form # 11: The RTI Team Report—to be used at the end of the RTI process and pull together everything that has been administered to the student including strategies, programs and interventionists. This form and all other documentation throughout the entire RTI process is collected. This documentation file is then sent to the special education eligibility team with a formal request for their review. All Due Process procedures are initiated after the formal request is initiated by the RTI Team.

CHAPTER 1

Auditory, Visual and Language Processing

This section is designed to increase understanding of Auditory, Visual and Language Processing and their effects on Language, Reading, Math, Spelling, Writing and all academic subjects. Processing disorders interfere with the way students understand the information presented to them.

What Is Auditory Processing?

Auditory processing involves integrating auditory information in the auditory pathways of the brain, resulting in the ability to comprehend auditory information accurately.

Key Characteristics of Auditory Processing Difficulties:

- Poor auditory sequencing skills
- Difficulty following conversations
- Poor sense of rhythm
- Poor auditory memory skills for words, sentences, numbers and directions
- Distracted by background noise
- Short auditory attention
- Difficulty localizing sound sources
- Misunderstanding what is said and asking for frequent verbal repetition
- Slow and/or inconsistent response to auditory stimuli
- Difficulty with phonemic awareness, phonics, reading and spelling
- Difficulty understanding and/or interpreting complex information
- Normal pure tone hearing results
- Fatigue resulting from auditory tasks
- Daydreaming
- Speech/Language impairments
- Disruptive behavior—impulsive, easily frustrated, frequently off-task

Area of Auditory Processing: Auditory Memory

Auditory Memory	Auditory Memory Tier 1
Auditory Memory—involves immediate and/or delayed recall of numbers, words, sentences, paragraphs, directions and spoken language. Examples of academic problems in this area: • Difficulty retrieving letters, words and numbers • Difficulty retrieving addresses and phone numbers • Failure to recognize sound-symbol relationship • Difficulty following multi-step oral directions **Accommodations and Modifications:** • Preferential seating • Short oral directions • Oral directions with written directions • Key points on the blackboard • Note-taker buddy • Teacher's copy of lecture outline • VAKT information presented together • Student repeats directions and assignments orally	**Suggested Interventionist: General Education Teacher with consultation from the Speech Pathologist/Special Education Teacher** **Suggested Session: Small group, explicit instruction within the CORE program, 2x a week within the classroom.** **Strategies/Activities for Auditory Memory:** • Student will be given a three-word sequence and then be asked to repeat back either the first word, the second word or the third word. • Student will remember the identified word: "Every time you hear the designated word in a paragraph, clap hands." • Student will name a word that is in a particular category. Student will have to name all of the words that were stated previously within the designated category. • Student will read a sentence and ask a basic fact question about the sentence. • Student will follow directions with fine motor responses. • Student will follow directions with gross motor responses. • Student will play the game, Does It Look the Same? Teacher describes a figure part by part. Student listens to the description and draws what it looks like. • Teacher will say a word and ask student to change the beginning, middle or last sound to a specific sound.

Auditory Memory Tier 2	Auditory Memory Tier 2
Suggested Interventionist: Speech Pathologist, Special Education Teacher **Suggested Session: 30 minutes 2 to 3x a week in a small group or individual basis in addition to the CORE program inside the classroom.** **Strategies/activities for Auditory Memory:** • Student will follow directions in a sequential order. Teacher gives two verbal commands. (Tap your head then clap your hands.) • Student will follow three step directions in a sequential order. Teacher gives three verbal commands and asks student to perform commands in order stated. • Student will repeat three words that are related. Student will repeat four words that are unrelated. • Student will repeat five words that are unrelated. • Student will repeat four words that include two categories and group the words in their appropriate category (cow, shoe, dress, dog, hat). • Student will identify a picture from a field of six pictures, giving a description that includes two descriptors. • Student will identify a picture from a field of six pictures, giving a description that includes three descriptors. • Student will repeat a tongue twister of three words. (Sally sells shells).	• Student will repeat a tongue twister of four words. • Student will repeat a tongue of five words. • Student will repeat a five-word sentence. • Student will repeat a six-word sentence. • Student will repeat a seven-word sentence. • Student will repeat an eight-word sentence. • Student will repeat a nine-word sentence. • Teacher will read a sentence twice. The second time the sentence is read, a word is omitted. Student will identify omitted word. • Teacher will say three words that are in the same category and then say two of the words. Student will identify the missing word. • Teacher will say four words that are in the same category (table, chair, bed, couch). Teacher will then say three of four words again, omitting one. Student will identify the missing word. • Teacher will say four words that are not in the same category (shoe, car, apple, dog). Teacher will say three of the words again. Student will identify the missing word.

Auditory Memory Tier 3	**Auditory Memory Tier 3**
Suggested Interventionist: Speech Pathologist, Special Education Teacher **Suggested Session: 60 minutes 5x a week in a small group or individual basis in addition to the CORE program outside of the classroom.** **Strategies/activities for Auditory Memory:** • Teacher will give two verbal commands. Student will follow directions. (Tap your head, then clap your hands) • Student will follow three-step directions in a sequential order. • Teacher will give three verbal commands and ask student to perform commands in order stated. • Student will repeat three words that are unrelated (horse, star, chair). • Student will repeat four words that are unrelated. • Student will repeat five words that are unrelated. • Student will repeat four words that include two categories and group the words in their appropriate category. • Student will identify a picture from a field of six pictures, giving a description that includes two descriptors. • Student will identify a picture from a field of six pictures, giving a description that includes three descriptors. • Student will repeat a tongue twister of three words. (Sally sells shells.)	• Student will repeat a tongue twister of four words. • Student will repeat a tongue twister of five words. • Student will repeat a five-word sentence. • Student will repeat a six-word sentence. • Student will repeat a seven-word sentence. • Student will repeat an eight-word sentence. • Student will repeat a nine-word sentence. • Teacher will read a sentence twice. The second time the sentence is read, a word is omitted. Student will identify omitted word. • Teacher will say three words that are in the same category (table, chair, bed). Teacher will say two of the words. Student will identify the missing word. • Teacher will say four words that are in the same category (table, chair, bed, couch). Teacher will say three of the words again. Student will identify the missing word. • Teacher will say four words that are not in the same category (shoe, car, apple, dog). Teacher will say three of the words again. Student will identify the missing word.

Area of Auditory Processing: Auditory Discrimination

<table>
<tr><th>Auditory Discrimination</th><th>Auditory Discrimination Tier 1</th></tr>
<tr><td>

Auditory Discrimination: involves differentiating individual sounds in words, words in sentences, and words in paragraphs; this skill also involves sounds in music, animal noises or environmental noises. Examples of academic problems in this area:

- Comprehension of oral directions
- Memorization of letter sounds and letter names
- Inadequate spelling, reading and writing skills
- Incorrect repetition of oral directions

Accommodations/Modifications:

- Preferential seating
- Short oral directions
- Oral directions with written directions
- Key points on the blackboard
- Note taker buddy
- Teacher's copy of lecture outline
- VAKT information presented together
- Students repeat directions and assignments orally

</td><td>

Suggested Interventionist: General Education Teacher with consultation from the Speech Pathologist/Special Education Teacher

Suggested Session: Small group, explicit instruction within the CORE program, 2x a week within the classroom.

Strategies/Activities for Auditory Discrimination:

- Student will discriminate among words that are the same or different (ball/ball; ball/tall).
- Student will discriminate initial sounds in words that are the same or different.
- Student will discriminate medial sounds in words that are the same or different.
- Student will discriminate final sounds in words that are the same or different.
- Student will discriminate notes in music that are the same or different.
- Student will discriminate words that have the same or different volume.
- Student will discriminate phrases that are the same or different (in the hat, in the vat).
- Student will listen to a specific sound and then listen to three words and identify the word that begins with the specific sound.
- Student will listen to a specific sound and then listen to three words and identify the word that ends with the specific sound.
- Student will listen to a word and then be instructed to think of another word that has the same vowel sound.

</td></tr>
</table>

Auditory Discrimination Tier 1	Auditory Discrimination Tier 1
• Student will listen to a word and identify whether a specific sound occurs in the beginning, middle or end of the word (Ship. Where does the p sound occur?). • Student will discriminate between the cognate sounds in words (Example: /s/ vs. /z/, /t/ vs. /d/, /k/ vs. /g/, /p/ vs. /b/, /m/ vs. /n/, /ch/ vs. /j/). • Student will distinguish between two sounds—same or different consonants. • Student will distinguish between two sounds—same or different long vowels. • Student will distinguish between two sounds—same or different short vowels. • Student will distinguish between two words—same or different with the initial sounds being same or different. • Student will distinguish between two words—same or different with the middle sounds being same or different. • Student will distinguish between two words—same or different with the final sounds being same or different. • Student will distinguish between three sounds—same or different consonants. • Student will distinguish between three sounds—same or different long vowels. • Student will distinguish between three sounds—same or different short vowels. • Student will distinguish between three words—two being the same and one being different in their initial sounds. • Student will distinguish between three words—two being the same and one being different in their medial sounds.	• Student will distinguish between three words—two being the same and one being different in their final sounds. • Teacher will say a targeted sound and then give two words with different initial consonant sounds. Student will identify the word that matches the target sound. • Teacher will present three words, two of which rhyme at the end. Student will pick out the two words that rhyme. • Teacher will present four words, three of which rhyme at the end. Student will pick out the three words that rhyme. • Teacher will present three words, two of which rhyme at the end. Student will pick out the word that does not rhyme. • Teacher will present four words, three of which rhyme at the end. Student will pick out the word that does not rhyme. • Teacher will create sentences with animal names that rhyme. Student will finish the sentence with a word that rhymes with the animal name. • Teacher will create sentences with toy names that rhyme. Student will finish the sentence with a word that rhymes with that name of a toy. • Teacher will create sentences with body part names that rhyme. Student will finish the sentence with a word that rhymes with that name of the body part • Teacher will say a targeted sound and then give three words with different initial consonant sounds. Student will identify the one word out of the three that matches the target sound. • Teacher will say a targeted sound and then give four words, three of which have a different initial consonant sound. Student will identify the word that matches the target sound.

Auditory Discrimination Tier 1	Auditory Discrimination Tier 2
• Teacher will say a word with a targeted short vowel sound in the medial position and then give two words with different medial short vowel sounds. Student will identify the word that matches the target medial sound. • Teacher will say a word with a targeted short vowel sound in the medial position and then give three words with different medial short vowel sounds. Student will identify the word that matches the target medial sound. • Teacher will say a word with a targeted short vowel sound in the medial position and then give four words with different medial short vowel sounds. Student will identify the word that matches the target medial sound.	**Suggested Interventionist: Speech Pathologist, Special Education Teacher** **Suggested Session: 30 minutes 2 to 3x a week in a small group or individual basis in addition to the CORE program inside the classroom.** **Strategies/Activities for Auditory Discrimination:** • Student will listen for a specific sound in a word (e.g., "Do you hear 't' in the word tell, take, bat, sweater?"). • Student will identify the position at which a sound occurs (e.g., "Where do you hear the 'ch' sound in the word 'witch'?") • Student will distinguish between two sounds—same and different consonants. • Student will distinguish between two sounds—same and different long vowels. • Student will distinguish between two sounds—same and different short vowels. • Student will distinguish between two words—same or different, with the initial sounds being same or different. • Student will distinguish between two words—same or different, with the middle sounds being same or different. • Student will distinguish between two words—same or different, with the final sounds being same or different. • Student will distinguish between three sounds—same or different consonants.

Auditory Discrimination Tier 2	Auditory Discrimination Tier 3
• Student will distinguish between three sounds—same or different long vowels. • Student will distinguish between three sounds—same or different short vowels. • Student will distinguish between three words—two with the same initial sound and one with a different initial sound. • Teacher will present three words, two of which rhyme at the end. Student will pick out the two words that rhyme. • Teacher will present four words, three of which rhyme at the end. Student will pick out the three words that rhyme. • Teacher will present three words, two of which rhyme at the end. Student will pick out the word that does not rhyme. • Teacher will present four words, three of which rhyme at the end. Student will pick out the word that does not rhyme.	**Suggested Interventionist: Speech Pathologist, Special Education Teacher** **Suggested Session: 60 minutes 5x a week in a small group or individual basis in addition to the CORE program outside the classroom.** **Strategies/Activities for Auditory Discrimination:** • Student will distinguish between two consonant sounds—same and different. • Student will distinguish between two long vowel sounds—same and different. • Student will distinguish between two short vowel sounds—same and different. • Student will distinguish between two words—with the initial sounds being same or different. • Student will distinguish between two words—with the middle sounds being same or different. • Student will distinguish between two words—with the final sounds being same or different. • Student will distinguish between three short vowel sounds—same or different. • Student will distinguish between three words—two being the same and one being different within their initial sounds.

Auditory Discrimination **Tier 3**	
• Teacher will present three words, two of which rhyme at the end. Student will pick out the two words that rhyme. • Teacher will present four words, three of which rhyme a the end. Student will pick out the two words that rhyme. • Teacher will present three words, two of which rhyme at the end. Student will pick out the word that does not rhyme. • Teacher will present four words, three of which rhyme at the end. Student will pick out the word that does not rhyme. • Teacher will create sentences with animal names that rhyme. Student will finish the sentence with a word that rhymes with the animal name. • Teacher will create sentences with toy names that rhyme. Student will finish the sentence with a word that rhymes with that toy. • Teacher will create sentences with body part names that rhyme. Student will finish the sentence with a word that rhymes with that name of the body part.	

Area of Auditory Processing: Auditory Discrimination

Auditory Closure	Auditory Closure Tier 1
Auditory Closure—involves the ability to "fill in" information or sounds that are not heard completely. Examples of academic problems in this area: • Auditory confusion while listening in a noisy environment • Vocabulary development below age level • Difficulty with syntax • Poor associations for sound recognition • Difficulty in blending complex sounds and words in phonics **Accommodations and Modifications:** • Preferential seating • Short oral directions • Oral directions with written directions • Key points on the blackboard • Note-taker buddy • Teacher's copy of lecture outline • VAKT information presented together • Student repeats directions and assignments orally	**Suggested Interventionist: General Education Teacher with consultation from the Speech Pathologist/Special Education Teacher** **Suggested Session: Small group, explicit instruction within the CORE program 2x a week within the classroom.** **Strategies/Activities for Auditory Closure:** • Student will finish a word when the last part of the word is missing (Bot-, Bottle). • Student fill in the middle of the word (bi---le, bicycle). • Student will fill in the beginning of the word (-ood bye, Goodbye). • Student will fill in the missing sounds of a phrase (peanut -utter and -elly, peanut butter and jelly). • Student will fill in the last word in a nursery rhyme. • Student will fill in the last word in a song title. • Student will fill in sentences that are missing an important word in order to complete the sentence. Student will figure out the word from the content of the sentence. • Student will fill in a story by using the Cloze technique. • Student will fill in a syllable from a two-syllable word in a sentence when half of the word is missing (pen---, pencil). • Teacher will say the word in parts. Student will say the whole word (tel e phone).

Auditory Closure Tier 1	Auditory Closure Tier 1
• Teacher will say a one-syllable word. Teacher adds a sound to the beginning of a word which completely changes the word. Student will identify the word that is formed after the new sound is added. • Teacher will say a one-syllable word. Teacher then adds a sound to the end of that word which completely changes the word. Student will identify the word that is formed after the new sound is added. • Teacher will say a one-syllable word. Teacher then deletes a sound at the beginning, which completely changes the word. Student will identify the word that is formed after the sound is deleted. • Teacher will say a one-syllable word. Teacher then deletes a sound at the end of that word which completely changes the word. Student will identify the word that is formed after the sound is deleted. • Teacher will say a one-syllable word. Teacher then changes the short vowel in the middle of the word which completely changes the word. Student will identify the word that is formed after the sound is changed. • Teacher will say a one-syllable word. Teacher then changes the long vowel sound in the middle of the word which completely changes the word. Student will identify the word that is formed after the sound is changed. • Teacher will repeat all of the previous activities using different colored tokens or counters to represent the individual phonemes in order to manipulate the different sounds.	• Student will use colored tokens to represent the different sounds in the words presented. Teacher says two words that have the same middle sounds. The second word spoken by the teacher has the first and last sounds switched. Student will listen to the second word and move the tokens to show how the sounds change position.

Auditory Closure Tier 2	Auditory Closure Tier 3
Suggested Interventionist: Speech Pathologist, Special Education Teacher **Suggested Session: 30 minutes 2 to 3x a week in a small group or individual basis in addition to the CORE program inside the classroom.** **Strategies/Activities for Auditory Closure:** • Student will finish a word. Then the last part of the word is missing (Can---, Candle). • Student will fill in the middle of the word (an-mal, animal). • Student will fill in the beginning of the word (-ather, father). • Student will fill in the missing pieces of a phrase (see -ou –ater, see you later). • Student will fill in the last word in a nursery rhyme. • Student will fill in the last word in a song title. • Student will fill in missing word in a sentence in order to complete the sentence. Student will use contextual clues. • Student will fill in a story by using the Cloze technique. • Student will fill in a syllable from a two-syllable word in a sentence when half of the word is missing. • Teacher will pick out a category and give the student three words within that category, leaving out the beginning, middle or final syllable of one of the words. Student will come up with the word. • Teacher will say parts of words to student who will say the whole word.	**Suggested Interventionist: Speech Pathologist, Special Education Teacher** **Suggested Session: 60 minutes 5x a week in a small group or individual basis in addition to the CORE program outside the classroom.** **Strategies/Activities for Auditory Closure:** • Student will finish a word when the last sound is missing. • Student will fill in the middle of the word when that sound is missing. • Student will fill in the beginning of the word when that sound is missing. • Student will fill in the missing pieces of a phrase (-it –own, sit down). • Student will fill in the last word of a nursery rhyme. • Student will fill in the last word of a song title. • Student will fill in missing words of a sentence, using contextual clues. • Student will fill in a story by using the Cloze technique. • Student will fill in a syllable from a two-syllable word in a sentence in which half of the word is missing. • Teacher will pick out a category and give the student three words within that category, leaving out the beginning, middle or final syllable of the word. Student will come up with the word. • Teacher will say words to students in parts. Student will say the whole word (puss y cat, pussy cat).

Area of Auditory Processing: Auditory Synthesis

Auditory Synthesis	Auditory Synthesis Tier 1
Auditory Synthesis—involves the ability to separate sounds in a word and the ability to hear separate sounds and form words from those sounds. Examples of academic problems in this area: • Difficulty with sequencing sounds into words • Poor ability remembering phonics • Poor ability correctly using grammar • Difficulty understanding the accents in words • Poor spelling skills **Accommodations and Modifications:** • Preferential seating • Short oral directions • Oral directions with written directions • Key points on the blackboard • Note-taker buddy • Teacher's copy of lecture outline • VAKT information presented together • Students repeat directions and assignments orally	**Suggested Interventionist: General Education Teacher with consultation from the Speech Pathologist/Special Education Teacher** **Suggested Session: Small group, explicit instruction within the CORE program 2x a week within the classroom.** **Strategies/Activities for Auditory Synthesis:** • Student will identify the picture of the word that the teacher says. • Student will say the word that these sounds make (p-air, pair). • Student will put sounds together to make a word (b-ee, bee). • Student will identify the number of syllables that are in a word the teacher says. • Teacher will identify a sound and then recite three words to the student, one of which has the targeted sound. Student must identify the word that includes the designated sound. • Teacher will say a word by its individual sounds and the student will say the blended word.

Auditory Synthesis Tier 1	Auditory Synthesis Tier 1
• Teacher will recite three words, two of which have the same sound in the initial position and the third word has a different sound (ball, bell, tell). Student will identify the word that has a different initial sound position from the other words. • Teacher will recite two- and three-syllable words, breaking the words into syllables. Student will blend words together. • Teacher will recite a sentence. Student will identify the beginning sounds of each word in the sentence. • Clapping syllables—Teacher will say words that have one to two syllables. Student will clap the syllables out. • Clapping syllables—Teacher will say words that have two to three syllables. Student will clap the number of syllables out. • Tapping syllables—Teacher will say words that have one to two syllables. Student will tap the syllables out. • Tapping syllables—Teacher will say words that have two to three syllables. Student will tap the number of syllables. • Snapping syllables—Teacher will say words that have one to two syllables. Student will snap the number of syllables. • Snapping syllables—Teacher will say words that have two to three syllables. Student will snap the number of syllables. • Teacher will give student different colored counters or mini blocks. Student will place a counter or block on the table for every syllable.	• Teacher will say a one-syllable word that has a short vowel and a consonant. Teacher will say the word fast and then slowly, isolating the two different sounds. Student will repeat the word fast and then in the two parts. Student will then be asked to do this after each word that the teacher presents. • Teacher will say two one-syllable words and ask the student to count the number of sounds. Student will be given chips to represent the number of phonemes that are in each word. Student will be asked to compare the two words and show that one word has more phonemes than the other. • Teacher will separate two-syllable words into two parts. Student will be asked to listen to the words in separate syllables and say the word at normal speed. • Teacher will separate three-syllable words into three parts. Student will be asked to listen to the words in separate syllables and say the word at normal speed.

Auditory Synthesis Tier 1	Auditory Synthesis Tier 2
• Student will be presented with two words, one of which has an additional letter in the initial position. Student will repeat the two words and identify the additional sound in the larger word (star, tar). • Student will be presented with three words in the same word family. Two words have an additional letter in the initial position. Student will be asked to repeat the words and identify the sounds that are different (at, cat, hat). • Teacher will say a one-syllable word. Student will be asked to isolate the first consonant sound of the word from the rest of the word and then segment the word. • Teacher will say a word and ask the student to isolate the first consonant blend of the word from the rest of the word. • Teacher will say a word twice that has a consonant, long vowel and consonant sound. Teacher will say the word fast the first time and then slowly, saying the individual sounds. Student will be asked to repeat the word fast and then slowly in parts. • Teacher will twice say a one-syllable word that has an initial long vowel sound followed by a consonant sound. Teacher will say the word fast the first time and then slowly, saying the individual sounds. Student will be asked to repeat the word fast and then slowly. Student will then be asked to do this after each word that the teacher presents.	**Suggested Interventionist: Speech Pathologist, Special Education Teacher** **Suggested Session: 30 minutes 2 to 3x a week in a small group or individual basis in addition to the CORE program inside the classroom.** **Strategies/Activities for Auditory Synthesis:** • Teacher will say words that have one to two syllables. Student will clap or tap the syllables out. • Teacher will say words that have two to three syllables. Student will clap or tap the number of syllables. • Teacher will say words that have one to two syllables. Student will say the number of syllables. • Teacher will say words that have two to three syllables. Student will say the number of syllables. • Teacher will give students different colored tokens or mini blocks. Student will place a token or block on the table for every syllable they hear. • Teacher will separate two-syllable words into two parts. Student will listen to the words in separate syllables and say the word at normal speed.

Auditory Synthesis Tier 2	Auditory Synthesis Tier 3
• Teacher will separate three-syllable words into three parts. Student will listen to the separate syllables of the word and say the word at normal speed. • Teacher will name a category such a number or a color, and then say a sentence that includes a word from the category, saying the targeted word in phoneme parts. Teacher starts with three-phoneme words and then move to four. Student will say the whole word.	**Suggested Interventionist: Speech Pathologist, Special Education Teacher** **Suggested Session: 60 minutes 5x a week in a small group or individual basis in addition to the CORE program outside the classroom.** **Strategies/Activities for Auditory Synthesis:** • Teacher will say words that have one to two syllables. Student will clap or tap the syllables out. • Teacher will say words that have two to three syllables. Student will clap or tap the number of syllables out. • Teacher will give students different colored tokens or mini blocks. Student will place a token or block on the table for every syllable. • Teacher will separate two-syllable words into two parts. Student will listen to the words in separate syllables and say the word at normal speed. • Teacher will say three-syllable words separated into parts. Student will listen to the words and then say the word at normal speed. • Teacher will name a category such as a number or a color, and then say a sentence that includes a word from the category, saying the targeted word in phoneme parts. Teacher starts with three-phoneme words and then moves to four. Student will say the whole word.

Area of Auditory Processing: Auditory Figure Ground

Auditory Figure Ground	Auditory Figure Ground Tier 1
Auditory Figure Ground—involves the ability to isolate sound within a noisy environment. Examples of academic problems in this area: • Not being able to pay attention • Internal and external distractibility • Frustration and irritability • Poor self-esteem due to failure in school and social environments **Accommodations and Modifications:** • Preferential seating • Short oral directions • Oral directions with written directions • Key points on the blackboard • Note taker buddy • Teacher's copy of lecture outline • VAKT information presented together • Students repeat directions and assignments orally	**Suggested Interventionist: General Education Teacher with consultation from the Speech Pathologist/Special Education Teacher** **Suggested Session: Small group, explicit instruction within the CORE program, 2x a week within the classroom.** **Strategies/Activities for Auditory Figure Ground:** • Student will identify a word dictated into a tape recorder with background noise. Background noise can be white noise, talking, music or traffic. • Student will perform an auditory listening task with instrumental music playing in the background. • Student will answer single-fact question with static noise in the background. • Student will do an auditory listening task with vocal music in the background. • Student will do an auditory listening task with cafeteria noise in the background. • Student will do an auditory task such as directions with a worksheet while playing a tape of someone reading a story in the background. • Teacher will read a story with background white noise. Student will be asked comprehension questions.

Auditory Figure Ground Tier 2	Auditory Figure Ground Tier 2
Suggested Interventionist: Speech Pathologist, Special Education Teacher **Suggested Session: 30 minutes 2 to 3x a week in a small group or individual basis in addition to the CORE program inside the classroom.** **Strategies/Activities for Auditory Figure Ground:** • Student will identify a word dictated into a tape recorder with background noise. Background noise can be white noise, talking, music or traffic. • Student will perform an auditory listening task with instrumental music playing in the background. • Student will answer single-fact question with static noise in the background. • Student will do an auditory listening task with vocal music playing in the background. • Student will do an auditory listening task with cafeteria noise in the background. • Student will do an auditory task such as directions with a worksheet while playing a tape of someone reading a story in the background. • Teacher will read a story with background white noise. Student will be asked comprehension questions.	• Student will do an auditory task with a radio talk show in the background. • Student will do auditory task with television show in the background. • Student will maintain a conversation with a peer for six minutes with white noise in the background. • Student will maintain a conversation with a peer for six minutes with music in the background. • Student will maintain a conversation with a peer for six minutes with a radio talk show in the background.

Auditory Figure Ground Tier 3

Suggested Interventionist: Speech Pathologist, Special Education Teacher

Suggested Session: 60 minutes 5x a week in a small group or individual basis in addition to the CORE program outside the classroom.

Strategies/Activities for Auditory Figure Ground:

- Student will identify a word dictated into a tape recorder with background noise. Background noise can be white noise, talking, music or traffic.
- Student will perform an auditory listening task with instrumental music playing in the background.
- Student will answer single-fact question with static noise in the background.
- Student will do an auditory listening task with vocal music playing in the background.
- Student will do an auditory listening task with cafeteria noise in the background.
- Student will do an auditory task such as directions with a worksheet while playing a tape of someone reading a story in the background.
- Teacher will read a story with background white noise. Student will be asked comprehension questions.

Auditory Figure Ground Tier 3

- Student will do an auditory task with a radio talk show in the background.
- Student will do auditory task with a television show in the background.
- Student will maintain a conversation with a peer for six minutes with white noise in the background.
- Student will maintain a conversation with a peer for six minutes with music in the background.
- Student will maintain a conversation with a peer for six minutes with a radio talk show in the background.

Area of Auditory Processing: Auditory Cohesion

<table>
<tr><th>Auditory Cohesion</th><th>Auditory Cohesion Tier 1</th></tr>
<tr><td>

Auditory Cohesion—involves a higher-level linguistic processing ability within a language environment. A person must be able to follow conversations, infer from language and understand jokes, understand inferences and draw conclusion. Examples of academic problems in this area:

- Inadequate note-taking ability
- Poor reading comprehension, not due to decoding difficulties
- Inappropriate behavior due to poor pragmatic skills
- Immature written expression

Accommodations and Modifications:

- Preferential seating
- Short oral directions
- Oral directions with written directions
- Key points on the blackboard
- Note taker buddy
- Teacher's copy of lecture outline
- VAKT information presented together
- Students repeat directions and assignments orally

</td><td>

Suggested Interventionist: General Education Teacher with consultation from the Speech Pathologist/Special Education Teacher

Suggested Session: Small group, explicit instruction within the CORE program 2x a week within the classroom.

Strategies/Activities for Auditory Cohesion:

- Student will be given two-step directions and asked to write down the five key words from those directions.
- Student will take notes using graphic organizers.
- Student will use a multiple meaning map to discuss the multiple meanings of the same word.
- Student will be given sentences that are written in the present tense and must change them to the past tense.
- Student will be given sentences that are written in the future tense and asked to change them to the present tense.
- Student will listen to a story or current event and will be asked to summarize it in writing using three sentences.
- Student will be given a simple sentence and a set of figurative language phrases. Student will add figurative language to the sentence to make it a complex sentence.
- Student will be asked to takes notes in a lecture situation when provided with a word bank at the top of the worksheet.
- Student will be given two to three directions and then asked to draw the appropriate object or scene from the directions.

</td></tr>
</table>

Auditory Cohesion Tier 2	Auditory Cohesion Tier 3
Suggested Interventionist: Speech Pathologist, Special Education Teacher **Suggested Session: 30 minutes 2 to 3x a week in a small group or individual basis in addition to the CORE program inside the classroom.** **Strategies/Activities for Auditory Cohesion:** • Student will be given three-step directions and asked to write down the five key words from those directions. • Student will take notes using graphic organizers. • Student will use a multiple meaning map to discuss the multiple meanings of the same word. • Student will be given two sentences that are written in the past tense and asked to change them to the present tense. • Student will be given sentences in the future tense and asked to change them it to the present tense. • Student will listen to a story or current event and will be asked to summarize it in writing. • Student will be given a simple sentence and asked to add figurative language to the sentence to make it a complex sentence. • Student will be asked to takes notes in a lecture situation when provided with a word bank at the top of the worksheet. • Student will be given directions and then asked to draw the appropriate object or scene from the directions.	**Suggested Interventionist: Speech Pathologist, Special Education Teacher** **Suggested Session: 60 minutes 5x a week in a small group or individual basis in addition to the CORE program outside the classroom.** **Strategies/Activities for Auditory Cohesion:** • Student will be given directions and asked to write down the key words from those directions. • Student will take notes using graphic organizers. • Student will use a multiple meaning map to discuss the multiple meanings of the same word. • Student will be given sentences that are written in the present tense and asked to change them to the past tense. • Student will be given sentences in the future tense and asked to change them to the present tense. • Student will listen to a story or current event and will be asked to summarize it in writing. • Student will be given a simple sentence and asked to add figurative language to the sentence to make it a complex sentence. • Student will be asked to take notes in a lecture situation when provided with a word bank at the top of the worksheet. • Student will be given directions and then asked to draw the appropriate object or scene from the directions.

Area of Auditory Processing: Auditory Binaural Integration

Auditory Binaural Integration	Auditory Binaural Integration Tier 1
Auditory Binaural Integration—involves the ability to transfer information between verbal and motor activities. Examples of academic problems in this area: • Difficulty playing a musical instrument • Difficulty taking notes in class while listening • Difficulty functioning well in a "whole language" reading environment • Difficulty copying correctly **Accommodations and Modifications:** • Preferential seating • Short oral directions • Oral directions with written directions • Key points on the blackboard • Note-taker buddy • Teacher's copy of lecture outline • VAKT information presented together • Students repeat directions and assignments orally	**Suggested Interventionist: General Education Teacher with consultation from the Speech Pathologist/Special Education Teacher** **Suggested Session: Small group, explicit instruction within the CORE program 2x a week within the classroom.** **Strategies/Activities for Auditory Binaural Integration:** • Student will sing while writing a sentence. • Student will pack his desk while singing a song. • Student will change the words in songs while listening to the song. • Student will identify an object while blindfolded. • Student will pick out a specific object from a bag of objects. • While walking around the room, student will identify a category of objects which are placed in a bag. • Student will draw an object or picture based on the directions of the teacher. Student must listen and draw at the same time. Teacher will provide three elements to include in the drawing.

Auditory Binaural Integration Tier 2	Auditory Binaural Integration Tier 3
Suggested Interventionist: Speech Pathologist, Special Education Teacher **Suggested Session: 30 minutes 2 to 3x a week in a small group or individual basis in addition to the CORE program inside the classroom.** **Strategies/Activities for Auditory Binaural Integration:** • Student will sing while jumping rope. • Student will bounce a ball while singing. • Student will identify an object while blindfolded. • Student will draw an object or picture. • Student will pick out a specific object from a bag of objects. • While walking around the room, student will identify a category of objects which are placed in a bag. • Student will draw an object or picture based on the directions of the teacher. Students must listen and draw at the same time. Teacher will provide four elements to include in the drawing.	**Suggested Interventionist: Speech Pathologist, Special Education Teacher** **Suggested Session: 60 minutes 5x a week in a small group or individual basis in addition to the CORE program outside the classroom.** **Strategies/Activities for Auditory Binaural Integration:** • Student will sing while jumping rope. • Student will bounce a ball while singing a song. • Student will change the words in songs. • Student will identify an object while blindfolded. • Student will pick out an object from a bag of objects. • Student will identify the category of objects which are in a bag. • Student will draw an object or picture based on the directions of the teacher. Student must listen and draw at the same time. Teacher will give five elements to include in the drawing.

Programs & Products for Auditory Processing (See Appendix C for web sites)

Product	Publisher	Tier	Type	Auditory Memory	Auditory Discrim.	Auditory Closure	Auditory Synthesis	Auditory Figure Ground	Auditory Cohesion	Auditory Binaural Integration
100% Listening	Linqui Systems	2,3	Supplemental						x	
50 Quick Play Listening Games	Lingui Systems	2,3	Supplemental						x	
Auditory Processing Game	Linqui Systems	2,3	Supplemental	x	x	x	x	x	x	x
Auditory Processing Activities	ECL	1,2,3	Supplemental				x			
Barnaby's Burrow Game	Linqui	2,3	Supplemental	x	x	x	x	x	x	x
Central Auditory Processing Kit	Linqui Systems	2,3	Sup	x	x	x	x	x	x	x
Differential Proc. Training: Acoustic Tasks	Linqui Systems	2,3	Supplemental							x
Differential Proc. Training	Linqui Systems	2,3	Supplemental							x
Earobics	CognitiveConcepts	1,2	Software	x	x	x	x	x	x	x
Fast for Word/Language/ Language to Reading	Scientific Learning Corp.	2,3	Software	x	x	x	x	x	x	x
Following Directions Series	Laureate	2,3	Supplemental		x					
Help for Auditory Processing.	Linqui Systems	2,3	Supplemental	x	x	x	x	x	x	x
Help!	Lingui Systems	2,3	Supplemental	x	x	x	x	x	x	x
Just for Kid	Linqui Systems	2,3	Supplemental	x	x	x	x	x	x	x
LIPS	Lindamood	3	Supplemental	x	x	x	x	x	x	x
No Glamour Auditory Proc.	Linqui Systems	2,3	Supplemental	x	x	x	x	x	x	x
No Glamour Auditory Proc.	Linqui Systems	2,3	Software	x	x	x	x	x	x	x
Nouns & Sounds	Laureate	2,3	Supplemental	x	x					
Smart Drive	Brain Train	2,3	Software		x					
Sound Smart Learning Fund	LocutourMultimedia	1,2	Software	x	x	x	x	x	x	x
Sound Smash	Locutour	2,3	Software	x	x					
Sounds Abound	Linqui Systems	1,2,3	Software				x			
The Source for Processing Disorders	Linqui Systems	1,2,3	Supplemental				x			

What Is Visual Processing ?

Visual processing involves the ability to detect and gain meaning from visual stimuli. The important concept to understand is the sequence in which visual-perceptual skills are developed and acquired through early developmental stages. These developmental stages affect different skills areas.

Key Characteristics for Visual Processing Difficulties:

- Poor visual discrimination of forms
- Inadequate figure-ground perception
- Difficulty judging spatially
- Poor visual memory for sequence form and directionality
- Difficulty forming visual images such as puzzles or geometric forms
- Difficulty perceiving and breaking down whole words into parts of words
- Difficulty perceiving and integrating parts of words into whole words
- Confusion with words that can be dynamically reversed (saw/was)
- Limited sight vocabulary
- Losing one's place while reading or calculating
- Limited memory for irregular words
- Difficulty spelling phonetically
- Ability to spell difficult phonemic words but not simple irregular words
- Labored or poor handwriting
- Confusion of sequences of letters and/or words such as reversals, inversions and transpositions during reading, writing and/or spelling
- Difficulty copying designs, geometric forms, and human figure drawing
- Poor balance and reaction time
- Poor fine motor control
- Poor movement in space (dancing, physical education classes)
- Confusion in right-left responses
- Difficulty imagining digits presented sequentially (phone numbers, addresses)

- Difficulty with visual-auditory integration
- Difficulty imagining the sequence of words
- Difficulty in problem solving; cannot visualize scenarios or endings of tasks
- Difficulty recognizing, recalling and manipulating visually presented material (addition, subtraction, multiplication, division, fractions, ratios)
- Difficulty recognizing and remembering geometric forms (geometry)
- Difficulty recognizing symbolic signs (/+/, /-/, /x/, /÷/)
- Difficulty sequencing steps in all forms of calculations
- Difficulty successfully lining up numbers either vertically or horizontally
- Difficulty staying within columns and rows in order to answer the problem
- Difficulty judging adequate space to complete a math problem
- Delays in learning how to write sentences, paragraphs, etc.
- Messy or incomplete worksheets
- Uneven spacing in writing
- Omitting letters from words and word from sentences
- Difficulty identifying errors in written work
- Difficulty copying from the board
- Saying words out loud while writing
- Writing ability neither commensurate with, nor reflective of understanding of information

Area of Visual Processing: Visual Discrimination

Visual Discrimination	Visual Discrimination Tier 1
Visual Discrimination—involves the ability to perceive similarities and differences in geometric forms; reading of letter symbols and math symbols; words and pictures. Examples of academic problems within this area: • Problems in all types of math • Difficulty understanding geometry • Problems recognizing math symbols • Problems recognizing, matching or comparing different shapes, sizes, colors, letters, words, objects and pictures • Reversals or inversions when writing numbers and letters • Poor or odd punctuation; misuse of capital letters • Problems in phonology • Problems in all levels of reading/writing • Difficulty with puzzles, maps **Accommodations and Modifications:** • Sit close to the board • Enlarge print; use print instead of script • Use of visual focusing aids on paper • Note taker for notes • Highlight notes • Oral directions with visual instructions • Use buddy reader • Color coding for words and directional markers • Use of books on tape • Write in text and worksheets	**Suggested Interventionist: General Education Teacher with consultation from the Occupational Therapist; COTA; Special Education Teacher** **Suggested Session: Small group, explicit instruction within the CORE program 2x a week within the classroom.** **Strategies/Activities for Visual Discrimination:** • Student will be examined by the school nurse for near and far visual acuity. • Student will be provided with enlarged images and reading materials. • Student will have modified worksheets which simplify and reduce non-essential visual stimuli. • Student will be seated close to the blackboard and/or in front of the room to reduce distractions of other students. • Area around/near the blackboard with be uncluttered. • Student will try blue overlays on printed/reading material to reduce glare from fluorescent lighting. • Student will be provided with index card, ruler or highlighted tracking strip for reading. • Teacher will write larger on blackboard or overhead projector. • Teacher will over-exaggerate spacing between words on all copy samples. • Student will utilize a slant board to decrease distance between eyes and writing/reading material. • Teacher will increase contrast—use black on white/white on black.

Visual Discrimination Tier 1	Visual Discrimination Tier 1
• Teacher will show pictures with different objects, people, etc. with missing parts. Student will point out the parts that are missing and name the object. • Teacher will present a series of designs, numbers or letters with one design, number or letter that is different in the series. Student will pick out the different one. • Teacher will present a series of designs, numbers or letters with one design, number or letter that is bigger or smaller than all the others. Student will identify the different one. • Teacher will present a series of symbols that are identical except for one of the symbols which is rotated. Student will pick out the different symbol and explain why. • Teacher will provide enlarged graph paper or turn composition notebook to provide vertical columns for math. • Teacher will reduce visual distractions in the room such as pictures on walls, mobiles or hanging objects. • Teacher will present a large colored picture with many objects in it. Student will point out the objects as the teacher names them. • Teacher will teach visual discrimination using different cards and filmstrips.	• Teacher will provide letter number strips on desks. • Teacher will utilize enlarged and exaggerated math symbols with titles (add, subtract, divide). • Teacher will utilize a different color to distinguish capital letters. • Teacher will provide instruction to confirm letter, number, and shape identification skills. • Teacher will group objects together and ask student to select the object which is different. • Teacher will give student an assortment of objects such as buttons, beads, and screws. Student will be asked to sort them into different egg carton sections according to size, color, shape or object. • Teacher will give student an assortment of letters and numbers. Student will be asked to sort them into different egg carton sections according to letter or number. • Teacher will make cards of geometric forms. Student will match the similar forms. • Teacher will teach size discrimination by showing pictures of different sizes. Student will discuss the difference in size between two cards placed in front of him.

Visual Discrimination Tier 2	Visual Discrimination Tier 2
Suggested Interventionist: Occupational Therapist, Occupational Therapy Assistant(COTA), Special Education Teacher **Suggested Session: 30 minutes 2 to 3x a week in a small group or individual basis inside the classroom** **Strategies/Activities for Visual Discrimination:** • Teacher will prepare a sheet consisting of a set of words. One word in each set will be different. Student will circle the word that is different. • Student will move in and out of different shapes on the floor. • Student will play matching games such as dominos. • Student will be given squares of various sizes and colors. Student will sort the squares according to size or color. • Teacher will group objects together. Student will select the object which is different. • Teacher will give student an assortment of objects such as buttons, beads, and screws. Student will sort them into different egg carton sections according to size, color, shape or object. • Teacher will give student an assortment of letters and numbers. Student will sort them into different egg carton sections according to letter or number. • Teacher will present a range of bead patterns. Student will copy the patterns. • Teacher will play the snap card game with the student. Student will visually discriminate a different card from other cards played.	• Teacher will present a series of identical letters written either print or cursive with one different letter. Student will pick out the odd letter and explain why. • Teacher will present a series of four words in which three words are the same and one is different. Student will pick the one that is different and explain why. • Teacher will present a series of words of varying complexity such as inversions, reversals, substitutions and transpositions. Student will pick out the word that is different from a series of four words and explain why (saw-was, saw-sam). • Teacher will present a series of symbols that are identical except for one of the symbols which is rotated. Student will pick out the different symbol and explain why. • Teacher will arrange a series of identical and similar pictures for the student to describe. • Teacher will make cards of geometric forms. Student will match the similar forms. • Teacher will teach size discrimination by using animal and form pictures of different sizes. Student will discuss the differences of size between the cards placed in front of him. • Teacher will teach picture discrimination by presenting a large colored picture with many objects in it. Teacher will ask the student to point out the objects as named by the teacher. • Teacher will teach visual discrimination through presenting different cards and filmstrips.

Visual Discrimination Tier 2	Visual Discrimination Tier 3
• Teacher will show pictures with different objects, people, etc., that are missing parts. Student will point out the different parts that are missing and name the object. • Teacher will present a series of designs, numbers or letters with one design, number or letter that is different in the series. Student will pick out the different design, number or letter. • Teacher will present a series of identical designs, numbers or letters with one design number or letter that is bigger or smaller than all the others. • Teacher will present a series of symbols that are identical except for one of the symbols, which has been rotated. Student will pick out the different symbol and explain why.	**Suggested Interventionist: Occupational Therapist, Occupational Therapy Assistant(COTA), Special Education Teacher** **Suggested Session: 60 minutes 5x a week in a small group or individual basis outside of the classroom.** **Strategies/Activities for Visual Discrimination:** • Teacher will prepare three-dimensional matching tasks with three objects, two of which are the same. Objects are presented in a linear array with explanation. • Teacher will prepare three-dimensional matching tasks with three objects, two of which are the same. Objects are presented in a scattered array with explanation. • Teacher will prepare two-dimensional matching tasks with three objects, two of which are the same. Objects are presented in a linear array with explanation. • Teacher will prepare two-dimensional matching tasks with three objects, two of which are the same. Objects are presented in a scattered array with explanation. • Teacher will designate a letter or number for the student is to find in the magazine. Student will be asked to circle as many different sizes or styles as possible. • Student will be asked to recognize objects, letters, numbers and shapes by touch alone. • Student will be given part of a newspaper. Student will be asked to circle certain letters, certain words, the first word in every sentence, the last word in every sentence or all the double letters in various words.

Area of Visual Processing: Visual Motor

<table>
<tr><th>Visual Motor</th><th>Visual Motor Tier 1</th></tr>
<tr><td>

Visual Motor—involves the ability to integrate the relationship between visual input and motor output as in copying tasks. It is the coordination of the visual information with motor processes. Examples of academic problems within this area are:

- Difficulty copying from the board
- Difficulty drawing a figure, geometric form or shape
- Difficulty playing an instrument
- Difficulty rapidly visualizing for writing and spelling
- Difficulty typing
- Difficulty performing well in gym, sports and playground skills
- Difficulty negotiating obstacles, clumsy
- Fear of movement in space
- Difficulty cutting and pasting
- Poor tool usage
- Poor handwriting

Accommodations and Modifications:

- Use of lined paper
- Note takers
- Use arrows for directions
- Use word processor
- Arrange test answers in vertical format
- Use markers to maintain place
- Directional clues
- Chart depicting letter formation
- Locker with key or punch numbered lock
- Use of manipulatives

</td><td>

Suggested Interventionist: General Education Teacher with consultation from the Occupational Therapist; COTA; Special Education Teacher

Suggested Session: Small group, explicit instruction , 2x a week within the CORE program within the classroom.

Strategies/activities for Visual Motor:

- Student will be given a reduced amount of required copying from the chalkboard.
- Teacher will write large letters on the chalkboard with space between lines.
- Teacher will provide student with paper to copy from, rather than copying from the board.
- Teacher will assign another student to copy information.
- Student will be assigned a helper/peer who will copy material from black board.
- Teacher will reduce amount of work required for completion of an assignment.
- Student will be given additional time for assignments.
- Student will be able to complete assignment in two or three sessions.
- Student will be given an external spacer.
- Student will be given primary lined paper with highlighted alternate lines.
- Teacher will enlarge cutting stimulus lines.

</td></tr>
</table>

<table>
<tr><th>Visual Motor Tier 1</th><th>Visual Motor Tier 2</th></tr>
<tr><td>
• Student will be given visual breaks.
• Teacher will color-code numbers.
• Teacher will provide student with a desk strip for left/right progression.
• Teacher will highlight margins for left/right progression.
• Teacher will seat student close to blackboard and/or in front of the room to reduce distractions of other students.
• Teacher will reduce clutter near/around the blackboard.
• Teacher will provide index card, ruler or highlighted tracking strip for reading.
• Teacher will exaggerate spacing between words on all copy samples.
• Student will utilize a slant board to decrease distance between eyes and writing/reading material.
• Teacher will provide enlarged graph paper or turn composition notebook to provide vertical columns for math problems.
• Teacher will encourage and facilitate handwriting throughout the school day.
• Teacher will provide student with mazes to complete.
• Teacher will encourage and facilitate handwriting throughout the day.
• Teacher will provide student with dot-to-dot picture.
</td><td>
Suggested Interventionist: Occupational Therapist, Occupational Therapy Assistant(COTA), Special Education Teacher

Suggested Session: 30 minutes 2 to 3x a week in a small group or individual inside the classroom

Strategies/activities for Visual Motor:
• Teacher will provide student with activity worksheets that strengthen visual discrimination skills.
• Teacher will provide student with activity worksheets that require visual discrimination with a motor output.
• Teacher will provide student with letter and number formation step worksheets.
• Teacher will provide student with geometric shape reproduction step worksheets.
• Teacher will provide student with mazes to complete.
• Teacher will provide student with dot-to-dot pictures.
• Teacher will provide student cut-and-paste copy projects.
• Teacher will provide student sequential drawing projects.
• Teacher will provide student pattern block reproduction project.
• Teacher will provide student 1” cube design reproduction activities.
• Teacher will provide student with geoboard reproduction activities.
• Teacher will provide student Tangram reproduction activities.
• Teacher will provide student with pegboard pattern reproduction activities.
</td></tr>
</table>

Visual Motor Tier 3	
Suggested Interventionist: Occupational Therapist, Occupational Therapy Assistant(COTA), Special Education Teacher **Suggested Session: 60 minutes 5x a week in a small group or individual outside of the classroom** **Strategies/Activities for Visual Motor:** • Teacher will provide student with activities that strengthen visual discrimination skills and require motor output. • Teacher will provide student with letter and number formation step worksheets. • Teacher will provide student with geometric shape reproduction step worksheets. • Teacher will provide student with mazes to complete. • Teacher will provide dot-to-dot pictures to student. • Teacher will provide student cut-and-paste copy projects. • Teacher will provide student sequential drawing projects. • Teacher will provide student pattern block reproduction projects. • Teacher will provide student 1" cube design reproduction activities. • Teacher will provide student with geoboard reproduction activities. • Teacher will provide student Tangram reproduction activities.	

Area of Visual Processing: Visual Spatial

<table>
<tr><th>Visual Spatial</th><th>Visual Spatial Tier 1</th></tr>
<tr><td>

Visual Spatial—involves the ability to integrate the relationship of space and the configuration of the objects seen within that space. It enables an individual to write in print and script quickly; and write sentences, paragraphs, etc. Examples of academic problems in this area:

- Difficulty picking out words on a page
- Difficulty reading text
- Difficulty focusing on math problems
- Difficulty copying/writing letters, shapes and spelling
- Poor directionality
- Difficulty drawing three-dimensional objects in art
- Difficulty reading and understanding maps
- Difficulty learning system of measures
- Difficulty understanding words designating spatial position
- Difficulty correctly positioning equipment
- Difficulty moving in space
- Difficulty tracking mazes
- Difficulty playing with LEGO

Accommodations and Modifications:

- Sit close to the board
- Enlarge print; use print instead of script
- Use of visual focusing aids on paper
- Note taker for notes
- Highlight text; color coding
- Oral directions
- Use verbal directions with visual instructions
- Write on text and workbooks
- Use directional markers

</td><td>

Suggested Interventionist: General Education Teacher with consultation from the Occupational Therapist; COTA; Special Education

Suggested Session: Small group, explicit instruction, 2x a week within the CORE program within the classroom

Strategies/activities for Visual Spatial Skills:

- Teacher will write large letters on the chalkboard with space between lines.
- Teacher will provide student with paper to copy from, rather than copying from the board.
- Student will be given an external spacer.
- Student will be given primary lined paper with highlighted alternate lines.
- Teacher will enlarge cutting stimulus lines.
- Teacher will color-code numbers.
- Teacher will provide student with a desk strip for left-right progression.
- Teacher will highlight margins for left-right progression.
- Teacher will provide left and right stickers for desktop.
- Teacher will reduce clutter near/around the blackboard.
- Teacher will provide index card, ruler or highlighted tracking strip for reading.

</td></tr>
</table>

Visual Spatial Tier 1	Visual Spatial Tier 2
• Teacher will exaggerate spacing between words on all copy samples. • Teacher will utilize a slant board to decrease distance between eyes and writing/ reading material. • Teacher will provide enlarged graph paper or rotate composition notebook to provide vertical columns.	**Suggested Interventionist: Occupational Therapist, Occupational Therapy Assistant(COTA), Special Education Teacher** **Suggested Session: 30 minutes 2 to 3x a week in a small group or individual basis inside the classroom** **Strategies/Activities for Visual Spatial Skills:** • Teacher will teach strategies/activities for left and right identification of self, others and inanimate objects. • Student will practice setting a table. • Teacher will utilize Legos to make three-dimensional buildings and then the students will be asked to make the same buildings. • Teacher will engage students in the following game activities: —Simon Says —Leapfrog —Cat and Mouse • Teacher will have students make a group sculpture in shapes such as diamond, circle, square, triangle. • Student will play games with hoops, beanbags, and boxes. • Teacher will provide dressing obstacle courses.

Visual Spatial Tier 3	
Suggested Interventionist: Occupational Therapist, Occupational Assistant(COTA), Special Education Teacher **Suggested Session: 60 minutes 5x a week in a small group or individual basis outside of the classroom.** **Strategies/Activities for Visual Spatial Skills:** • Teacher will engage students in the following game activities: —Simon Says —Leapfrog —Cat and Mouse • Teacher will have students make a group sculpture in shapes such as diamond, circle, square, triangle. • Student will play games with hoops, beanbags, and boxes. • Student will practice setting a table. • Student will wash and dry up. • Student will be asked to make collages or origami. • Teacher will utilize Legos to make three-dimensional buildings and then the student will be asked to make the same buildings. • Teacher will ask the student to draw different shapes on top of other shapes.	

Area of Visual Processing: Visual Coordination

<table>
<tr><th>Visual Coordination and Eye-Hand Coordination</th><th>Visual Coordination and Eye-Hand Coordination Tier 1</th></tr>
<tr><td>

Visual Coordination and Eye-Hand Coordination—involves the ability to follow and track objects and symbols with coordinated eye movement. A further example of visual coordination is eye-hand coordination. Examples of academic problems in this area:

- Difficulty reading a sentence, paragraph or book
- Difficulty reading a math problem
- Difficulty following written information
- Difficulty playing sports
- Poor gym and playground skills
- Difficulty with skilled manipulation
- Difficulty with arts and crafts, home activities, wood shop, playing an instrument
- Difficulty cutting and pasting
- Difficulty crossing the midline
- Poor development of hand dominance
- Poor gross coordination
- Difficulty recognizing the concepts of vertical, horizontal, diagonal and curved lines

Accommodations and Modifications:

- Use of lined paper (use every other line)
- Note-takers
- Use arrows for directions
- Use word processor
- Arrange test answers in vertical format
- Use markers to maintain place
- Chart depicting letter formation
- Locker with key or punch numbered lock
- Use manipulatives

</td><td>

Suggested Interventionist: General Education Teacher with consultation from the Occupational Therapist; COTA; Special Education Teacher

Suggested Session: Small group, explicit instruction 2x a week within the CORE program within the classroom

Strategies/Activities for Visual Coordination and Eye-Hand Coordination:

- Teacher will provide index card, ruler or highlighted tracking strip for reading.
- Student will utilize a slant board to decrease distance between eyes and writing/ reading material.
- Teacher will provide student with paper to copy from, rather than copying from the board.
- Student will be given primary lined paper with highlighted alternate lines.
- Teacher will color-code numbers.
- Teacher will highlight margins for left-right progression.
- Teacher will reduce clutter near/around the blackboard.
- Teacher will provide enlarged graph paper or rotate composition notebook to provide vertical columns for math problems.
- Teacher will enlarge cutting stimulus lines.

</td></tr>
</table>

Visual Coordination and Eye-Hand Coordination Tier 1	Visual Coordination and Eye-Hand Coordination Tier 2
• Teacher will engage students in the following game activities using one eye at a time then two eyes: Pirate or Tube Flashlight Tag—the student will follow the teacher flashlight around the room with his/her flashlight. • Student will play Letter or Word Scavenger Hunt on a page or in a room. • Student will trace lines.	**Suggested Interventionist: Occupational Therapist, Occupational Therapy Assistant(COTA), Special Education Teacher** **Suggested Session: 30 minutes 2 to 3x a week in a small group or individual inside the classroom** **Strategies/Activities for Visual Coordination and Eye-Hand Coordination:** • Student will engage in the following games: —Ball in Tube —Changing Sizes —Penny Drop —Flash Card —Noisy Button —Motifs —Mountain Climbing —Road Driving Game —Pin Tin Rotations • Student will copy and use geo boards. • Student will use visual tracking worksheets. • Student will use fine motor workbooks. • Student will use pattern reproduction worksheets such as follow the dots. • Student will complete mazes. • Student will copy from board. • Student will catch balls of different sizes: basketball, football, baseball, etc.

Visual Coordination and Eye-Hand Coordination Tier 3	
Suggested Interventionist: Occupational Therapist, Occupational Therapy Assistant(COTA), Special Education Teacher **Suggested Session: 60 minutes 5x a week in a small group or individual outside of the classroom.** **Strategies/Activities for Visual Coordination and Eye-Hand Coordination:** • Student will engage in the following games: —Ball in Tube —Changing Sizes —Penny Drop —Flash Card —Noisy Button —Motifs —Mountain Climbing —Road Driving Game —Pin Tin Rotations • Students will copy and use geo boards. • Students will use visual tracking worksheets. • Students will use fine motor workbooks. • Students will use pattern reproduction worksheets such as follow the dots. • Students will complete mazes. • Students will copy from board. • Students will catch balls of different sizes: basketball, football, baseball, etc.	

Area of Visual Processing: Visual Figure-Ground

Visual Figure-Ground	Visual Figure-Ground Tier 1
Visual Figure-Ground—involves the ability to perceive objects in the foreground and background and separate them meaningfully. Examples of academic problems in this area: • Difficulty isolating a word in text • Difficulty isolating a math problem • Difficulty isolating an object or figure from text • Difficulty isolating information on graphs • Difficulty isolating names of cities, countries from a map • Difficulty concentrating on relevant visual stimuli or ignoring irrelevant stimuli • Difficulty shifting attention appropriately • Difficulty noticing all the relevant words in a question, identifying key words or developing "skim and scan" skills • Difficulty keeping place when reading, completing a worksheet or copying from the board • Difficulty organizing written work and labeling diagrams **Accommodations and Modifications:** • Sit close to the board • Enlarge print; use print instead of script • Use of visual focusing aids on paper • Notetaker for notes • Highlight text; color coding • Oral directions with visual instructions • Use buddy reader • Use of books on tape • Write on text or worksheet • Use directional markers	**Suggested Interventionist: General Education Teacher with consultation from the Occupational Therapist; COTA; Special Education Teacher** **Suggested Session: Small group,explicit instruction 2x a week within the CORE program within the classroom.** **Strategies/Activities for Visual Figure-Ground:** • School nurse will examine student's near visual acuity. • Teacher will provide enlarged images and reading materials. • Teacher will modify worksheets by simplifying and reducing non-essential visual stimuli. • Student will sit close to blackboard and/or in front of the room to reduce distractions of other students. • Teacher will reduce clutter near/around the blackboard. • Teacher will provide index card, ruler or highlighted tracking strip for reading. • Teacher will write larger on blackboard or overhead projector. • Teacher will exaggerate spacing between words on all copy samples. • Student will utilize a slant board to decrease distance between eyes and writing/reading material. • Teacher will increase contrast (use black on white/white on black). • Teacher will provide enlarged graph paper or rotate composition notebook to provide vertical columns for math. • Teacher will reduce visual distractions in the room such as pictures on walls, mobiles or hanging objects.

Visual Figure-Ground Tier 2	Visual Figure-Ground Tier 2
Suggested Interventionist: Occupational Therapist, Occupational Therapy Assistant(COTA), Special Education Teacher **Suggested Session: 30 minutes 2 to 3x a week in a small group or individual inside the classroom** **Strategies/activities to Improve Visual Figure-Ground:** • Student will set a table, finding the right items in the drawer or cupboard. • Student will complete word searches. • Student will complete activity workbooks that focus on spotting differences. • Student will solve jigsaws and paint-by-numbers exercises. • Student will find hidden objects on an activity sheet. • Student will circle the same word in text. • Student will find words that begin with a designated letter in text. • Student will outline a specific object from a worksheet containing overlapping objects. • Student will sort designated objects from a bag full of different objects. • Student will play computer games requiring sorting or matching or use a letter chart to cross out a designated letter. • Student will engage in board games such as Monopoly, Chutes and Ladders. • Teacher will provide students with a worksheet containing several rows of designs; each row also contains a word which the student will circle.	• Teacher will provide the student with a worksheet containing multiple replicas of design. Student will color only a specified portion of design. • Teacher will present a picture that has objects in the background and foreground. Student will pick out the objects in the background and foreground. • Teacher will ask the student to pick out objects within the classroom that are square, round or triangular shaped. • Teacher will present stencils with designs to the student. Student will trace the stencils on a piece of paper. Student will color the figure and the background in different colors. • Teacher will present puzzles that have both foreground and background in the picture. Student will complete the puzzle, pointing out both foreground objects and background objects. • Teacher will present materials that have pictures of objects or people that have parts missing. Student will point out where the parts are missing. • Teacher will create a collage with the student. Student will place pictures that represent the background first on the collage. Student will place pictures or objects representing the foreground on top of the background pictures. Student will point out the objects that are in the background and foreground. • Teacher will present drawings with overlapping mixed figures and designs. Student will discriminate the background and foreground.

Visual Figure-Ground Tier 3	Visual Figure-Ground Tier 3
Suggested Interventionist: Occupational Therapist, Occupational Therapy Assistant(COTA), Special Education Teacher **Suggested Session: 60 minutes 5x a week in a small group or individual outside of the classroom** **Strategies/activities to improve Visual Figure-Ground:** • Student will set a table, finding the right items in the drawer or cupboard. • Student will complete word searches. • Student will complete activity workbooks that focus on spotting the difference. • Student will solve jigsaws and paint-by-numbers activities. • Student will find hidden objects on an activity sheet. • Student will circle the same word in a text. • Student will find words that begin with a designated letter in text. • Student will outline a specific object from a worksheet containing overlapping objects. • Student will sort designated objects from a bag full of different objects. • Student will play computer games requiring sorting or matching. • Teacher will use a letter chart to cross out a designated letter. • Student will engage in board games such as Monopoly, Chutes and Ladders.	• Teacher will provide the student with a worksheet containing multiple replicas of design. Student will color only a specified portion of design. • Teacher will present a picture that has objects in the background and foreground. Student will pick out the objects in the background and foreground. • Teacher will ask the student to pick out objects that are square, round or triangular shaped within the classroom. • Teacher will present student with stencils with designs. Student will trace the stencils on a piece of paper. Student will color both the figure and the background in different colors. • Teacher will present puzzles that have both foreground and background in the picture. Student will complete the puzzle, pointing out both foreground objects and background objects. • Teacher will present materials that have pictures of objects or people that have parts missing. Student will point out the parts that are missing. • Teacher will create a collage with the students. Student will first place pictures that represent the background on the collage. Students will then place foreground pictures or objects on top of the background. Student will point out the objects that are in the background and foreground. • Teacher will present drawings with overlapping mixed figures and designs. Student will discriminate the background and foreground upon request.

Area of Visual Processing: Visual Memory and Visual Sequential Memory

<table>
<tr><th>Visual Memory and Visual Sequential Memory</th><th>Visual Memory and Visual Sequential Memory Tier 1</th></tr>
<tr><td>

Visual Memory and Visual Sequential Memory—includes the ability to remember prior visual experiences. Visual sequential memory is the skill that enables a student to spell and read. This skill enables one to remember the sequence of a word. Examples of academic problems in this area:

- Difficulty copying from a board or book accurately
- Difficulty remembering an item/picture/symbol/words/forms/numbers and their orientation once they have been removed from sight.
- Difficulty concentrating or paying attention to tasks
- Difficulty to remember math facts/equations
- Difficulty to remember a foreign language
- Difficulty to decode in reading/encode in spelling
- Poor sight word accuracy
- Difficulty to pair grapheme-phoneme association
- Difficulty to function well with rote learning
- Difficulty reproducing data from a book/board
- Slow processing of visual stimulus

Accommodations and Modifications:

- Sit close to the board
- Enlarge print; Use print instead of script
- Use of visual focusing aids on paper
- Note-taker for notes
- Highlight text; color coding
- Oral directions with visual instructions
- Use buddy reader or books on tape
- Write on text
- Use directional markers

</td><td>

Suggested Interventionist: General Education Teacher

Suggested Session: Small group, explicit instruction within the classroom with consultation of the Occupational Therapist/COTA.

Strategies/Activities for Visual Memory and Visual Sequential Memory:

- School nurse will examine student's near and far visual acuity.
- Student will sit close to blackboard and/or in front of the room to reduce distractions of other students.
- Teacher will provide letter number strips on desk.
- When student is required to copy from the board the teacher will:
  - —Number each line to provide an extra visual clue
  - —Write each line on the board in a different color
  - —Seat student close to blackboard
  - —Provide student with a photocopy of teacher's notes
  - —Ask student to verbalize what he sees on blackboard or what is written on notes
- Student will recall familiar objects on a tray.
- Student will play concentration.
- Student will draw a picture of a day's event.
- Student will be shown a picture or card and asked to remember what is on it. The picture or card is removed from view and student will be asked to give a detailed description of it or ask specific questions about the picture.

</td></tr>
</table>

Visual Memory and Visual Sequential Memory Tier 1	Visual Memory and Visual Sequential Memory Tier 1
• Student will complete word searches or find the difference between pictures. • Student will participate in timed exercises copying from a board or book to paper. • Student will complete mazes working from left to right. • Student will be shown designs on the overhead projector. The design will be removed and student will be asked to reproduce it. • Student will be asked to study part of a room and then leave it. Objects are removed or changed in position. Student must identify what has changed or is different. • Student will be given sentence to read and then given a worksheet containing the words of the sentence in a random order. Student is asked to cut out the words and glue them to a page in the correct order. • Student will be encouraged to visualize and verbalize what he has seen, such as the route that he takes coming to school. • Student will complete matching figure worksheets. Figures can be geometric forms, words, words backwards, words with lower- and upper-case letters in both words. • Student will reproduce templates or parquetry blocks from memory after the template is shown.	• Student will complete word searches. • Student will identify the different letter in two words (ex: cot, cat). • Student will copy movements or body sequences. • Student will thread beads in a color or shape from a model sequence. • Teacher will give student sequences of items to remember. • Student will discuss the day's events in order. • Student will fill in the missing letter for word worksheet. • Student will circle the correct spelling from a list of familiar words. • Student will identify contextual changes. (A group of students sit in a row. One student looks at everyone's position and leaves the room. Two students swap places. Who has moved?) • Teacher will show a row of toys or objects, mix them up and then ask the student to put them back in sequential order. • Teacher will make a large card showing a sequence of shapes, symbols, letters or numbers. Teacher will make smaller cards with the individual shapes, etc. Student will put them in the correct sequence.

Visual Memory and Visual Sequential Memory Tier 1	Visual Memory and Visual Sequential Memory Tier 2
• Student will engage in sequencing games, with increasing the movements to be copied (e.g., bounce the ball, bounce the ball and clap, bounce the ball, clap then jump). • Teacher will place identical spot mats on the floor close to each other. Teacher will jump on a sequence of colored mats and ask the student to copy the sequence. • Student will look for patterns or groups when remembering a sequence (e.g., phone numbers). • Teacher will emphasize visualization by encouraging the student to look at a word and write it in the air before writing on a piece of paper. • Student will recreate a mental picture of a sequential image, such as a layout of a golf course or Tachistoscope. • Student will play Concentration. • Student will use a geo board.	**Suggested Interventionist: Occupational Therapist, Occupational Therapy Assistant (COTA), Special Education Teacher** **Suggested Session: 30 minutes 2 to 3x a week in a small group or individual inside the classroom** **Strategies/activities for Visual Memory and Visual Sequential Memory:** • Student will recall familiar objects on a tray. • Student will play concentration. • Student will draw a picture of a day's event. • Student will be shown a picture or card and asked to remember what is on it. The picture or card is removed from view and student will be asked to give a detailed description of it or will be asked specific questions about the picture. • Student will complete word searches or find the difference. • Student will participate in timed exercises copying from a board or book to paper. • Student will complete mazes working from left to right. • Student will be shown designs on the overhead projector. The design will be removed and the student will be asked to reproduce it. • Student will be asked to study part of a room and then leave it. Objects are removed or changed in position. Student will return and identify what has changed or what is different.

Visual Memory and Visual Sequential Memory Tier 2	Visual Memory and Visual Sequential Memory Tier 3
• Student will be given sentence to read. This is removed and then student is given a worksheet containing the words of the sentence in a random order. Student will cut out the words and glue them to the page in the correct order. • When student is required to copy from a board the teacher will: —Number each line to provide an extra visual clue —Write each line on the board in a different color —Seat students close to blackboard —Provide student with a photocopy of teacher's notes —Ask student to verbalize what he sees on blackboard or what is written on notes • Student will be encouraged to visualize and verbalize what he has seen, such as the route that he takes coming to school. • Student will complete matching figure worksheets. Figures can be geometric forms, words, words backwards, words with lower- and upper-case in both words. • Student will reproduce templates or parquetry blocks from memory after the template is shown. • Student will play concentration.	**Suggested Interventionist: Occupational Therapist, Occupational Therapy Assistant (COTA), Special Education Teacher** **Suggested Session: 60 minutes 5x a week in a small group or individual outside of the classroom.** **Strategies/Activities for Visual Memory and Visual Sequential Memory:** • Student will engage in sequencing games that increase the movements to be copied: (bounce the ball; bounce the ball and clap; bounce the ball, clap, then jump). • Teacher will place identical spot mats on the floor close to each other, jump on a sequence of colored mats and ask the student to copy the sequence. • Student will look for patterns or groups when remembering a sequence (phone numbers). • Teacher will emphasize visualization by encouraging the student to look at a word and write it in the air before writing on a piece of paper. • Student will recreate a mental picture of a sequential image, such as a layout of a golf course or Tachistoscope.

Visual Memory and Visual Sequential Memory Tier 3	Visual Memory and Visual Sequential Memory Tier 3
• When student is required to copy from a board the teacher will: —Number each line to provide an extra visual clue —Write each line on the board in a different color —Seat student close to blackboard —Provide student with a photocopy of their notes —Ask student to verbalize what he sees on blackboard or what is written on notes • Student will be encouraged to visualize and verbalize what he has seen, such as the route that he takes coming to school. • Student will complete matching figure worksheets. Figures can be geometric forms, words, words backwards, words with lower- and upper-case in both words. • Student will reproduce templates or parquetry blocks from memory after the template is shown. • Student will play concentration. • Student will use a Geo board.	• Student will complete word searches. • Student will identify the different letter in two words (cot, cat). • Student will copy movements or body sequences. • Student will thread beads in a color or shape from a model sequence. • Teacher will give student sequences of items to remember in sequence. • Student will discuss the day's events in order. • Student will fill in the missing letter for words worksheet. • Student will circle the correct spelling from a list of familiar words. • Student will identify contextual changes. (A group of students sit in a row. One student looks at everyone's position and then leaves the room. Two students swap places. The student returns to the room and identifies who has moved.) • Teacher will show a row of toys or objects, mix them up and ask the child to put them back in sequential order. • Teacher will make a large card showing a sequence of shapes, symbols, letters or numbers, and smaller cards with the individual shapes etc. Student will put small cards in the correct sequence.

Area of Visual Processing: Visual Closure

Visual Closure	Visual Closure Tier 1
Visual Closure—involves the ability to recognize a symbol, word or object by only seeing parts of that symbol, word or object. Visual closure is a foundation skill for fluency and speed in reading and spelling. Examples of academic problems within this area: • Difficulty identifying a visual object when looking at an incomplete or unclear image • Difficulty visualizing images • Difficulty applying spelling patterns; decoding words • Difficulty blending letters into words visually • Difficulty completing mathematical calculations/ facts • Difficulty developing a sight word vocabulary • Difficulty using Cloze techniques • Difficulty finishing math problems and predicting the answer • Difficulty going from part to whole words and whole words to their segmented parts • Difficulty completing puzzles • Slow processing of visual stimulus **Accommodations and Modifications:** • Sit close to the board • Enlarge print ;Use print instead of script • Use of visual focusing aids on paper • Note taker for notes • Highlight text; color coding • Oral directions with visual instructions • Use buddy reader or books on tape • Write on text • Use directional markers	**Suggested Interventionist: General Education Teacher with consultation from the Occupational Therapist; COTA; Special Education Teacher** **Suggested Session: Small group, explicit instruction 2x within the CORE program within the classroom.** **Strategies/Activities for Visual Closure:** • School nurse will examine student's near and far visual acuity. • Teacher will provide enlarged images and reading materials. • Teacher will modify worksheets by simplifying and reducing non-essential visual stimuli. • Student will sit close to blackboard and/or in front of the room to reduce distractions of other students. • Teacher will reduce clutter near/around the blackboard. • Teacher will write larger on blackboard or overhead projector. • Teacher will increase contrast—use black on white/white on black. • Teacher will provide letter/number strips on desk. • Teacher will provide enlarged graph paper or rotate composition notebook to provide vertical columns for math. • Teacher will reduce visual distractions in the room such as pictures on walls, mobiles or hanging objects. • Teacher will utilize enlarged and exaggerated math symbols with titles (add, subtract, divide).

Visual Closure Tier 2	Visual Closure Tier 3
Suggested Interventionist: Occupational Therapist, Occupational Therapy Assistant (COTA), Special Education Teacher **Suggested Session: 30 minutes 2 to 3x a week in a small group or individual inside the classroom** **Strategies/activities for Visual Closure:** • Student will complete jigsaws. • Student will complete dot-to-dots. • Student will color in pictures. • Student will complete word searches. • Student will write or draw in sand. • Student will fill in the missing letter or word. • Student will match complete and incomplete shapes. • Student will engage in construction games. • Student will play Scrabble. • Student will use stencils. • Student will engage in model making. • Student will build three-dimensional models. • Student will identify the whole from a partially covered picture. • Student will find the matching object, geometric form, shape, pictures, etc.. Top row on worksheet has a figure drawn. The bottom row has the parts of the picture. The student will pick out the correct parts to the picture. • Student will complete puzzles. • Student will guess the word after being shown words that have part of the letter form missing. • Student will guess the object after being shown the object with some parts missing.	**Suggested Interventionist: Occupational Therapist, Occupational Therapy Assistant (COTA), Special Education Teacher** **Suggested Session: 60 minutes 5x a week in a small group or individual outside the classroom** **Strategies/activities for Visual Closure:** • Student will complete jigsaws. • Student will complete dot-to-dots. • Student will color in pictures. • Student will complete word searches. • Student will write or draw in sand. • Student will fill in the missing letter or word. • Student will match complete and incomplete shapes. • Student will engage in construction games. • Student will play Scrabble. • Student will use stencils. • Student will engage in model making. • Student will build three-dimensional models. • Student will identify the whole from a partially covered picture. • Student will find the matching object, geometric form, shape, pictures, etc. Top row on worksheet has a figure drawn. The bottom row has the parts of the picture. The student will pick out the correct parts to the picture. • Student will complete puzzles. • Student will guess the word after being shown words that have part of the letter form missing. • Student will guess the object after being shown the object with some parts missing.

Area of Visual Processing: Visual Form Constancy

Visual Form Constancy	Visual Form Constancy Tier 1
Visual Form Constancy—involves the ability to recognize forms that are alike and different. These objects can be different in size, shape, thicknesses and color. Examples of academic problems within this area: • Difficulty cooking and following directions • Difficulty understanding geometry; attributes • Difficulty understanding the concepts of thicker/thinner; bigger/smaller. • Difficulty making Lego from instructions • Difficulty judging size, height, width and distance • Difficulty categorizing and classifying objects/shapes/colors/materials • Difficulty recognizing everyday objects when put in unusual positions or in a different size • Difficulty mislaying items and being unable to find them • Difficulty recognizing/reading the same words in different fonts, typefaces, etc. • Difficulty transferring from the printed form to cursive handwriting • Difficulty organizing self and objects • Slow processing of visual stimulus **Accommodations and Modifications:** • Sit close to the board • Enlarge print; Use print instead of script • Use of visual focusing aids on paper • Note taker for notes • Highlight text; color coding • Oral directions with visual instructions • Use buddy reader or books on tape • Write on text • Use directional markers	**Suggested Interventionist: General Education Teacher** **Suggested Session: Small group, explicit instruction within the classroom with consultation of the Occupational Therapist/COTA.** **Strategies/activities for Visual Form Constancy:** • School nurse will examine student's near and far visual acuity. • Teacher will provide enlarged images and reading materials. • Teacher will modify worksheets by simplifying and reducing non-essential visual stimuli. • Student will sit close to blackboard and/or in front of the room to reduce distractions of other students. • Teacher will reduce clutter near/around the blackboard. • Student will use blue overlays on printed/reading material to reduce glare from fluorescent lighting. • Teacher will provide index card, ruler or highlighted tracking strip for reading. • Teacher will write larger on blackboard or overhead projector. • Teacher will exaggerate spacing between words on all copy samples. • Student will utilize a slant board to decrease distance between eyes and writing/reading material. • Teacher will increase contrast—use black on white/white on black. • Teacher will provide enlarged graph paper or turn composition notebook to provide vertical columns.

Visual Form Constancy **Tier 2**

Suggested Interventionist: Occupational Therapist, Occupational Therapy Assistant (COTA), Special Education Teacher

Suggested Session: 30 minutes 2 to 3x a week in a small group or individual inside the classroom

Strategies/activities for Visual Form Constancy:

- Student will touch, feel, and talk about three-dimensional objects when their size or orientation may alter.
- Student will color three-dimensional drawings and models.
- Student will copy three-dimensional patterns and shapes, such as brick designs or origami.
- Student will match three-dimensional objects, for size, shape, volume and density.
- Student will make models.
- Student will compare and contrast the size and shape of objects.
- Student will build up three-dimensional geometric shapes.
- Student will make three-dimensional models from two-dimensional diagrams such as Lego.
- Student will work with solid objects to identify objects seen from different angles such as above, below, underneath, behind.
- Teacher will select a shape from a sorting box and place it at a distance in the room. Student will be asked to find a similar sized ball from the box.
- Teacher will write the same word in many styles, colors and prints together with other words. Student will underline the same word in its different forms.

Visual Form Constancy **Tier 2**

- Student will outline jigsaws to see how individual parts fit together to make a whole.
- Student will fill in outlines with geometric shapes, progressing from matching a shape to its outline to a stage where several shapes are needed to fill an outline.
- Student will play shape lotto.
- Student will make shapes with arithmetic sticks.
- Student will identify shapes, numbers, letters, words, pictures and objects when a portion is missing.
- Student will look at a design made from parquetry blocks with one piece missing. Student will find the appropriate block to complete the pattern.
- Teacher will show a picture with multiple shapes of varied sizes. There should be many shapes of the same size. Student will tell how many of one particular shape there are.
- Teacher will show a picture with multiple words that have the same word family. Student will write how many times he sees a designated word.
- Teacher will show a picture with multiple numbers, repeating the same numbers multiple times. Student will write how many times they see the designated number.
- Teacher will reduce visual distractions in the room such as pictures on walls, mobiles or hanging objects.
- Student will utilize enlarged and exaggerated math symbols with titles (e.g., add, subtract, divide).
- Teacher will utilize a different color for capital letters.
- Teacher will provide letter, number and shape instruction to confirm letter, number and shape identification skills.

Visual Form Constancy Tier 3	Visual Form Constancy Tier 3
Suggested Interventionist: Occupational Therapist, Occupational Therapy Assistant (COTA), Special Education Teacher **Suggested Session: 60 minutes 5x a week in a small group or individual outside the classroom** **Strategies/activities for Visual Form Constancy:** • Student will touch, feel, and talk about three-dimensional objects when their size or orientation may alter. • Student will color three-dimensional drawings and models. • Student will copy three-dimensional patterns and shapes, such as brick designs or origami. • Student will match three-dimensional objects, for size, shape, volume and density from boards varying in presentation. • Student will make models. • Student will compare and contrast the size and shape of objects. • Student will build up three-dimensional geometric shapes. • Student will make three-dimensional models from two-dimensional diagrams such as Lego. • Student will work with solid objects to identify objects seen from different angles such as above, below, underneath, behind. • Teacher will select a shape from a sorting box and place it at a distance in the room. Student will be asked to find a similar sized ball from the box. • Teacher will write the same word in many styles, colors and prints, together with other words. Student will underline the same word in its different forms.	• Student will underline the same word in its different forms. Student will outline jigsaws to see how individual parts fit together to make a whole. • Student will fill in outlines with geometric shapes. Progress from matching a shape to its outline to a stage where several shapes are needed to fill an outline. • Student will play shape lotto. • Student will make shapes with arithmetic sticks. • Student will identify shapes, numbers, letters, words, pictures and objects when a portion is missing. • Student will look at a design made from parquetry blocks with one piece missing. Students will find the appropriate block to complete the pattern. • Teacher will show a picture with multiple shapes of varied sizes. There should be many shapes of the same size. Students will tell how many of one particular shape there are. • Teacher will show a picture with multiple words that have the same word family. Students will write how many times he sees a designated word. • Teacher will show a picture with multiple numbers, repeating the same numbers multiple times. Students will write how many times they see the designated number.

Programs & Products for Visual Processing (See Appendix C for web sites)

Product	Publisher	Tier	Type	Visual Discrim.	Visual Motor	Visual Spatial	Visual Coord.	Visual Fig Gr	Visual Memory	Visual Closure	Visual Form Constancy
ABC Mazes	Ann Arbor	2,3	Supplemental/ Workbook	x	x	x	x	x	x	x	x
Amazing Mazes	Kumon	2,3	Supplemental/ Workbook		x	x					
BuildingPerspective	Sunburst	2,3	Software	x	x	x		x	x	x	x
Calcudraw	BUKI books	2,3	Supplemental/ Workbook		x	x				x	
Chalkboard	Laura Sena	2,3	Supplemental/ Workbook		x	x					
Color by Letter	BUKI Pub.	2,3	Supplemental/ Workbook	x							
Color by Number	BUKI Pub.	2,3	Supplemental/ Workbook	x							
Creating Line Designs	CLD	2,3	Supplemental/ Workbook		x						
Creating Patterns	Sunburst	2,3	Software	x		x		x		x	x
Dot to Dot	Proof Slinky Science	2,3	Supplemental/ Workbook	x							
Eye Hand Coordination Boosters	Exceptional Teaching Inc.	2,3	Supplemental/ Workbook		x						
Eye-Hand Puzzles	Pearson	2,3	Supplemental/ Workbook	x	x	x	x	x		x	x
Find It Games	Find It Games	2,3	Supplemental/ Workbook					x			

Programs & Products for Visual Processing (See Appendix C for web sites)

Product	Publisher	Tier	Type	Visual Discrim.	Visual Motor	Visual Spatial	Visual Coord.	Visual Fig Gr	Visual Memory	Visual Closure	Visual Form Constancy
Half n Half Design	Ann Arbor	2,3	Supplemental/ Workbook	x	x	x	x	x	x	x	x
Hands on Geoboards	Creative Publications	2,3	Supplemental/ Workbook		x	x					
I Spy Eagle Eye Game	Briar Patch	2,3	Supplemental/ Workbook					x			
I Spy Game	Briar Patch	2,3	Supplemental/ Workbook					x			x
Investigating with Pattern Blocks	Learning Resources	2,3	Supplemental/ Workbook		x	x					
Let's Do It-	Gail Kushnir	2,3	Supplemental/ Workbook		x						
Magic Picture Hide & Seek	Buki Books	2,3	Supplemental/ Workbook					x			
Memory Challenge	Critical Thinking	2,3	Supplemental/ Workbook	x				x	x	x	x
Memory Fun	Sunburst	2,3	Software	x				x	x	x	x
Mosaic Hidden Pictures	Proof Slinky	2,3	Supplemental/ Workbook					x		x	
Mosaic Picture Patterns	BUKI Pub.	2,3	Supplemental/ Workbook	x							
My First Book of Mazes	Kumon	2,3	Supplemental/ Workbook		x	x					
My Hidden Pictures	Highlights for Children	2,3	Supplemental/ Workbook					x			
Perceptual Activities	Ann Arbor	2,3	Supplemental/ Workbook	x	x	x	x	x	x	x	x

Programs & Products for Visual Processing (See Appendix C for web sites)

Product	Publisher	Tier	Type	Visual Discrim.	Visual Motor	Visual Spatial	Visual Coord.	Visual Fig Gr	Visual Memory	Visual Closure	Visual Form Constancy
Primary Geoboards/Primary	Learning Resources	2,3	Supplemental/ Workbook		X	X					
Puzzles for Pattern Blocks	Learning Resources	2,3	Supplemental/ Workbook		X	X					
Read-n-Draw	CLD	2,3	Supplemental/ Workbook		X						
Sentence Tracking	AnnArbor	2,3	Supplemental/ Workbook	X			X	X	X	X	X
Sequencing Fun	Sunburst	2,3	Software	X		X	X	X		X	X
SmartDriver	Brain Train	2,3	Software	X	X	X	X	X	X	X	X
Spatial Relationships	Sunburst	2,3	Software	X				X		X	X
Stare Jr.	Game Dev. Group Inc.	2,3	Supplemental/ Workbook					X		X	
Symbol Disc. Series	Ann Arbor	2,3	Supplemental/ Workbook	X			X	X	X	X	X
Symbol LetterTracking	AnnArbor	2,3	Supplemental/ Workbook	X			X	X	X	X	X
The Maze Book	Ann Arbor	2,3	Supplemental/ Workbook	X	X	X	X	X	X	X	X
Think-a-Minutes	Critical Thinking	2,3	Supplemental/ Workbook	X	X	X	X	X	X	X	X
Thinker Doodles	Critical Thinking	2,3	Supplemental/ Workbook	X	X			X	X	X	X
Three Pigs, One Wolf, Seven Magic Shapes	Scholastic	2,3	Supplemental/ Workbook		X						
Training That Makes Sense	Ann Arbor	2,3	Supplemental/ Workbook	X			X	X	X	X	X

Programs & Products for Visual Processing (See Appendix C for web sites)

Product	Publisher	Tier	Type	Visual Discrim.	Visual Motor	Visual Spatial	Visual Coord.	Visual Fig Gr	Visual Memory	Visual Closure	Visual Form Constancy
Visual Perception Skill Bldg.1&2	Critical Thinking	2,3	Supplemental/ Workbook	x	x	x	x	x	x	x	x
Visual ClosureWorkbook	Your Therapy Source	2,3	Supplemental/ Workbook							x	
Visual Disc.	Remedia	2,3	Supplemental/ Workbook	x							
Visual Disc. For all	KLIK Enterprises	2,3	Supplemental/ Workbook	x							
Visual Disc.& Memory	Kay Pictures	2,3	Supplemental/ Workbook	x							
Visual Discrimination: Noting Differences	Achieve Publications	2,3	Supplemental/ Workbook	x							
Visual Motor Workbook	Your Therapy Source Inc	2,3	Supplemental/ Workbook		x						
Visual Tracking Workbook	Bernell	2,3	Supplemental/ Workbook				x				
What's Different	BUKI Pub.	2,3	Supplemental/ Workbook	x							
Word Tracking	Ann Arbor	2,3	Supplemental/ Workbook	x			x	x	x	x	x

What is Language Processing?

Language processing is the acquisition, comprehension or expression of spoken or written language. Language processing may involve all, one, or some of the phonologic, morphologic, semantic, syntactic, or pragmatic components of the linguistic system. Students with language processing difficulties frequently have problems in sentence processing or in abstracting information meaningfully for storage and retrieval from short-and long term memory (ASHA, 1980, p. 317-318).

Key Characteristics for Language Processing Difficulties:

- Difficulty using language for different social purposes such as greeting, informing, commenting, questioning and/or demanding
- Difficulty changing language structures to adjust to a specific situation and/or listener
- Difficulty following conversational rules as a speaker and/or listener
- Difficulty telling a story either structurally or semantically in terms of people and events
- Limited vocabulary
- Limited recognition of word meaning
- Delays in structural aspects of language such as: the use of complex sentences, the use of passive constructive, the use of negative constructions and the use of question forms
- Delays in the development of grammatical morphemes such as irregular verbs, articles, past tense, pronouns and conjunctions
- Difficulty explaining, inferring and interpreting words, sentences and narratives
- Difficulty with non-literal meanings such as humor, figurative language and analogies

Area of Language Processing: Pragmatics

Pragmatics	Pragmatics Tier 1
Pragmatics—involves the ability to use language for social purposes. Student can regulate language structures to meet the needs of listeners and ensure listener comprehension. Student can use language to convey a range of communicative functions, demonstrating understanding and speaking in social contexts. Examples of problems in this area are: • Inappropriate comments • Poor social judgment • Misinterpreting of the verbal and non-verbal behavior of peers • Difficulty taking turns during conversation • Interrupting other people when they are speaking • Difficulty providing related information and/or staying appropriately on topic • Providing irrelevant or unrelated information **Accommodations/Modifications:** • Provide extra time on answers • Fill in the blanks orally by asking specific questions • Use written projects • Use notes with oral reports • Small group discussions	**Suggested Interventionist: General Education Teacher with consultation from the Speech Pathologist/Special Education Teacher** **Suggested Session: Small group, explicit instruction within the CORE program 2x a week within the classroom.** **Strategies/Activities for Pragmatics:** • Teacher will establish classroom rules for "good" conversations, such as: Take Turns, Do Not Interrupt, Be Polite, Use Social Greetings and Stay On Topic. • Teacher will post the rules. • Student will role-play a conversational exchange on a specific topic as a way of practicing the rules. • Teacher will have two students role-play a conversation on a specific topic, but make several conversational mistakes. Student will identify the errors. • Teacher will identify specific conversational topics that are practiced so that progress can be measured. • Teacher will introduce new topics intermittently and compare how student performs on the practice conversations versus new conversations. • Teacher will immediately reinforce the student for following the rules of "good conversation." • Teacher will teach student how to ask questions by developing who, what, when, where, why and how questions. Student will then answer those questions.

Pragmatics Tier 1	Pragmatics Tier 2
• Teacher will provide students with routine phrases that can be used to initiate either conversation or social interaction, such as: —How's it going? —Can I help you? —Are you okay? —I don't understand. —Can you help me? —I don't like that. —What are you doing? —Where are you going? —Can I come along? —Can I do that with you? • Teacher will reinforce the student for generalizing information from one situation to another by: giving the student an intangible reward for work well done (handshake, high-five, pat on the back), or giving the student a tangible reward for work well done (ten minutes free time, line leading, more classroom privileges). • Teacher will ask the student to list major categories of objects, beginning with broad categories and then generalizing into more specific categories. • Teacher will ask the student to list subcategories which fit into larger categories (plant/flowers, bushes/trees). • The teacher will ask the student to respond to "What if?" questions within the classroom. • Teacher will explain how the rules in the classroom generalize to real life situations (being on time for school is like being on time for work).	**Suggested Interventionist: Speech Pathologist, Special Education Teacher** **Suggested Session: 30 minutes 2 to 3x a week in a small group or individual basis in addition to the CORE program inside the classroom.** **Strategies/Activities for Pragmatics:** • Student will practice the following pragmatic functions: —Requesting an object —Politely responding to a question —Expressing gratitude —Requesting help —Expressing regret —Greeting another person —Asking a question —Requesting directions —Answering a phone call —Welcoming a new person —Asking for information —Giving someone else directions to complete a task —Making introductions —Asking for clarification —Requesting permission —Introducing one person to another —Interrupting a conversation politely —Providing an explanation for poor behavior —Apologizing —Adjusting conversation to meet the needs of a situation

Pragmatics Tier 2	Pragmatics Tier 2
• Teacher will encourage peer learning by assigning another student to act as a role model. • Teacher will identify concepts that are related and explain the relationship (heating oil to heat; sentences to paragraphs; money to food). • Teacher will ask the student to play analogy games, initially using multiple-choice possibilities. After the student understands how to do this, student will play analogy games without the use of multiple choices. • Teacher will ask the student to explain the definition of words/concepts in his or her own language, building comprehension and generalization. • Teacher will scramble sentences for generalization purposes. Student will unscramble the sentences into correct sentence structure and help with generalization. • Teacher will ask the student to role-play real life situations, such as riding a horse, making a sandwich, making a bed, cooking a meal. • Teacher will ask the student to take verbal messages to different personnel within the school. Student will return to the classroom with the new message. • Student will learn to identify irrelevant, unrelated and/or repetitive responses during conversational exchanges that are scripted in class. For example: —Student will create Mr. Blooper, a character who engages in conversational mistakes or bloopers, and will practice being Mr. Blooper, and/or identifying when Mr. Blooper makes mistakes.	—Student will create conversational cartoons using Mr. Blooper and his mistakes. —Teacher will discuss the impact of Mr. Blooper's mistakes with the class. —Student will write about how they feel about Mr. Blooper's mistakes. —Teacher will use role-playing techniques to facilitate social learning. • Teacher will focus on specific social problems, such as a new child entering the class, catching someone stealing, bullying, lying, helping another child who gets lost. • Teacher will use comic strips to present different social problems followed by classroom discussion concerning various solutions to these problems. • Teacher will have student find stories from newspapers and magazines that highlight specific problems such as bullying, stealing, lying and cheating. • Teacher will facilitate classroom discussion to develop problem-solving skills. • Teacher will present an idiom or a joke every day for students to discuss. Teacher will elicit meaning of the idiom or joke. • Teacher will have the student echo what the teacher or another student says. Student must use the right inflectional patterns and facial expression as well as repeat words exactly.

Pragmatics Tier 3	Pragmatics Tier 3
Suggested Interventionist: Speech Pathologist, Special Education Teacher **Suggested Session: 60 minutes 5x a week in a small group or individual basis in addition to the CORE program outside the classroom.** **Strategies/activities for Pragmatics:** • Teacher will reinforce the student with tangible and intangible rewards for verbal interactions that are spontaneous, original and contain variety. • Teacher will encourage and direct student to use facial expressions, gestures, actions and no action in order to communicate without using words. • Students will practice using certain phrases/words within social situations in school. Teacher will limit the amount of times the student can use particular words/phrases. • Teacher will give a list of common words for which the student will look up antonyms and synonyms. Student will use the new words in conversational sentences. • Teacher will identify the student-limited utterances and expand the student's sentences in order to demonstrate how to expand sentences and mean the same thing. • Teacher will encourage "think out-loud" planning when a student has to respond.	• Student will continue to practice the following pragmatic functions using expanded sentences: —Requesting an object —Politely responding to a question —Expressing gratitude —Requesting help —Expressing regret —Greeting another person —Asking a question —Requesting directions —Answering a phone call —Welcoming a new person —Asking for information —Giving someone else directions to complete a task —Making introductions —Asking for clarification —Requesting permission —Introducing one person to another —Interrupting a conversation politely —Providing an explanation for poor behavior —Apologizing —Adjusting conversation to meet the needs of the listener —Adjusting conversation to meet the needs of a situation —Determining whether a listener is following a conversation • Teacher will use puppets to retell a story or act out an activity. Student will follow the teacher's lead and do the exact same thing. • Teacher will ask the student to be someone else and role-play the conversation.

Pragmatics Tier 3	Pragmatics Tier 3
• Teacher will continue to use routine phrases to initiate either conversation or social interaction. The student will expand the routine phrases to include more complex sentences, such as: —How's it going this morning in school? —Can I help you with getting your lunch? —Are you okay or do you feel sick? —I don't understand what you want. —Can you help me get my coat on? —I don't like your attitude. —What are you doing with all of the papers? —Where are you going on the weekend? —Can I come along for the ride to the store? —Can I do that with you or do you want to do it alone? • Teacher will continue to teach student to identify irrelevant, unrelated and/or repetitive responses in class during scripted conversational exchanges. • Student will alternate playing the character of Mr. Blooper in the classroom. —Create Mr. Blooper, a character who engages in conversational mistakes or bloopers. —Have students practice being Mr. Blooper, and/or identifying when Mr. Blooper makes mistakes. —Have students create conversational cartoons using Mr. Blooper and his mistakes. —Discuss with the class the impact of Mr. Blooper's mistakes. —Have students write about how they feel about Mr. Blooper's mistakes.	• Teacher will ask the student to bring in pictures of himself/herself at various stages of their development. Teacher will ask the student to create a story centered around the pictures reacting to targeted situations that the teacher creates. • Teacher will focus on specific social problems, such as a new child entering the class, catching someone stealing, bullying, lying, helping another child who gets lost. • Teacher will use comic strips to teach different social problems followed by classroom discussion concerning various solutions to these problems. Teacher will remove the captions and the student will write his or her own captions. • Teacher will teach student to ask questions. For every topic being taught, student will develop who, what, when, where, why and how questions. Then let other students answer questions. • Teacher will have student find stories from newspapers and magazines that highlight specific problems such as bullying, stealing, lying and cheating. Utilize classroom discussion to develop problem-solving skills for students. • Teacher will present an idiom or a joke every day for students to discuss. • Teacher will elicit the meaning of the idiom or joke. • Teacher will highlight ambiguous language that might be used in jokes.

Area of Visual Processing: Semantics

<table>
<tr><th>Semantics</th><th>Semantics Tier 1</th></tr>
<tr><td>

Semantics—involves the ability to conceptualize and formulate ideas about objects, events and relations. Examples of difficulties in this area:

- Delays in vocabulary development
- Word confusions and mispronunciations
- Limited understanding of multiple word meanings
- Poor word associations
- Limited understanding of idioms, non-literal and figurative language
- Difficulty expressing feelings appropriately
- Poor problem-solving skills in social settings considered rude by peers
- Difficulty retrieving, remembering or generalizing words and their meaning in multiple contexts
- Difficulty extracting word meaning or using new words in spoken and written context
- Difficulty conceptualizing "the big idea"
- Difficulty integrating new information
- Difficulty seeing connections between words, sentences, events and experiences
- Difficulty learning from others and/or from natural context

Accommodations/Modifications:

- Provide extra time on answers
- Fill in the blanks orally by asking specific questions
- Use written projects
- Use notes with oral reports
- Small group discussions

</td><td>

Suggested Interventionist: General Education Teacher with consultation from the Speech Pathologist

Suggested Session: Small group, explicit instruction within the CORE program, 2x a week within the classroom.

Strategies/Activities for Semantics:

- Teacher will develop a Word Bank adding new words on a daily basis, and having student look up the meanings and put the words in sentences for homework.
- Student will always go home with new vocabulary words. At the end of every week the class is divided into teams for a word competition.
- Teacher will have a peer work specifically with the student on a Vocabulary Development Box. Set aside time for independent reading during which peers identify unknown words. The words are looked up and the student must put new words into sentences for homework.
- Teacher will ensure that other teachers are aware of the weekly words and the student's Vocabulary Development Box. All teachers will use the student's vocabulary words in their conversations with the student.
- Teacher will emphasize important vocabulary words by increased stress and volume during class instruction.
- Teacher will use "turtle talk" by slowing down his rate of speech when talking.
- Teacher will pause frequently when presenting new content information.

</td></tr>
</table>

Semantics Tier 1	Semantics Tier 1
• Teacher will utilize visual and auditory materials to reinforce learning. • Teacher will have a peer make an audiotape of a text book that is being used in class. Student listens to tape. • Teacher will audiotape her lessons and send the tape home with the student as a reinforcer to what was taught in class. • Teacher will provide student not only with written materials but with pictures and key words when introducing a new topic. • Teacher will use objects and/or pictures when teaching new vocabulary words and ask the student to draw pictures of the new words. • Teacher will develop Word Webs emphasizing how information is associated and connected. • Student will brainstorm characteristics or attributes that describe the word and write each attribute within a graphic organizer. • Teacher will develop Word Tree, with the root of the tree being the base word which will be discussed in class: tempt. The branches of the tree contain variations of the word: attempt, tempting and temptation. • Teacher will teach word roots so that student can learn how words become more complex and how meaning changes. • Teacher will teach absurdities through pictures such as someone walking on the ceiling.	• Student will help with an answer, providing cues and clues, teaching facts, testing and developing quizzes. • Teacher will pre-teach new vocabulary words before words are used in a content lesson. • Teacher will pre-teach by writing words on the board, defining them and giving examples of how they are used. Pre-teaching should occur the day before the words are used in a lesson. • Teacher will present the wrong answer and have student correct the information. • Teacher will draw attention to the key aspects of auditory communication by pointing out the key words and phrases related to the instructions. • Teacher will write a contract for the student specifying what behavior is expected with the re-inforcers that will be used. • Teacher will explain the importance of comprehending absurdities within pictures and verbal information. Teacher will explain humor and use examples through absurdities. • Teacher will teach student the differences between fantasy and reality by discussing movies, stories, TV programs, books, newspaper articles. • Teacher will teach the difference between nonsense and sensible situations by role-playing.

Semantics Tier 2	Semantics Tier 2
Suggested Interventionist: Speech Pathologist **Suggested Session: 30 minutes 2 to 3x a week in a small group or individual basis in addition to the CORE program inside the classroom.** **Strategies/Activities for Semantics:** • Teacher will explain to the student how to classify new vocabulary words by category, function, antonym, synonym and sub-category. • Teacher will direct student to label persons, places, things and pick out verbs that could be used with those persons, places and things. • Teacher will direct student to define the meanings of the persons, places and things that were labeled. • Teacher will direct student to add adjectives to explain further the persons, places and things. • Teacher will direct student to add adverbs to further explain verbs that are used with the persons, places or things. • Teacher will ask the student to picture a specific location like a clothing store and name as many objects, actions, persons that are connected to the specific location. • Teacher will create novel or absurd situations to teach new vocabulary words. • Teacher will have the student create a vocabulary notebook with definitions of words that the student does not know. • Teacher will teach new vocabulary words within the context of known information to help the student remember the new vocabulary words.	• Teacher will have student make up stories using newly introduced and learned vocabulary words. • Teacher will continue to develop a Word Bank, adding new words on a daily basis. Students will look up the meanings and put the words into sentences for homework. • Teacher will have a peer work specifically with the student on a Vocabulary Development Box. Set aside time for independent reading during which peers identify unknown words. The words are looked up and the student must put these new words into sentences for homework. • Teacher will emphasize important vocabulary words by increasing stress and volume during instruction. • Teacher will use "turtle talk" by slowing down rate of speech. • Teacher will pause frequently when presenting new content information. • Teacher will look directly at the targeted student, rephrase and repeat questions, key words and ideas. • Teacher will use new words in a sentence completion activity. Teacher will explain how the use of different words changes the meaning of the sentence. Student will change targeted words within the sentence to change its meaning. • Teacher will have student read a story. Teacher will provide the student with true/false statements that reflect the main points of the story in order to get the "Big Idea" of the story. • Teacher will have a student read a story and provide student with statements about the story out of sequence. Student has to place the statement in sequence.

Semantics Tier 2	Semantics Tier 2
• Teacher will utilize visual, auditory and tactile materials to reinforce learning. • Teacher will provide student not only with written materials but with pictures and key words when introducing a new topic. • Teacher will use objects and/or pictures when teaching new vocabulary words. Teacher will ask the student to draw pictures of the new words. • Teacher will develop Word Webs in order to emphasize how information is associated and connected. • Student will brainstorm characteristics or attributes that describe the word and write each attribute within a graphic organizer. • Student will compare a term's meaning and its features to those of other terms that fall into the same category. • Student will use a Semantic Map graphic organizer to activate and draw on prior knowledge, recognize important components of different concepts and see the relationships among these components. • Teacher will put vocabulary words onto 3x5 cards, including pairs of cards that include the following: word and definition; word and analogy; word and synonyms; words and antonyms. Student will match pairs.	• Teacher will teach word roots so that student can learn how words become more complex and how meaning changes. • Teacher will teach absurdities through pictures such as someone walking on the ceiling. • Teacher will present the wrong answer and have student correct the information. • Teacher will provide instructional modification, providing answers to the targeted student and helping with an answer by providing cues and clues, teaching facts, testing and developing quizzes. • Teach will pre-teach new vocabulary words before they are used in a content lesson. This includes exposing a student to the words by writing them on the board, defining them and giving examples of how words are used. • Teacher will use the Frayer Model, a word categorization activity that helps learners develop their understanding of concepts. Student will provide a definition, list characteristics or facts, and provide examples and non-examples of the concept. • Student will study words or terms by relating one concept to another, forming a concept circle. Student will identify common relationship that exists among several terms. • Student will use a concept definition map that is a graphic organizer which helps students understand the essential attributes, qualities or characteristics of a concept.

Semantics Tier 3	Semantics Tier 3
Suggested Interventionist: Speech Pathologist, Special Education Teacher **Suggested Session: 60 minutes 5x a week in a small group or individual basis in addition to the CORE program outside the classroom.** **Strategies/Activities for Semantics:** • Teacher will provide student with situations which elicit particular emotions and assist the student in expressing those emotions. • Teacher will provide the student with a list of questions involving opinions, feelings and/or emotions. Teacher will assist the student in answering those question orally. • Teacher will prompt student to express the consequence or outcome of a statement or situation explained by the teacher. • Teacher will read stories involving morals and asks the student to give his or her opinion about the outcome of the story. • Teacher will show the student pictures of dangerous situations and ask the student why it is dangerous and what a solution may be. • Student will make rules for the classroom and connect the appropriate consequences for those rules. • Teacher will ask the student to illustrate a story that contains emotional overtones. Teacher will list the emotions portrayed in the story.	• Teacher will look directly at the targeted student, rephrase and repeat questions, key words and important ideas. • Teacher will provide student not only with written materials but with pictures and key words when introducing a new topic. • Teacher will use objects and/or pictures when teaching new vocabulary words. Teacher will ask the student to draw pictures of the new words. • Teacher will develop word webs, always emphasizing how information is associated and connected. • Student will continue to brainstorm characteristics or attributes that describe the word and write each attribute on graphic organizers. Student will fill in the graphic organizers independently. • Student will compare a term's meaning and its features to those of other terms that fall into the same category. • Student will use a semantic map graphic organizer to activate and draw on prior knowledge, recognize important components of different concepts and see the relationships among thee components. • Teacher will put vocabulary words onto 3x5 cards, including pairs of cards that include the following: word and definition; word and analogy; word and synonyms; and words and antonyms. Students will match pairs.

Semantics Tier 3	Semantics Tier 3
• Teacher will use the Frayer Model, which is a word categorization activity that helps learners develop their understanding of concepts. Student will provide a definition; list characteristics or facts; examples; and non-examples of the concept. • Student will study words or terms by relating one concept to another, forming a concept circle. Students will identify common relationship that exists among several terms. • Students will use a concept definition map that is a graphic organizer which helps students understand the essential attributes, qualities or characteristics of a concept • Teacher will set up a situation in which the students can role-play different emotions and explain them. • Teacher will provide students with pictures of people with happy, sad, angry, disappointed, fearful faces. Student will create a story about each of those faces, explaining the emotion perceived. • Teacher will develop a unit on figurative language. The student will pick the more interesting of the sentence pairs. (Mary speaks too much or Mary shoots off her mouth at a moments notice.) • Teacher will have the student identify idioms in everyday reading material and determine the meaning of the idiom from the context of the story. • Teacher will write a paragraph and then give the student a list of idioms and ask the student to pick one that would make a good ending for the paragraph.	• Teacher will identify similes and metaphors in everyday reading. Students will pick similes and metaphors from additional reading. • Teacher will emphasize that similes and metaphors are figurative language and are not meant to be interpreted literally. • Teacher will have the student match idioms, similes and metaphors to their definitions and examples. • Teacher will ask student to illustrate an idiom, simile or metaphor according to the literal translation and explain why it is funny. • Teacher will direct student to find commercials on TV that use figurative language and then write about the different commercials that they viewed. • Teacher will explain what a proverb is and then read a fable and have the student use the context of the story to choose an appropriate "moral" of the story. • Teacher will ask student to create greeting cards using idioms, similes, metaphors and proverbs for different situations.

Area of Language Processing: Syntactics

<table>
<tr><th>Syntactics</th><th>Syntactics Tier 1</th></tr>
<tr><td>

Syntactics—involves the ability to learn linguistic form and understand and use phonological, morphological and syntactic rules. Examples of problems within this area are:

- Consistent production of simple sentence structure
- Difficulty with complex, compound and/or embedded clauses
- Reading one sentence at a time
- Needing additional time to interpret and understand classroom conversation, lectures and instruction
- Confusion with word order in both spoken and written language
- Difficulty with contractions, prefixes, suffixes, pronouns, prepositions and noun and verb endings

Accommodations and Modifications:

- Provide extra time on answers
- Fill in the blanks orally by asking specific questions
- Use written projects
- Use notes with oral reports
- Small group discussions

</td><td>

Suggested Interventionist: General Education Teacher with consultation from the Speech Pathologist

Suggested Session: Small group, explicit instruction within the CORE program, 2x a week within the classroom.

Strategies/Activities for Syntactics:

- Teacher will teach grammar directly as a daily lesson. Teacher will teach the student to understand the concept of "subject" and "verb" by demonstrating with objects, pictures and sample written sentences.
- Teacher will utilize a traditional linguistic approach so that every student has a grammar box. Student will start with subject, verb as parts of speech, which are color coded.
- Teacher will use pictures to represent the subject or verb in order to help student create simple sentences.
- Teacher will show student that sentences express thoughts about a subject and what that subject is and what it does.
- Teacher will explain and demonstrate that certain forms of verbs go with certain subjects and that correct subject-verb agreement requires the correct match.
- Teacher will provide student with correct examples of subject-verb agreement which are most commonly used incorrectly.
- Teacher provides a list of those verbs the student most often uses incorrectly.

</td></tr>
</table>

Syntactics Tier 1	Syntactics Tier 1
• Teacher will teach different sentence types so that student understands the difference between a negative sentence, a passive sentence, a question sentence and a compound sentence. • Teacher will have the student complete written worksheets in which the student must choose the sentence that is complete or incomplete. • Student will complete sentences that are incomplete with the appropriate subject or verb. • Teacher will have the student write descriptive sentences using the proper form of the subjects and verbs. • Teacher will give the student a series of sentences, both written and oral, and have the student identify which sentence is grammatically incorrect and which sentence is grammatically correct. • Teacher will use comic strips with captions deleted and ask the student to complete the captions in grammatically correct sentences, using subject and verbs. • Teacher will use a book with pictures only and no words. The student will complete the book writing complete sentences under each of the pictures. • Teacher will teach the difference between telling and asking in sentence structure. Teacher will provide a written model for the student to demonstrate how statements can be changed into questions. • Teacher will ask the student to change simple sentences into sentences that ask questions. • Teacher will provide the student with the vocabulary to answer who, what, where, and why questions.	• Teacher will provide real life activities within the classroom that prompt students to ask questions. • Teacher will provide student with sentences that are out of order. Student will complete the activity by putting the words in the sentences into proper word order. • Teacher will teach the different pronouns that are used in a sentence. Teacher will make sure that the student understands the use of pronouns within sentences. • Teacher will provide the student with worksheets for which the student must choose the correct pronoun forms. • Teacher will provide the student with worksheets for which the student must change the noun with the proper pronoun. • Teacher will teach the student the concept of time, which effects verb tenses. Teacher will provide the student with a list of words that denote time, such as yesterday, today tomorrow, before or later. • Teacher will provide students with sentences that include verbs in the present, future and past tense. Students will be asked to pick certain verb tenses within the sentences. • Teacher will copy a paragraph which is written in the present tense. The verbs within the paragraph will be highlighted. The student will change the verbs to the past tense and then to the future tense.

Syntactics Tier 2	Syntactics Tier 3
Suggested Interventionist: Speech Pathologist **Suggested Session: 30 minutes 2 to 3x a week in a small group or individual basis in addition to the CORE program inside the classroom.** **Strategies/Activities for Syntactics:** • Teacher will teach grammar, parts of speech as well as sentence structure directly as a daily lesson. • Teacher will utilize a traditional linguistic approach so that every student has a grammar box. Start with subject, verb and object parts of speech, which are color coded. Use pictures to allow students to create simple sentences. Each part of speech should be defined and students should be encouraged to collect additional words for homework. • Teacher will teach different sentence types by demonstration and illustration so that student understands the difference between a negative sentence, a passive sentence, a question sentence and a compound sentence. • Teacher will determine if the student's errors are a result of dialectical differences. • Teacher will ensure that the student understands the concept of "subject" and "verb" by depicting scenes with pictures. • Teacher will make a list of verbs that student uses incorrectly. • Student will complete written worksheets in which he identifies sentences with appropriate and inappropriate word order. • Student will use comic strips with captions deleted and describe with correct word order the characters' actions.	**Suggested Interventionist: Speech Pathologist** **Suggested Session: 60 minutes 5x a week in a small group or individual basis in addition to the CORE program outside the classroom.** **Strategies/Activities for Syntactics:** • Teacher will routinely tape record the student's speech and review errors with student. • Student will point out his own errors after the conversation has been taped. • Student will construct sentences verbally and in written form that have correct subject-verb agreement. • Student will demonstrate acceptable and unacceptable speech by using complete/incomplete statements. • Teacher will make a list of common incomplete sentences used by the students. • Student will practice descriptive statements when speaking, describing objects, pictures, activities, etc. • Teacher will videotape the student and his classmates engaging in conversation. Student will critique the video tape. • Teacher will determine whether the student understands the difference between a statement and a question. Student will change statements into questions and questions into statements. • Teacher will plan a mystery activity and have the student come up with five "wh" questions pertaining to the activity.

Syntactics **Tier 3**	
• Teacher will demonstrate acceptable and unacceptable speech by using correct/incorrect word order. Student will critique the statements. • Teacher will make sure the student understands the different pronoun forms as they are used in sentences. Demonstrate through the use of objects, pictures and written sentences.	

Programs & Products for Language Processing (See Appendix C for web sites) pg. 1 of 1

Product	Publisher	Tier	Type	Pragmatics	Semantics	Syntax
100% Grammar	Lingui Systems	2,3	Supplemental			x
Grammar for the Real World	Knowledge Adventure	2,3	Software		x	
Grammar Interactive	Lingui Systems	2,3	Software		x	x
HELP 2	Lingui Systems	2,3	Supplemental	x	x	x
HELP 3	Lingui Systems	2,3	Supplemental	x	x	x
HELP 4	Lingui Systems	2,3	Supplemental	x	x	x
HELP 5	Lingui Systems	2,3	Supplemental	x	x	x
HELP for Grammar	Lingui Systems	2,3	Supplemental		x	x
Just for Kids	Lingui Systems	2,3	Supplemental			x
Languagelinks	Laureate	1,2	Supplemental			x
Missing Links	Sunburst	2,3	Software		x	x
Prepositions	Laureate	1,2	Supplemental			x
Pronoun Perspective	Laureate	1,2	Supplemental			x
Question Structure	Lingui Systems	2,3	Supplemental			x
Sentence Structure Interactive	Lingui Systems	2,3	Software			x
Simple Sentence Structure	Laureate	1,2,	Supplemental			x
Social Language Training	Lingui Systems	2,3	Supplemental	x		
Social Lang. Behavior Interactive	Lingui Systems	2,3	Software	x		
Spotlight on Grammar	Lingui Systems	2,3	Supplemental		x	x
Spotlight on Social Skills	Lingui Systems	2,3	Supplemental	x		

CHAPTER 2

What Is Reading?

Reading is the understanding of how the symbols (letters) of written language represent the sounds of spoken language (phonemes). The critical prerequisites for recognizing the connection between letters and sounds are the skills that are learned through phonemic awareness and phonics. Students are able to associate specific letters and sounds and blend those letter-sounds to read words through the structured and sequential presentation of phonics. They begin to translate written words into spoken words through their increased knowledge of sound-symbol association. This sequential process leads to automaticity, which is achieved when students recognize words as whole units by sight. When they achieve automaticity in word recognition, they are able to read fluently. The key to comprehension is the ability to read with fluency which allows the students to make sense of text that is being read. This happens in the reader's mind and requires complex interaction between the reader and the text. The following two phases must occur.

Phase One—in the primary grades (K-3), when students learn the sequential process of reading, they move from phonemic awareness and letter-sound knowledge to automaticity and fluency. This first process must be completed by third grade otherwise the second phase cannot happen. If a student reads too slowly, that student cannot comprehend what is being read.

Phase Two—from fourth grade forward, students read to learn as they continue their academic career. They should be able to recognize sequence, identify cause and effect, compare and contrast, identify the main ideas and the supporting details, distinguish fact from opinion, predict, make inferences, and draw conclusions.

Key Characteristics of Reading Problems:

- Poor retrieval of letters and words
- Poor spelling skills
- Poor sound-symbol associative skills
- Poor ability to rhyme words
- Poor ability to segment words
- Poor ability to blend words together
- Difficulty discriminating the differences or likenesses between sounds/words
- Difficulty recognizing word families

- Difficulty with sequencing sounds into words
- Difficulty with phonics
- Difficulty understanding the accents in words
- Difficulty in sounding out words in syllables and multi-syllabic words
- Poor ability to distinguish the different sounds at the beginning, middle and end of words
- Difficulty separating words into their component parts and putting words from their component parts into whole words
- Difficulty with decoding and encoding words
- Difficulty reading text
- Poor sight word vocabulary
- Poor vocabulary
- Poor writing skills
- Difficulty "playing" with the language
- Slow fluency skills
- Poor comprehension ability
- Difficulty retrieving meaning of the text
- Poor listening skills
- Difficulty sequencing or retelling a story
- Difficulty identifying cause and effect from reading
- Difficulty comparing and contrasting ideas read
- Difficulty identifying fact from opinion
- Difficulty predicting ideas in reading
- Difficulty making inferences
- Difficulty drawing conclusions
- Difficulty creating visual images from reading

Areas of Reading: Phonemic Awareness

<table>
<tr><th>Phonemic Awareness: Awareness of Gross Differences</th><th>Phonemic Awareness: Awareness of Gross Differences Tier 1</th></tr>
<tr><td>Awareness of Gross Differences—involves both word and sound discrimination. Examples of reading problems in this area:
• Difficulty discriminating the differences between two sounds that are the same or different
• Difficulty discriminating the differences between two words that are the same or different
• Difficulty discriminating a sound difference given three sounds two of which are the same
• Difficulty discriminating the different word given three words, two of which are the same</td><td>Suggested Interventionist: General Education Teacher with consultation from the Special Education teacher/Speech Pathologist/ Reading Specialist

Suggested Session: small group explicit instruction within the CORE reading instruction program 2x a week within the classroom

Strategies/Activities for Awareness of Gross Differences:
• Student will discriminate between two sounds—same and different consonants.
• Student will discriminate between two sounds—same and different long vowels.
• Student will discriminate between two sounds—same and different short vowels.
• Student will discriminate between two words—same or different with the initial sounds being same or different.
• Student will discriminate between two words—same or different with the middle sounds being same or different.
• Student will discriminate between two words—same or different with the final sounds being same or different.</td></tr>
</table>

Phonemic Awareness: Awareness of Gross Differences Tier 2	Phonemic Awareness: Awareness of Gross Differences Tier 3
Suggested Interventionist: Speech Pathologist, Special Education Teacher, Reading Teacher **Suggested Session: 30 minutes 2 to 3x a week in small group or individual basis in addition to the CORE reading program within the classroom** **Strategies/Activities for Awareness of Gross Differences**: • Student will discriminate between three sounds—same or different consonants. • Student will discriminate between three sounds—same or different long vowels. • Student will discriminate between three sounds—same or different short vowels. • Student will discriminate between three words—two being the same and one being different within their initial sounds. • Student will discriminate between three words—two being the same and one being different within their medial sounds. • Student will discriminate between three words—two being the same and one being different within their final sounds.	**Suggested Interventionist: Speech Pathologist, Special Education Teacher, Reading Teacher** **Suggested Session: 60 minutes 5x a week in small group or individual basis in addition to the CORE reading program within the classroom outside the classroom** **Strategies/Activities for Awareness of Gross Differences:** • Student will discriminate between three sounds—same or different consonants. • Student will discriminate between three sounds—same or different long vowels. • Student will discriminate between three sounds—same or different short vowels. • Student will discriminate between three words—two being the same and one being different within their initial sounds. • Student will discriminate between three words—two being the same and one being different within their medial sounds. • Student will discriminate between three words—two being the same and one being different within their final sounds.

Phonemic Awareness: Awareness of Rhyme	Phonemic Awareness: Awareness of Rhyme Tier 1
Awareness of Rhyme—involves the ability to match words that rhyme. Examples of reading problems in this area: • Difficulty producing words that rhyme • Difficulty rhyming words in sentences and producing poems • Difficulty recognizing word families • Poor associations for sound recognition • Difficulty blending complex sounds and words in phonics	**Suggested Interventionist: General Education Teacher with consultation of the Special Education teacher/Speech Pathologist/ Reading Specialist** **Suggested Session: small group explicit instruction within the CORE reading instruction program 2x a week within the classroom** **Strategies/Activities for Awareness of Rhyme:** • Teacher will present two words that rhyme at the end. Student will indicate whether those words rhyme. • Teacher will present three words, two of which rhyme at the end. Student will pick out the two words that rhyme. • Teacher will present four words, three of which rhyme at the end. Student will pick out the two words that rhyme. • Teacher will present three words, two of which rhyme at the end. Student will pick out the word that does not rhyme.

Phonemic Awareness: Awareness of Rhyme Tier 2	Phonemic Awareness: Awareness of Rhyme Tier 3
Suggested Interventionist: Speech Pathologist, Special Education Teacher, Reading Specialist **Suggested Session: 30 minutes 2 to 3x a week in a small group or individual basis in addition to the CORE reading instruction program inside the classroom** **Strategies/Activities for Awareness of Rhyme:** • Teacher will present four words, three of which rhyme at the end. Student will pick out the word that does not rhyme. • Teacher will create sentences with words that rhyme. Teacher says a sentence with an animal name. Student will finish the sentence with a word that rhymes with the animal name. • Teacher will create sentences with words that rhyme. Teacher says sentences with the name of a toy in it. Student will finish the sentence with a word that rhymes with that name of a toy. • Teacher will create sentences with words that rhyme. Teacher says a sentence with the name of a body part in it. Student will finish the sentence with a word that rhymes with that name of the body part.	**Suggested Interventionist: Speech Pathologist, Special Education Teacher, Reading Specialist** **Suggested Session: 60 minutes 5x a week in a small group or individual basis in addition to the CORE reading instruction program outside the classroom** **Strategies/Activities for Awareness of Rhyme:** • Teacher will present four words, three of which rhyme at the end. Student will pick out the word that does not rhyme. • Teacher will create sentences with words that rhyme. Teacher says a sentence with an animal name. Student will finish the sentence with a word that rhymes with the animal name. • Teacher will create sentences with words that rhyme. Teacher says a sentence with the name of a toy in it. Student will finish the sentence with a word that rhymes with that name of a toy. • Teacher will create sentences with words that rhyme. Teacher says a sentence with the name of a body part in it. Student will finish the sentence with a word that rhymes with that name of the body part.

Phonemic Awareness: Segmenting Words Into Syllables	Phonemic Awareness: Segmenting Words into Syllables Tier 1
Segmenting Words Into Syllables—involves the ability to separate sounds in a word and the ability to hear separate syllables that form words from those sounds. Examples of reading problems in this area: • Difficulty with sequencing sounds into words • Difficulty in remembering phonics • Poor ability to read words in syllables • Difficulty understanding the accents in words • Difficulty sounding out words in syllables • Difficulty spelling multi-syllabic words	**Suggested Interventionist: General Education Teacher with consultation from Special Education teacher/Speech Pathologist** **Suggested Session: small group explicit instruction within the CORE reading instruction program 2x a week within the classroom** **Strategies/Activities for Segmenting Words into Syllables:** • Clapping syllables—Teacher will say words that have one to two syllables. Student will clap the syllables out. • Clapping syllables—Teacher will say words that have two to three syllables. Student will clap the number of syllables out. • Tapping syllables—Teacher will say words that have one to two syllables. Student will tap the syllables out. • Tapping syllables—Teacher will say words that have two to three syllables. Student will tap the number of syllables out. • Snapping syllables—Teacher will say words that have one to two syllables. Student will snap the number of syllables. • Snapping syllables—Teacher will say words that have two to three syllables. Student will snap the number of syllables. • Teacher will give student different colored counters or mini blocks. Student will place a counter or block on the table for every syllable he hears.

Phonemic Awareness: Segmenting Words into Syllables Tier 2	Phonemic Awareness: Segmenting Words into Syllables Tier 3
Suggested Interventionist: Speech Pathologist, Special Education Teacher, Reading Specialist **Suggested Session: 30 minutes 2 to 3x a week in a small group or individual basis in addition to the CORE reading instruction program inside the classroom** **Strategies/Activities for Segmenting Words Into Syllables:** • Clapping syllables—Teacher will say words that have one to two syllables. Student will clap the syllables out. • Clapping syllables—Teacher will say words that have two to three syllables. Student will clap the number of syllables out. • Tapping syllables—Teacher will say words that have one to two syllables. Student will tap the syllables out. • Tapping syllables—Teacher will say words that have two to three syllables. Student will tap the number of syllables out. • Snapping syllables–Teacher will say words that have one to two syllables. Student will snap the number of syllables. • Snapping syllables—Teacher will say words that have two to three syllables. Student will snap the number of syllables. • Teacher will give student different colored counters or mini blocks. Student will place a counter or block on the table for every syllable he hears.	**Suggested Interventionist: Speech Pathologist, Special Education Teacher, Reading Specialist** **Suggested Session: 60 minutes 5x a week in a small group or individual basis in addition to the CORE reading instruction program outside the classroom** **Strategies/Activities for Segmenting Words Into Syllables:** • Clapping syllables—Teacher will say words that have one to two syllables. Student will clap the syllables out. • Clapping syllables—Teacher will say words that have two to three syllables. Student will clap the number of syllables out. • Tapping syllables—Teacher will say words that have one to two syllables. Student will tap the syllables out. • Tapping syllables—Teacher will say words that have two to three syllables. Student will tap the number of syllables out. • Snapping syllables–Teacher will say words that have one to two syllables. Student will snap the number of syllables. • Snapping syllables—Teacher will say words that have two to three syllables. Student will snap the number of syllables. • Teacher will give student different colored counters or mini blocks. Student will place a counter or block on the table for every syllable he hears.

Phonemic Awareness: Awareness of Consonant Segments	Phonemic Awareness: Awareness of Consonant Segments Tier 1
Awareness of Consonant Segments—involves the ability to isolate sounds in the beginning and ending of words. Examples of reading problems in this area: • Difficulty recognizing words that are different when listening to words that have different initial consonants • Difficulty recognizing words that are different when listening to words that have different final consonants • Difficulty rhyming words • Difficulty focusing on the differences between words presented • Difficulty with sound-symbol relationships	**Suggested Interventionist: General Education Teacher with consultation from the Special Education Teacher/Speech Pathologist/ Reading Specialist** **Suggested Session: small group explicit instruction within the CORE reading instruction program 2x a week within the classroom** **Strategies/activities for Awareness of Consonant Segments and Medial Short Vowel Sounds:** • Teacher will present a targeted sound. Teacher will give two words with different initial consonant sounds. Student will identify the word that matches the target sound. • Teacher will present a targeted sound. Teacher will give three words with different initial consonant sounds. Student will identify the word that matches the target sound • Teacher will present a targeted short vowel sound in the medial position. Teacher will give two words with different medial short vowel sounds. Student will identify the word that matches the target medial sound. • Teacher will present a targeted short vowel sound in the medial position. Teacher will give three words with different medial short vowel sounds. Student will identify the word that matches the target medial sound. • Teacher will present a targeted consonant sound in the final position. Teacher will give two/three words with different final consonant sounds. Student will identify the word that matches the target final consonant sound.

Phonemic Awareness: Awareness of Consonant Segments Tier 2	Phonemic Awareness: Awareness of Consonant Segments Tier 2
Suggested Interventionist: Speech Pathologist, Special Education Teacher, Reading Specialist **Suggested Session: 30 minutes 2 to 3x a week in a small group or individual basis in addition to the CORE reading instruction program inside the classroom** **Strategies/Activities for Awareness of Consonant Segments and Medial Short Vowel Sounds:** • Teacher will present a targeted sound. Teacher will give two words with different initial consonant sounds. Student will identify the word that matches the target sound. • Teacher will present a targeted sound. Teacher will give three words with different initial consonant sounds. Student will identify the word out of the three words that matches the target sound. • Teacher will present a targeted sound. Teacher will give four words with different initial consonant sounds on three of the words. Student will identify one word out of the four words that matches the target sound. • Teacher will present a targeted short vowel sound in the medial position. Teacher will give two words with different medial short vowel sounds. Student will identify the word that matches the target medial sound. • Teacher will present a targeted short vowel sound in the medial position. Teacher will give three words with different medial short vowel sounds. Student will identify the word that matches the target medial sound.	• Teacher will present a targeted short vowel sound in the medial position. Teacher will give four words with different medial short vowel sounds. Student will identify the word that matches the target medial sound. • Teacher will present a targeted consonant sound in the final position. Teacher will give two words with different final consonant sounds. Student will identify the word that matches the target final consonant sound. • Teacher will present a targeted consonant sound in the final position. Teacher will give three words with different final consonant sounds. Student will identify the word that matches the target final consonant sound. • Teacher will present a targeted consonant sound in the final position. Teacher will give four words with different final consonant sounds. Student will identify the word that matches the target final consonant sound.

Phonemic Awareness: Awareness of Consonant Segments Tier 3	Phonemic Awareness: Awareness of Consonant Segments Tier 3
Suggested Interventionist: Speech Pathologist, Special Education Teacher, Reading Specialist **Suggested Session: 60 minutes 5x a week in a small group or individual basis in addition to the CORE reading instruction program outside the classroom** **Strategies/Activities for Awareness of Consonant Segments and Medial Short Vowel Sounds:** • Teacher will present a targeted sound. Teacher will give two words with different initial consonant sounds. Student will identify the word that matches the target sound. • Teacher will present a targeted sound. Teacher will give three words with different initial consonant sounds. Student will identify one word out of the three words that matches the target sound. • Teacher will present a targeted sound. Teacher will give four words with different initial consonant sound on three of the words. Student will identify one word out of the four words that matches the target sound. • Teacher will present a targeted short vowel sound in the medial position. Teacher will give two words with different medial short vowel sounds. Student will identify the word that matches the target medial sound. • Teacher will present a targeted short vowel sound in the medial position. Teacher will give three words with different medial short vowel sounds. Student will identify one word that matches the target medial sound.	• Teacher will present a targeted short vowel sound in the medial position. Teacher will give four words with different medial short vowel sounds. Student will identify one word that matches the target medial sound. • Teacher will present a targeted consonant sound in the final position. Teacher will give two words with different final consonant sounds. Student will identify one word that matches the target final consonant sound. • Teacher will present a targeted consonant sound in the final position. Teacher will give three words with different final consonant sounds. Student will identify one word that matches the target final consonant sound. • Teacher will present a targeted consonant sound in the final position. Teacher will give four words with different final consonant sounds. Student will identify one word that matches the target final consonant sound.

Phonemic Awareness: Awareness of Alliteration	Phonemic Awareness: Awareness of Alliteration Tier 1
Awareness of Alliteration—involves the ability to "play" with the language. Student must be able to recognize the beginning of words and know when those words begin with the same sound. Examples of reading problems in this area: • Inadequate sound/symbol associative skills • Difficulty discriminating different and same sounds • Problems in decoding words for reading • Difficulty decoding words for spelling and writing	**Suggested Interventionist: General Education Teacher with consultation from the Special Education Teacher/Speech Pathologist/ Reading Specialist** **Suggested Session: small group explicit instruction within the CORE reading instruction program 2x a week within the classroom** **Strategies/Activities for Awareness of Alliteration:** • Teacher will give a two-word sequence with the identical consonant sound in the initial position. Student will present a third word with the same initial consonant sound. • Teacher will give a three-word sequence with the identical consonant sound in the initial position. Student will present a fourth word with the same initial consonant sound. • Teacher will give a two-word nonsense sequence with the identical consonant sound in the initial position. Student will present a third word with the same initial consonant sound. • Teacher will give a three-word sequence with the identical consonant sound in the initial position. Student will present a fourth word with the same initial consonant sound.

Phonemic Awareness: Awareness of Alliteration Tier 2	Phonemic Awareness: Awareness of Alliteration Tier 3
Suggested Interventionist: Speech Pathologist, Special Education Teacher, Reading Specialist **Suggested Session: 30 minutes 2 to 3x a week in a small group or individual basis in addition to the CORE reading instruction program inside the class** **Strategies/Activities for Awareness of Alliteration:** • Teacher will give a two-word nonsense sequence with the identical consonant sound in the initial position. Student will present a third word with the same initial consonant sound. • Teacher will give a three-word sequence with the identical consonant sound in the initial position. Student will present a fourth word with the same initial consonant sound. • Teacher will give a two-word sequence with the identical consonant sound in the initial position. Student will present a third word with the same initial consonant sound. • Teacher will give a three-word sequence with the identical consonant sound in the initial position. Student will present a fourth word with the same initial consonant sound.	**Suggested Interventionist: Speech Pathologist, Special Education Teacher, Reading Specialist** **Suggested Session: 60 minutes 5x a week in a small group or individual basis in addition to the CORE reading instruction program outside the classroom** **Strategies/Activities for Awareness of Alliteration:** • Teacher will give a two-word sequence with the identical consonant sound in the initial position. Student will present a third word with the same initial consonant sound. • Teacher will give a three-word sequence with the identical consonant sound in the initial position. Student will present a fourth word with the same initial consonant sound. • Teacher will give a two-word nonsense sequence with the identical consonant sound in the initial position. Student will present a third word with the same initial consonant sound. • Teacher will give a three-word sequence with the identical consonant sound in the initial position. Student will present a fourth word with the same initial consonant sound. • Teacher will give a two-word sequence with the identical consonant sound in the initial position. Student will present a third word with the same initial consonant sound.

Phonemic Awareness: Segmentation of Onset and Rhyme	Phonemic Awareness: Segmentation of Onset and Rhyme Tier 1
Segmentation of Onset and Rhyme—involves the ability to blend words. Examples of reading problems in this area: • Difficulty in segmenting individual phonemes • Difficulty discriminating different and same sounds • Difficulty in decoding words for reading and spelling • Difficulty separating words into their component parts and put words in their component parts into whole words	**Suggested Interventionist: General Education Teacher with consultation from the Special Education Teacher/Speech Pathologist/ Reading Specialist** **Suggested Session: small group explicit instruction within the CORE reading instruction program 2x a week within the classroom** **Strategies/Activities for Segmentation of Onset and Rhyme:** • Teacher will present two words, one of which has an additional letter in the initial position. Student will repeat the two words and identify the sound that is different in the larger word. Student will identify the sound that is eliminated from the first word in order to form the second word. • Teacher will present three words that have the same word family. Two words have an additional letter in the initial position. Student will be asked to repeat the words and identify the sounds that are different. • Teacher will say a word. Student will isolate the first consonant sound of the word from the rest of the word. Student will segment the one syllable word. • Teacher will say a word. Student will isolate the first consonant blend of the word from the rest of the word.

Phonemic Awareness: Segmentation of Onset and Rhyme Tier 2	Phonemic Awareness: Segmentation of Onset and Rhyme Tier 3
Suggested Interventionist: Speech Pathologist, Special Education Teacher, Reading Specialist **Suggested Session: 30 minutes 2 to 3x a week in a small group or individual basis in addition to the CORE reading instruction program inside the class** **Strategies/Activities for Segmentation of Onset and Rhyme:** • Teacher will present with two words, one of which has an additional letter in the initial position. Student will repeat the two words and identify the sound that is different in the larger word. Student will identify the sound that is eliminated from the first word in order to form the second word. • Teacher will present three words. The three words have the same word family. Two words have an additional letter in the initial position. Student will repeat the words and identify the sounds that are different. • Teacher will say a word. Student will isolate the first consonant sound of the word from the rest of the word. Student will segment the one syllable word. • Teacher will say a word. Student will isolate the first consonant blend from the rest of the word.	**Suggested Interventionist: Speech Pathologist, Special Education Teacher, Reading Specialist** **Suggested Session: 60 minutes 5x a week in a small group or individual basis in addition to the CORE reading instruction program outside the classroom** **Strategies/Activities for Segmentation of Onset and Rhyme:** • Teacher will present with two words, one of which has an additional letter in the initial position. Student will repeat the two words and identify the sound that is different in the larger word. Student will identify the sound that is eliminated from the first word in order to form the second word. • Teacher will present three words. The three words have the same word family. Two words have an additional letter in the initial position. Student will repeat the words and identify the sounds that are different. • Teacher will say a word. Student will isolate the first consonant sound of the word from the rest of the word. Student will segment the one syllable word. • Teacher will say a word. Student will isolate the first consonant blend from the rest of the word.

Phonemic Awareness: Phoneme Segmentation	Phonemic Awareness: Phoneme Segmentation Tier 1
Phoneme Segmentation—involves the ability of a student to segment a syllable into its component phonemes. Examples of reading problems in this area: • Difficulty in decoding words • Difficulty in spelling words • Difficulty in discriminating the beginning of words • Difficulty in discriminating the endings of words	**Suggested Interventionist: General Education Teacher with consultation from the Special Education Teacher/Speech Pathologist/ Reading Specialist** **Suggested Session: small group explicit instruction within the CORE reading instruction program 2x a week within the classroom** **Strategies/Activities for Phoneme Segmentation:** • Teacher will twice present a word that has a consonant, long vowel and consonant sound. The first time the teacher says the word quickly. The second time the teacher says the word slowly saying the individual sounds. Student will repeat the word quickly and then slowly in parts. • Teacher will present a one-syllable word twice that has a long vowel sound first and a consonant sound second. The first time the teacher says it quickly; the second time slowly saying the individual sounds. Student will repeat the word quickly and then slowly in parts. • Teacher will present a one-syllable word that has a short vowel and a consonant. The first time the teacher says the word quickly; the second time slowly saying the individual sounds. Student will repeat the word quickly and then slowly in parts. • Teacher will present two one-syllable words. Student will count the number of sounds. Student will be given chips to place in front of him for the number of phonemes that are in each word. Student will compare the two words and show that one word has more phonemes than the other.

Phonemic Awareness: Phoneme Segmentation Tier 2	Phonemic Awareness: Phoneme Segmentation Tier 3
Suggested Interventionist: Speech Pathologist, Special Education Teacher, Reading Specialist **Suggested Session: 30 minutes 2 to 3x a week in a small group or individual basis in addition to the CORE reading instruction program inside the class** **Strategies/Activities for Phoneme Segmentation:** • Teacher will present a word that has a consonant, long vowel and consonant sound twice. The first time the teacher says the word quickly. The second time the teacher says the word slowly saying the individual sounds. Student will repeat the word quickly and then slowly in parts. • Teacher will present a one syllable word twice that has a long vowel sound first and a consonant sound second. The first time the teacher says it quickly; the second time slowly saying the individual sounds. Student will repeat the word quickly and then slowly in parts. • Teacher will present a one syllable word that has a short vowel and a consonant. The first time the teacher says the word quickly; the second time slowly saying the individual sounds. Student will repeat the word quickly and then slowly in parts. • Teacher will present two one syllable words. Student will count the number of sounds. Student will be given chips to place in front of him for the number of phonemes that are in each word. Student will compare the two words and show that one word has more phonemes than the other.	**Suggested Interventionist: Speech Pathologist, Special Education Teacher, Reading Specialist** **Suggested Session: 60 minutes 5x a week in a small group or individual basis in addition to the CORE reading instruction program outside the classroom** **Strategies/Activities for Phoneme Segmentation:** • Teacher will present a word that has a consonant, long vowel and consonant sound twice. The first time the teacher says the word quickly; the second time the teacher says the word slowly saying the individual sounds. Student will repeat the word quickly and then slowly in parts. • Teacher will present a one syllable word twice that has a long vowel sound first and a consonant sound second. The first time the teacher says it quickly; the second time slowly saying the individual sounds. Student will repeat the word quickly and then slowly in parts. • Teacher will present a one syllable word that has a short vowel and a consonant. The first time the teacher says the word quickly; the second time slowly saying the individual sounds. Student will repeat the word quickly and then slowly in parts. • Teacher will present two one syllable words. Student will count the number of sounds. Student will be given chips to place in front of him for the number of phonemes that are in each word. Student will compare the two words and show that one word has more phonemes than the other.

Phonemic Awareness: Blending of Syllables and Phonemes	Phonemic Awareness: Blending of Syllables and Phonemes Tier 1
Blending of Syllables and Phonemes—involves the ability of a student to separate words into syllables or words into individual sounds and blend those sounds. This ability also is necessary in order to spell words. Examples of reading problems in this area: • Difficulty decoding words • Difficulty spelling words • Difficulty reading text • Difficulty with sound/symbol associative skills	**Suggested Interventionist: General Education Teacher with consultation from the Special Education Teacher/Speech Pathologist/ Reading Specialist** **Suggested Session: small group explicit instruction within the CORE reading instruction program 2x a week within the classroom** **Strategies/Activities for Blending of Syllables and Phonemes:** • Teacher will separate two syllable words into two separate parts. Students will listen to the words in separate syllables and say the word at normal speech speed. • Teacher will separate three syllable words into three separate parts. Student will listen to the words in separate syllables and say the word at normal speech speed. • Teacher will name a category such a number or a color. Teacher will say a sentence incorporating the color or number but say the color or number in individual phoneme. Teacher will start with three phoneme words. Student will tell the teacher what the whole word is. • Teacher will name a category such as a fruit or animal. Teacher will say a sentence incorporating the fruit or animal but say the fruit or animal in its individual phoneme. Teacher will start with four phoneme words. Student will tell the teacher what the whole word is.

Phonemic Awareness: Blending of Syllables and Phonemes Tier 2	Phonemic Awareness: Blending of Syllables and Phonemes Tier 3
Suggested Interventionist: Speech Pathologist, Special Education Teacher, Reading Specialist **Suggested Session: 30 minutes 2 to 3x a week in a small group or individual basis in addition to the CORE reading instruction program inside the class** **Strategies/Activities for Blending of Syllables and Phonemes:** • Teacher will separate two syllable words into two separate parts. Student will listen to the words in separate syllables and say what the word really is at normal speech speed. • Teacher will separate three syllable words into three separate parts. Student will listen to the words in separate syllables and say what the word really is at normal speech speed. • Teacher will name a category such a number or a color. Teacher will say a sentence incorporating the color or number but say the color or number in individual phoneme. Teacher will start with three phoneme words. Student will tell the teacher what the whole word is. • Teacher will name a category such as a fruit or animal. Teacher will say a sentence incorporating the fruit or animal but say the fruit or animal in its individual phoneme. Teacher will start with four phoneme words. Student will tell the teacher what the whole word is.	**Suggested Interventionist: Speech Pathologist, Special Education Teacher, Reading Specialist** **Suggested Session: 60 minutes 5x a week in a small group or individual basis in addition to the CORE reading instruction program outside the classroom** **Strategies/Activities for Blending of Syllables and Phonemes:** • Teacher will separate two syllable words into two separate parts. Student will listen to the words in separate syllables and say what the word really is at normal speech speed. • Teacher will separate three syllable words into three separate parts. Student will listen to the words in separate syllables and say what the word really is at normal speech speed. • Teacher will name a category such a number or a color. Teacher will say a sentence incorporating the color or number but say the color or number in individual phoneme. Teacher will start with three phoneme words. Student will tell the teacher what the whole word is. • Teacher will name a category such as a fruit or animal. Teacher will say a sentence incorporating the fruit or animal but say the fruit or animal in its individual phoneme. Teacher will start with four phoneme words. Student will tell the teacher what the whole word is.

Phonemic Awareness: Phoneme Manipulation	Phonemic Awareness: Phoneme Manipulation Tier 1
Phoneme Manipulation—enables a student to segment and blend words efficiently. Student should be able to add, delete, substitute and switch sounds in words. Examples of reading problems in this area: • Difficulty in decoding words • Difficulty in spelling words • Difficulty in reading text • Difficulty in sound/symbol associative skills • Difficulty in discrimination of like/differences in words	**Suggested Interventionist: General Education Teacher with consultation from the Special Education Teacher/Speech Pathologist/ Reading Specialist** **Suggested Session: small group explicit instruction within the CORE reading instruction program 2x a week within the classroom** **Strategies/activities for Phoneme Manipulation:** • Teacher will say a one-syllable word and then will add a sound to the beginning of the word which completely changes the word. Student will say the word that is formed after the new sound is added. • Teacher will say a one-syllable word and then will add a sound to the end of that word which completely changes the word. Student will say the word that is formed after the new sound is added. • Teacher will say a one-syllable word and then will delete a sound at the beginning, which completely changes the word. Student will say the word that is formed after the sound is deleted. • Teacher will say a one-syllable word and then will delete a sound at the end of that word which completely changes the word. Student will say the word that is formed after the sound is deleted. • Teacher will say a one-syllable word and then will change the short vowel in the middle of the word which completely changes the word. Student will say the word that is formed after the sound is changed. • Teacher will say a one-syllable word and then will change the long vowel sound in the middle of the word which completely changes the word. Student will say the word that is formed after the sound is changed.

Phonemic Awareness: Phoneme Manipulation Tier 2	Phonemic Awareness: Phoneme Manipulation Tier 2
Suggested Interventionist: Speech Pathologist, Special Education Teacher, Reading Specialist **Suggested Session: 30 minutes 2 to 3x a week in a small group or individual basis in addition to the CORE reading instruction program inside the class** **Strategies/Activities for Phoneme Manipulation:** • Teacher will say a one syllable word and then will add a sound to the beginning of a word which completely changes the word. Student will say the word that is formed after the new sound is added. • Teacher will say a one syllable word and then will add a sound to the end of that word which completely changes the word. Student will say the word that is formed after the new sound is added. • Teacher will say a one-syllable word and then will delete a sound at the beginning, which completely changes the word. Student will say the word that is formed after the sound is deleted. • Teacher will say a one-syllable word and then will delete a sound at the end of that word which completely changes the word. Student will say the word that is formed after the sound is deleted. • Teacher will say a one-syllable word and then will change the short vowel in the middle of the word which completely changes the word. Student will say the word that is formed after the sound is changed.	• Teacher will say a one-syllable word and then will change the long vowel sound in the middle of the word which completely changes the word. Student will say the word that is formed after the sound is changed. • Teacher will repeat all of the above activities using different colored tokens or counters to represent the individual phonemes in order to manipulate the different sounds. • Teacher will give student colored tokens. Teacher will then say two words. There is one sound that is different between the two words but the same number of phonemes. Student will use different colored tokens to correspond to different sounds. Student will point to the token that represents the different sound between the two words. • Student will use colored tokens to represent the different sounds in the words presented. Teacher will say two words that have the same middle sounds. The second word spoken by the teacher represents the first and last sound switched. Student will listen to the second word and move their tokens to show how the sounds change position.

Phonemic Awareness: Phoneme Manipulation Tier 3	Phonemic Awareness: Phoneme Manipulation Tier 3
Suggested Interventionist: Speech Pathologist, Special Education Teacher, Reading Specialist **Suggested Session: 60 minutes 5x a week in a small group or individual basis in addition to the CORE reading instruction program outside the classroom** **Strategies/Activities for Phoneme Manipulation:** • Teacher will say a one-syllable word and then will add a sound to the beginning of a word which completely changes the word. Student will say the word that is formed after the new sound is added. • Teacher will say a one-syllable word and then will add a sound to the end of that word which completely changes the word. Student will say the word that is formed after the new sound is added. • Teacher will say a one-syllable word and then will delete a sound at the beginning, which completely changes the word. Student will say the word that is formed after the sound is deleted. • Teacher will say a one-syllable word and then will delete a sound at the end of that word which completely changes the word. Student will say the word that is formed after the sound is deleted. • Teacher will say a one-syllable word and then will change the short vowel in the middle of the word which completely changes the word. Student will say the word that is formed after the sound is changed. • Teacher will say a one-syllable word and then will change the long vowel sound in the middle of the word which completely changes the word. Student will say the word that is formed after the sound is changed.	• Teacher will repeat all of the above activities using different colored tokens or counters to represent the individual phonemes in order to manipulate the different sounds. • Teacher will give student colored tokens and then will say two words. There is one sound that is different between the two words but the same number of phonemes. Students will use different colored tokens to correspond to different sounds. Students will point to the token that represents the different sound between the two words. • Student will use colored tokens to represent the different sounds in the words presented. Teacher will say two words that have the same middle sounds. The second word spoken by the teacher represents the first and last sound switched. Student will listen to the second word and move their tokens to show how the sounds change position.

Area of Reading: Phonics

Phonics: Letter-Naming Skills	Phonics: Letter-Naming Skills Tier 1
Letter-Naming Skills—enables a student to understand the alphabetic principle. It is an awareness that letters have something to do with written language; ability to recognize and name letters; realization that letters stand for sounds, and that letters from left to right in a printed word represent the sounds from beginning to end. Examples of reading problems in this area: • Difficulty with sound/symbol association • Difficulty decoding words • Difficulty developing a sight words • Difficulty discriminating the same/different letters **Accommodations and Modifications:** • Color highlighting • Use reading partners • Use objects and pictures for letter recognition • Use animated presentation of mnemonic clues for letter names • Use of index cards • Review frequently • Use rules of the English Language • Read assignments orally to student • Allow student to read out loud • Use assistive technology • Use word banks • Color code sound and word patterns	**Suggested Interventionist: General Education Teacher with consultation from the Special Education Teacher/Speech Pathologist/ Reading Specialist** **Suggested Session: small group explicit instruction within the CORE reading instruction program 2x a week within the classroom** **Strategies/Activities to develop Letter-Naming Skills:** • Teacher will prepare a sheet consisting of a group of letters. One letter in each group will be different. Student will circle the letter that is different and name the letter. • Teacher will name a letter that the student is to find in his magazine. Student will circle as many different sizes or styles of the designated letter found within a magazine. • Teacher will cut various size letters from different colored papers. Student will sort the same letters together. Student will select which letter is different either by shape or color or both and name the letter. • Teacher will group four of the same letter and one different letter in a row. Student will select which letter is different and name the letter. • Student will use letter cards and letter tiles to verbalize the new letters. • Student will trace letters on cards, sand paper and sand. • Student will make letters with different materials such as clay, play dough, etc.

Phonics: Letter-Naming Skills Tier 2	Phonics: Letter-Naming Skills Tier 3
Suggested Interventionist: Speech Pathologist, Special Education Teacher, Reading Specialist **Suggested Session: 30 minutes 2 to 3x a week in a small group or individual basis in addition to the CORE reading instruction program inside the class** **Strategies/Activities for Letter-Naming Skills:** • Teacher will name a letter that the student is to find in his magazine. Student will circle as many different sizes or styles of the designated letter found within a magazine. • Teacher will cut various size letters from different colored papers. Student will sort the same letters. Student will name the letter that is different either by shape or color or both and name the letter. • Teacher will group four of the same letter and one different letter in a row. Student will select which letter is different and name the letter. • Student will sort various letters into different egg carton sections according to size, color and shape or object. Student will name the letter in each section. • Teacher will create a range of bead letter patterns. Student will be asked to copy the patterns and name the letters while copying the pattern.	**Suggested Interventionist: Speech Pathologist, Special Education Teacher, Reading Specialist** **Suggested Session: 60 minutes 5x a week in a small group or individual basis in addition to the CORE reading instruction program outside the classroom** **Strategies/Activities for Letter-Naming Skills:** • Teacher will name a letter that the student is to find in his magazine. Student will circle as many different sizes or styles of the designated letter found within a magazine. • Teacher will cut various size letters from different colored papers. Student will sort the same letters. Student will name the letter that is different either by shape or color or both and name the letter. • Teacher will group four of the same letter and one different letter in a row. Student will select which letter is different and name the letter. • Student will sort various letters into different egg carton sections according to size, color and shape or object. Student will name the letter in each section. • Teacher will create a range of bead letter patterns. Student will copy the patterns and name the letters while copying them.

Phonics: Letter-Sound Correspondence Skills	Phonics: Letter-Sound Correspondence Skills Tier 1
Letter-Sound Correspondence Skills- involves the ability to match the corresponding sound of a letter with that letter. This skill combines the ability to use phonemic awareness and phonics in reading and spelling. Examples of reading problems within this skill area: • Difficulty segmenting letter-sound activities • Difficulty blending phonemes into words • Difficulty manipulating phonemes into words • Difficulty playing with words by adding • Difficulty decoding and encoding words • Difficulty reading words in text • Difficulty reading and writing sentences or paragraphs **Accommodations and Modifications:** • Color highlighting • Use objects and pictures for sound recognition • Use of index cards and review frequently • Use animated presentation of mnemonic clues for consonants, short vowels, blends, diphthongs, digraphs, controlled r sounds • Read assignments orally to student • Books on tape • Allow student to read out loud • Use computer program that student • Use rules of the English language • Color code sound and word patterns • Use assistive technology programs	**Suggested Interventionist: General Education Teacher with consultation from the Special Education Teacher/Speech Pathologist** **Suggested Session: small group explicit instruction within the CORE reading instruction program 2x a week within the classroom** **Strategies/Activities for Letter-Sound Correspondence:** • **Segmentation**—Teacher will say a word (cvc) and repeat the same word saying the individual sounds of the letters. Teacher will show the letter that corresponds to the sound. Student will repeat the individual sounds while pointing to the corresponding letters. • **Blending Sounds**—Teacher will show letters to the student and ask the student to say each individual corresponding sound of the letters presented. The letters shown spell out a word. Student will look at the letters that spell the word and say the sounds quickly. • **Manipulating Phonemes**— —**Adding Letter/Sound**—Teacher will spell a word. Student and teacher read it together. Teacher will add a letter (either in the beginning or end of the word). Student will read the new word. —**Deleting Letter/Sounds**—Teacher will spell a word. Student and teacher will read it together. Teacher will take a letter away (from the beginning, end or middle of the word). Student will read the new word.

Phonics- Letter-Sound Correspondence Skills Tier 1	Phonics: Letter-Sound Correspondence Skills Tier 2
—**Substituting Letter/Sound**—Teacher will spell a new word. Teacher will change a letter in the new word to spell a new word. Student will sound out the new word and read it. —**Rearranging Letter/Sound**—Teacher will show some letters. Student will tell the teacher the sound of each independent letter. Teacher will arrange the letters into a word. Student will say the word. Teacher will rearrange the letters to form another word. Student will then say the new word.	**Suggested Interventionist: Speech Pathologist, Special Education Teacher, Reading Specialist** **Suggested Session: 30 minutes 2 to 3x a week in a small group or individual basis in addition to the CORE reading instruction program inside the class** **Strategies/Activities for Letter-Sound Correspondence:** • **Visual Sound Presentation:** Teacher will present sound cards visually for the student to recognize and say. Sounds will be presented individually and the teacher will follow a prescribed sequence of sounds. • **Auditory/Kinesthetic Presentation:** Teacher will say the sounds. Student repeats the sound and writes the letter down on a piece of paper. • **Sounds are taught within a sequence and one at a time.** After each sound is taught, the sound will be added to the previous sounds and reviewed together during the Visual Sound Presentation. • **Visual Word Presentation:** Teacher will present the word cards that follow the sequence of sounds visually and the student will read each word. These words will have only one new sound in them and is a review of the previously taught sounds. • **Auditory/Kinesthetic Presentation:** Teacher will dictate the words. Student will repeat the words and will write them on a piece of paper. • **Visual Presentation of Phrases:** Phrases will be presented visually by the teacher for the student to read.

Phonics: Letter-Sound Correspondence Skills Tier 2	Phonics: Letter-Sound Correspondence Skills Tier 3
• **Auditory/Kinesthetic Presentation:** Teacher will dictate the phrases to the student. Student will repeat the phrase and write it down. • **Visual Presentation of Sentences:** Teacher will show the sentences to the student and the student will read the sentences out loud. • **Auditory/Kinesthetic Presentation:** Teacher will dictate the sentences to the student. Student will repeat the sentence and write the sentence down on a piece of paper. • Teacher will present all sounds in the above sequence until all consonants, short vowels, blends, dipthongs, digraphs, controlled /r/ sounds and double vowel teams are learned.	**Suggested Interventionist: Speech Pathologist, Special Education Teacher, Reading Specialist** **Suggested Session: 60 minutes 5x a week in a small group or individual basis in addition to the CORE reading instruction program outside the classroom** **Strategies/Activities for Letter-Sound Correspondence:** • **Visual Sound Presentation:** Teacher will present sound cards visually for the student to recognize and say. Sounds will be presented individually and the teacher will follow a prescribed sequence of sounds. • **Auditory/Kinesthetic Presentation:** Teacher will say the sounds. Student repeats the sound and writes the letter down on a piece of paper. • **Sounds are taught within a sequence and one at a time.** After each sound is taught, the sound will be added to the previous sounds and reviewed together during the Visual Sound Presentation. • **Visual Word Presentation:** Teacher will present the word cards that follow the sequence of sounds visually and the student will read each word. These words will have only one new sound in them and is a review of the previously taught sounds. • **Auditory/Kinesthetic Presentation:** Teacher will dictate the words. Student will repeat the words and will write them on a piece of paper. • **Visual Presentation of Phrases:** Phrases will be presented visually by the teacher for the student to read.

Phonics: Letter-Sound Correspondence Skills Tier 3	Phonics: Word Study
• **Auditory/Kinesthetic Presentation:** Teacher will dictate the phrases to the student. Student will repeat the phrase and write it down. • **Visual Presentation of Sentences:** Teacher will show the sentences to the student and the student will read the sentences out loud. • **Auditory/Kinesthetic Presentation:** Teacher will dictate the sentences to the student. Student will repeat the sentence and write the sentence down on a piece of paper. • Teacher will present all sounds in the above sequence until all consonants, short vowels, blends, dipthongs , digraphs, controlled r sounds and double vowel teams are learned.	**Word Study**—is the automatic recognition of high frequency words. It is the ability to decode regular words quickly and accurately, using spelling patterns and orthographic units which in turn allow student to process the meaning of what they are reading. Students build their sight-word vocabulary as well as develop word recognition. Examples of reading problems within this skill area: • Difficulty decoding words • Difficulty spelling words • Difficulty reading words in text • Difficulty writing sentences or paragraph correctly • Difficulty visually recognizing words such as sight words • Difficulty using context clues in reading • Difficulty recognizing words by their visual outline. **Accommodations and Modifications:** • Review new vocabulary • Color highlighting • Use reading partners/ students read out loud • Illustrate vocabulary • Use objects and pictures for word chunk recognition • Color code sound and word patterns • Use word banks • Use Word Walls with word families • Read assignments orally to student • Use rules of the English Language • Use technology programs

Phonics: Word Study Tier 1	Phonics: Word Study Tier 2
Suggested Interventionist: General Education Teacher with consultation from the Special Education Teacher and the Reading Specialist. **Suggested Session: small group, explicit instruction 2x a week within the CORE reading program within the classroom.** **Strategies/Activities for Word Study:** • Teacher will introduce words that have the same outline as other words for memorization. • Teacher will introduce on 3x5 same colored cards sight words repetitively several times a day. Student will write their own same color cards. Student will write the sight words on different surfaces to help memory. • Teacher will create a Word Wall with different word families written on the charts. Student will create his own Word Wall as he learns the different words within the word family one word by one word. • Student will sort words by vowel teams and say the words as they are sorted. • Student will play word games with different word families or familiar "chunks" of words. • Teacher will create a Language Experience Chart. • Teacher will use a K-W-L Charts using words from core subject areas such as Social Studies and Science. • Teacher will facilitate Literacy Centers with word sorts, reread books, write responses to stories, Guided Reading. • Teacher will conduct Choral Reading.	**Suggested Interventionist: Speech Pathologist; Sp. Ed. Teacher; Reading Specialist** **Suggested Session: 30 minutes 2 to 3x a week in a small group or individual basis in addition to the CORE reading instruction program inside the class** **Strategies/activities for Word Study:** • Teacher will introduce different kinds of letter chunks and spelling patterns: such as commonly occurring word stems (-et, -ake,); endings (/-s/, /-ed/, /-ing/, /-er/, /-est/); suffixes and prefixes and root words. • Teacher will introduce the importance of context clues to help in decoding an unfamiliar word. • Teacher will create a Word Wall with contractions, spelling demons, homophones. Teacher will include pictures of the words next to the words. • Teacher will visually introduce words to the student. Students will write sentences on the subsequent days for the student to reread the words in a different format. • Teacher will play concentration with syllables that make up two syllable compound words. Students will play a game such as Concentration. • Teacher will introduce the /-ck/, /-tch/, /-dge/ rule and will create words with the rule and the endings. • Teacher will create Word Walls with words that have silent letters in them.

Phonics: Word Study Tier 2	**Phonics: Word Study Tier 3**
• Teacher will give a combination of letters to the student in order to create his own words. • Student will create new words from root words by adding prefixes and suffixes • Student will be asked to create their own word list with designated spelling patterns • Teacher will use pocket charts to model words that turn into contractions • Teacher will create K-W-L Charts using words from core subject areas such as Social Studies and Science • Teacher will create Language Experience Chart • Teacher will create Literacy Centers with word sorts, reread books, write responses to stories, Guided Reading • Teacher will facilitate Choral Reading • Teacher will create a Word Wall with different word families written on the charts. Student will create his own Word Wall as he learns the different words within the word family one word by one word. • Teacher will create a Word Wall with contractions, spelling demons, homophones. Teacher will include pictures of the words next to the words.	**Suggested Interventionist: Speech Pathologist; Sp. Ed. Teacher; Reading Specialist** **Suggested Session: 60 minutes 5x a week in a small group or individual basis in addition to the CORE reading instruction program outside the classroom** **Strategies/activities for Word Study:** • Teacher will introduce different kinds of letter chunks and spelling patterns: such as commonly occurring word stems (-et, -ake,); endings (/-s/, /-ed/, /-ing/, /-er/, /-est/); suffixes and prefixes and root words. • Teacher will introduce words that have the same outline as other words for memorization. • Teacher will present on 3x5 colored cards sight words several times a day. Student will write his own cards and also write the sight words on different surfaces to help memory. • Teacher will introduce the importance of context clues to help in decoding an unfamiliar word. • Teacher will create a Word Wall with different word families written on the charts. Student creates his own Word Wall as he learns the different words within the word family one word by one word. • Teacher will create a Word Wall with contractions, spelling demons, homophones, including pictures of the words next to the words.

Phonics: Word Study Tier 3	Phonics: Word Study Tier 3
• After words are visually introduced to the student, the student will write sentences on the subsequent days. The student will reread the words in a different format. • Teacher will give student a familiar combination of letters and student will make up his own words. • Student will sort words by vowel teams and say the words as he sorts them. • Student will play word games with different word families or familiar "chunks" of words. • Student will create new words from root words by adding prefixes and suffixes. • Student will be asked to create his own word list with designated spelling patterns. • Teacher will use pocket charts to model words that turn into contractions. • Teacher will play Concentration with syllables that make up two syllable compound words. Students are asked to pick up two cards and see if the two cards make up a compound word. • Teacher will introduce the /-ck/, /-tch/, /-dge/ rule and create words with the rule and the endings. • Teacher will create Word Walls with words that have silent letters. • Teacher will use K-W-L Charts using words from core subject areas such as Social Studies and Science.	• Teacher will facilitate language experience chart. • Teacher will facilitate literacy centers with word sorts, reread books, write responses to stories, guided reading. • Teacher will facilitate choral reading.

Area of Reading: Fluency

Fluency	Fluency Tier 1
Fluency—involves the ability to recognize words quickly and accurately. When student no longer has to concentrate on decoding words, his attention is freed to focus on the meaning of the text. Examples of reading problems within this skill area: • Difficulty reading with comprehension skills • Difficulty reading quickly and automatically • Difficulty reading with expression, tone, emphasis and word phrasing. **Accommodations and Modifications:** • Review new vocabulary • Color highlighting • Use reading partners • Illustrate vocabulary • Use outlining/webbing • Use index cards • Summarize main points • Frequent review/ frequent questioning • Allow student to read out loud • Use assistive technology programs • Use word banks • Use rules of the English language • Color-code sound and word patterns	**Suggested Interventionist: General Education Teacher with consultation from the Special Education Teacher and the Reading Specialist.** **Suggested Session: small group explicit instruction within the CORE reading instruction program 2x a week within the classroom** **Strategies/Activities for Fluency:** • Teacher will choose three sight words and write them on the Word Wall. Student will practice these words on 3x5 cards, in sentences and in paragraphs. • Teacher will sort words into word families, controlled words or spelling generalizations. Examples of these categories are: /-ild/, /-old/, /-old/, /-ind/, /-ing/, /-ank/, /-unk/, /-onk/. • The teacher will sort multiple sounds word sorts by the different sounds that the spelling generalizations make. The rules for the spelling generalizations must also be taught while doing this exercise. (See Spelling section) • Teacher will illustrate spelling patterns by teaching the different sounds that all the single consonants and short vowels make as well as the spelling rules for /-ck/, /-tch/ and /-dge/ combinations.

Fluency Tier 1	Fluency Tier 2
• Student will learn the inflectional ending of words by creating a base word plus the following endings: -es, -ed, -ing, -er, est, -est. • Teacher will demonstrate that two words can be changed into one word (a contraction) by taking away a letter and adding an apostrophe. • Teacher will write the two parts of compound words on two different 3x5 cards. Student will sound out each part of the word and then say them together. • Student will be taught the six types of syllables. The six syllable rules are: (1) Closed Syllable; (2) Open Syllable); (3) Silent /e/ syllable; (4) Double Vowel Team Syllable; (5) Controlled /r/ syllable and (6) Consonant /le/ syllable. Each syllable rule is taught, words are written on folded 3x5 cards. The first syllable is in green and the second syllable is in black. Students will read the green syllable and then the black syllable. Syllabication should be taught first with compound words and then with multi-syllabic words that are not compound words.	**Suggested Interventionist: Sp. Ed. Teacher; Reading Specialist** **Suggested Session: 30 minutes 2 to 3x a week in a small group or individual basis in addition to the CORE reading instruction program inside the class** **Strategies/Activities for Fluency:** • Teacher will present the Letter Combination Word Making approach. Students will create sight words out of individual sounds. Most of the word chosen is presented in connected letters. The student will be given another letter to place inside the word to create a sight word. This activity can be used with single sounds, consonant digraphs and consonant blends. • Teacher will sort word families, controlled words or spelling generalizations. Examples of these categories are: /-ild/, /-old/, /-old/, /-ind/, /-ing/, /-ank/, /-unk/, /-onk/. • Teacher will sort words by multiple different sounds that spelling generalizations make; sounds such as /ci/, /ce/, /cy/, /s/. The rules for those sound combinations must also be taught while doing this exercise.

Fluency Tier 2	Fluency Tier 3
• Teacher will illustrate spelling patterns by teaching the different sounds that all the single consonants and short vowels make as well as the spelling rules for /-ck/, /-tch/ and /-dge/ combinations. • Student will learn the following inflectional endings to words by creating a base word plus the following endings: /-s/, /-es/, /-ed/, /-ing/, /-er/, /-est/. • Teacher will demonstrate that two words can be changed into one word (a contraction) by taking away a letter and adding an apostrophe. • Teacher will write the two parts of compound words on two different 3x5 cards. Students will sound out each part of the word and then say them together. • Teacher will add prefixes to words. Students will read the word. Teacher then adds suffixes to words. Students will read the words. Lastly, the teacher adds prefixes and suffixes to the same words. Student will read those words. • Students will learn the six types of syllables. The six syllable rules are: (1) Closed Syllable; (2) Open Syllable); (3) Silent /e/ syllable; (4) Double Vowel Team Syllable; (5) Controlled /r/ syllable and (6) Consonant /le/ syllable. Each syllable rule will be taught and written on folded 3x5 cards. The first syllable is in green and the second syllable is in black. First students will read the green syllable and then the black syllable. Syllabication will be taught first with compound words and then with words that are not compound words.	**Suggested Interventionist: Special Education Teacher; Reading Specialist** **Suggested Session: 60 minutes 5x a week in a small group or individual basis in addition to the CORE reading instruction program outside the classroom** **Strategies/Activities for Fluency:** • Teacher will create sight words out of individual sounds. Words chosen will be presented in connected letters. Student will be given a letter to place inside the word to create a sight word. This activity will be used with single sounds, consonant digraphs and consonant blends. • Teacher will sort words by word families, controlled words or spelling generalizations. Examples of these categories are: /-ild/, /-old/, /-old/, /-ind/, /-ing/, /-ank/, /-unk/, /-onk/. • Teacher will sort sounds such as /ci/, /ce/, /cy/, /s/ by the different sounds that the spelling generalizations make. Teacher presents the rules for those sound combinations while doing this exercise. • Students will learn the spelling patterns that the different sounds make. These sound patterns are: /-ck/, /-tch/, /-dge/ combinations.

Fluency Tier 3	
• Student will learn the following inflectional endings to words by cre--ating a base word plus the following endings: s, es, ed, ing, er, est. • Teacher will give the student letter cards. Teacher will write two words with the letter cards. Students will learn that two words can be one word (a contraction) by taking away a letter and adding an apostrophe. • Teacher will write the two parts of compound words on two different 3x5 cards. Students will sound out each part of the word and then say them together. Teacher will explain that compound words are formed when two real words are joined to create a new word. Each part of the compound word will be a word by itself. • Prefixes and suffixes are added to words to form new words. Teacher will add prefixes to words. Students will read the word. Teacher will add suffixes to words. Students will read the words. Lastly, the teacher adds prefixes and suffixes to the same words. Student reads words. • Students will learn the six types of syllables. The six syllable rules are: (1) Closed Syllable; (2) Open Syllable); (3) Silent /e/ syllable; (4) Double Vowel Team Syllable; (5) Controlled /r/ syllable and (6) Consonant /le/ syllable. Each syllable rule will be taught and written on folded 3x5 cards. The first syllable is in red and the second syllable is in black. Students will read the words in syllables. First students read the red syllable and then the black syllable.	

Area of Reading: Vocabulary

Vocabulary	Vocabulary Tier 1
Vocabulary—involves the ability to know what words mean so that what is read can be understood. Students learn vocabulary by indirect and direct word learning methods. There are four types of vocabulary: listening vocabulary; speaking vocabulary; reading vocabulary and writing vocabulary. Examples of reading problems within this area: • Difficulty in reading comprehension • Difficulty in deriving meaning from context • Difficulty in writing, spelling, speaking, listening skills **Accommodations and Modifications:** • Review new vocabulary • Color highlighting • Illustrate vocabulary • Use outlining/webbing • Summarize main points • Review and question frequently • Read assignments orally to student • Allow student to read out loud • Use word banks • Use rules of the English language • Use technology programs	**Suggested Interventionist: General Education Teacher with consultation from the Special Education Teacher/Speech Pathologist/ Reading Specialist** **Suggested Session: small group explicit instruction within the CORE reading instruction program 2x a week within the classroom** **Strategies/Activities for vocabulary development:** • Teacher will create vocabulary word walls by placing a targeted word on the Word Wall. Student will look up antonyms in the dictionary for the targeted word. • Student will provide associations for targeted words. • Teacher will point out words that have multiple meanings. Student will use each word appropriately in different contexts. • Student will use the new vocabulary words in a sentence completion activity. • Teacher will repeat phrases using an expanded vocabulary. Student will repeat the new expanded sentence. • Teacher will give student a new vocabulary word of the day. Students will receive points every time he uses the targeted new vocabulary word in a sentence. • Student will be assigned a designated category. Student will list the words that can be associated with that category. • Teacher will set up a role-playing activity that the student acts out. The activity prompts new words.

Vocabulary Tier 1	Vocabulary Tier 1
• Student will act out different targeted words. • Teacher will write a new vocabulary word on an envelope. Pictures will be placed inside that do and do not go with the new vocabulary word. Student will identify the pictures that match the targeted word. • Teacher will make a list of unfamiliar vocabulary words that belong to the reading assignment. Student will look up those words in a dictionary. • Teacher will model how to use the context clues surrounding the new vocabulary words in order to know the meaning of the new word. • Teacher will explain how to classify or file new words as to category, function, antonym and synonym in order to remember the new vocabulary words. • Student will study words or terms by relating one concept to another, and by creating concept circles. Student will identify common relationship that exists among several terms. • Teacher will present concept definition maps as a graphic organizer to help students understand the essential attributes, qualities or characteristics of a concept. Student will describe what the concept is, make comparisons, tell what it is like and give examples of it. • Teacher will use the Frayer Model to help student develop his understanding of concepts. Student will provide a definition, list characteristics or facts, and provides examples and non-examples of the concept.)	• Student will compare a term's meaning and its features to those of other terms that fall into the same category by filling in a semantic feature analysis organizer. • Student will use a semantic mapping graphic organizer to activate and draw on prior knowledge, recognize important components of different concepts and see the relationships among components.

Vocabulary Tier 2	Vocabulary Tier 2
Suggested Interventionist: Special Education Teacher; Reading Specialist; Speech Pathologist **Suggested Session: 30 minutes 2 to 3x a week in a small group or individual basis in addition to the CORE reading instruction program inside the classroom** **Strategies/activities for Vocabulary Development:** • Teacher will create vocabulary word walls by placing a targeted word on the Word Wall. Student will look up antonyms in the dictionary for the targeted word. • Student will provide associations for targeted words. • Teacher will point out words that have multiple meanings. Student will use each word appropriately in different contexts. • Student will use the new vocabulary words in a sentence completion activity. • Teacher will repeat phrases that the student will say using an expanded vocabulary. Student will repeat the new expanded sentence. • Teacher will give student a new vocabulary word of the day. Student will receive points every time he uses the targeted new vocabulary word in a sentence during the school day. • Student will be assigned a designated category. Student will list the words that can be associated with that category. • Teacher will set up a role playing activity that the student act out. The activity prompts new words.	• Student will act out different targeted words. • Teacher will write a new vocabulary word on an envelope. Pictures will be placed inside that do and do not go with the new vocabulary word. Student will separate the right pictures out that match the vocabulary word targeted. • Teacher will make a list of unfamiliar vocabulary words that belong to the reading assignment. Student will look up those words in a dictionary. • Teacher will model how to use the context clues surrounding the new vocabulary words in order to know the meaning of the new word. • Teacher will explain how to classify or file new words as to category, function, antonym and synonym in order to remember the new vocabulary words. • Student will study words or terms by relating one concept to another by creating concept circles. Student will identify common relationship that exists among several terms. • Teacher will present concept definition maps as a graphic organizer to help student understand the essential attributes, qualities or characteristics of a concept. Student will describe what the concept is, make comparisons, tell what it is like and give examples of it. • Teacher will use the Frayer Model to help student develop his understanding of concepts. Student will provide a definition, list characteristics or facts, and provides examples and non-examples of the concept.

Vocabulary Tier 2	Vocabulary Tier 3
• Student will compare a term's meaning and its features to those of other terms that fall into the same category by filling in a semantic feature analysis organizer. • Student will use a semantic mapping graphic organizer to activate and draw on prior knowledge, recognize important components of different concepts and see the relationships among three components. • Student will put vocabulary words onto 3x5 cards. The pairs of cards that are made are the following: word and definition; word and analogy; word and synonyms and words and antonyms. Student will match up one of the pairs to the targeted vocabulary words in a game of Concentration.	**Suggested Interventionist: Special Education Teacher; Reading Specialist, Speech Pathologist** **Suggested Session: 60 minutes 5x a week in a small group or individual basis in addition to the CORE reading instruction program outside the classroom** **Strategies/Activities for Vocabulary Development:** • Teacher will create vocabulary word walls by placing a targeted word on the Word Wall. Student will look up antonyms in the dictionary for the targeted word. • Student will provide associations for targeted words. • Teacher will point out words that have multiple meanings. Student will use each word appropriately in different contexts. • Student will use the new vocabulary words in a sentence completion activity. • Teacher will repeat phrases that the student will say using an expanded vocabulary. Student will repeat the new expanded sentence. • Teacher will give student a new vocabulary word of the day. Student will receive points every time he uses the targeted new vocabulary word in a sentence during the school day. • Student will be assigned a designated category. Student will list the words that can be associated with that category. • Teacher will set up a role playing activity that the student acts out. The activity prompts new words.

Vocabulary Tier 3	Vocabulary Tier 3
• Student will act out different targeted words. • Teacher will write a new vocabulary word on an envelope. Pictures will be placed inside that do and do not go with the new vocabulary word. Student will separate the right pictures out that match the vocabulary word targeted. • Teacher will make a list of unfamiliar vocabulary words that belong to the reading assignment. Student will look up those words in a dictionary. • Teacher will model how to use the context clues surrounding the new vocabulary words in order to know the meaning of the new word. • Teacher will explain how to classify or file new words as to category, function, antonym and synonym in order to remember the new vocabulary words. • Student will study words or terms by relating one concept to another by creating concept circles. Student will identify common relationship that exists among several terms. • Teacher will present concept definition maps as a graphic organizer to help student understand the essential attributes, qualities or characteristics of a concept. Student will describe what the concept is, make comparisons, tell what it is like and give examples of it. • Teacher will use the Frayer Model to help students develop understanding of concepts. Student will provide a definition, list characteristics or facts, and provides examples and non-examples of the concept.	• Student will compare a term's meaning and its features to those of other terms that fall into the same category by filling in a semantic feature analysis organizer. • Student will use a semantic mapping graphic organizer to activate and draw on prior knowledge, recognize important components of different concepts and see the relationships among three components. • Student will put vocabulary words onto 3x5 cards. The pairs of cards that are made are the following; word and definition; word and analogy; word and synonyms and words and antonyms. Student will match up one of the pairs to the targeted vocabulary words in a game of Concentration.

Area of Reading: Comprehension

<table>
<tr><th>Comprehension</th><th>Comprehension Tier 1</th></tr>
<tr><td>

Comprehension—involves the interaction between reader and text so that meaning can be derived. Examples of comprehension problems within this area:

- Difficulty recognizing the sequence of events
- Difficulty identifying cause and effect relationships
- Difficulty comparing and contrasting information
- Difficulty identifying the main idea and supporting details
- Difficulty identifying between fact and opinion
- Difficulty predicting what idea comes next
- Difficulty making inferences from what is read
- Difficulty drawing conclusions
- Difficulty relating text material to prior information
- Difficulty prioritizing important information
- Difficulty developing questions on text based material
- Difficulty creating visual images
- Difficulty retelling information

Accommodations and Modifications:

- Review new vocabulary by illustration
- Color highlighting
- Use reading partners
- Use outlining and webbing
- Summarize main points
- Question and review frequently
- Books on tape
- Allow student to read out loud
- Use computer program that reads for the student
- Use word banks
- Use rules of the English language
- Use comprehension technology programs

</td><td>

Suggested Interventionist: General Education Teacher with consultation from the Special Education Teacher and the Reading Specialist.

Suggested Session: small group explicit instruction within the CORE reading instruction program 2x a week within the classroom

Strategies/Activities for Reading Comprehension:

- Student will draw a visual image of the characteristics for the character map.
- Student will pre-read the title, look at the illustrations and read the introductory paragraph of the story in order to predict the story. At the end of the story, the student will discuss whether the prediction was right or wrong and adjust the prediction.
- Student will compare and contrast two targeted concepts within the story using a Venn diagram.
- Student will fill in the four columns of the KWL chart by writing the answers to: What they already know; What they think they know; What they think they will learn and What they have learned.
- Student will participate in a group summarizing activity identifying the major topics from the reading. A four-column chart is written on the board and categories of important concepts are placed as headings. Student will contribute concepts for each category. After the chart is filled in, student will write a summary based on these facts.
- Student will create a paragraph frame that can either be a process paragraph or a contrast frame. The process paragraph and contrast paragraph have sentence starters that correspond to the topic being read.

</td></tr>
</table>

Comprehension Tier 1	Comprehension Tier 2
• Student will engage in "pair up" activity. A better reader (reads) will work with a poorer reader (retells). • Teacher will identify a central word from the reading. Student will write all the associations for that word and write a sentence stating what those associations mean. • Teacher will design a situation similar to the text being read. The student will work in groups and discuss possible solutions to the situations. • Teacher will model each of the following skills: summarizing, questioning, clarifying, and predicting to improve comprehension. Groups will be formed and student will participate in one of the four skills. • Teacher will depict a story that contains visual imagery details. As the story is read, student will be asked to answer the following questions: What does it look like? What does it smell like? What does it feel like? What does it taste like? • Teacher will read a text; the student will fill out a visual framework organizer. • Teacher will model thinking process by verbalizing her thoughts out loud. Students will practice think-aloud with other students in class. • Teacher will read different versions of the same story. Student will work with fellow classmates to discuss possible solutions to the problems that are central to the plot. • Teacher will read a story. Student will draw what is imagined during the reading.	**Suggested Interventionist: Special Education Teacher, Reading Specialist** **Suggested Session: 30 minutes 2 to 3x a week in a small group or individual basis in addition to the CORE reading instruction program inside the class** **Strategies/Activities for Reading Comprehension:** • Student will pre-read the title, look at the illustrations and read the introductory paragraph of the story in order to predict the story. At the end of the story, the student will collaborate with other students whether they are right or wrong and adjust their prediction. • Student will predict the story elements by setting, characters, problems, events and resolution into categories. Student will write a paragraph and compare what he wrote (pre-read) to what was read. • Student will complete a story frame graphic organizer by sequencing the story with sentence starters such as: The problem begins with……; after that…..' then…..; the problem is solved when….; the story ends when…… • Student will identify a story's structure, literary elements, setting, theme, conflicts, resolutions, events and their relationship to each other within a story grammar map or other graphic organizer.

Comprehension Tier 2	Comprehension Tier 2
• Student will fill in a circular framework graphic organizer. The graphic text boxes will have the following titles; beginning scene, next event, next event, until the story ending. • Teacher will predict the major concepts and creates four sentences that address these concepts. In front of the statements the teacher places two columns, one that says Me and other that says Text. Student will either agree or disagree with the statements and place a check in the Me column. After the reading, student looks at his answers and revise any answer that is not correct. • Student will create a paragraph frame from either a process paragraph or a contrast paragraph. Each paragraph will have sentence starters that correspond to the topic being read. • Teacher will select one important concept and develop questions on all three levels of questioning (literal, interpretive & applied). Student will answer the appropriate level questions developed by the teacher in the reflection question chain. • Student will generate the QAR (Question-Answer-Relationship) questions from the following questions: Right There questions (literal level); Think and Search questions (relationship of information relating to each other); Author and You (inferential questions); and On My Own (background knowledge of student not from the text).	• Teacher will identify a central word from the reading. Student will write all his associations for that word and then write a sentence stating what those associations mean in a pre-reading activity. • Teacher will design a situation similar to the text being read. The student will collaborate in groups and discuss possible solutions to the problematic situations. • Teacher will model each of the following skills: summarizing, questioning, clarifying, and predicting to improve comprehension in a reciprocal teaching activity. Groups are formed and student will participate in one of the four skills. • Student will review the text; write questions; read the passage; answer their questions; summarize what they have read; create graphic organizer and write a summary at the end of this SQ3R (Survey, Question, Read, Recite and Review) method. • Teacher will use a semantic map organizer and write the key concept word on the board from the text. Lines are projected out from the word that have the following categories: Where; How; What it looks like; Features of the concept; and How the features are used. • Teacher will read a story that contains visual imagery details. As the story is read, student will be asked to answer the following questions: (1) What does it look like? (2) What does it smell like? (3) What does it feel like? (4) What does it taste like?

Comprehension Tier 3	Comprehension Tier 3
Suggested Interventionist: Special Education Teacher, Reading Specialist **Suggested Session: 60 minutes 5x a week in a small group or individual basis in addition to the CORE reading instruction program outside the classroom** **Strategies/activities for Reading Comprehension:** • Student will draw a visual image of the characteristics for the characters on a character map. • Student will pre-read the title, look at the illustrations and read the introductory paragraph of the story in order to predict the story. At the end of the story, the student will discuss whether he is right or wrong and adjust his prediction. • Student will categorize the story elements by setting, characters, problems, events and resolution. Student will write a paragraph and compare what they wrote (predict) to what was read. • Student will identify a story frame graphic organizer by sequencing the story with the following sentence starters such as: The problem begins with......; after that....; then....; the problem is solved when....; the story ends when...... • Student will identify a story's structure, literary elements, setting, theme, conflicts, resolutions, events and their relationship to each other within the story grammar graphic organizer map.	• Student will fill in a circular framework graphic organizer. The graphic text boxes will have the following titles; beginning scene, next event, next event,... until the story ending. • Student will compare and contrast two targeted concepts within the story using a Venn diagram. • Teacher will identify the major concepts of a story and create four sentences that address these concepts. In front of the statements the teacher places two columns, one that says Me and other that says Text. Student will either agree or disagree with the statements and place a check in the Me column. After the reading, student looks at the answers and revises any answer that is not correct. • Student will fill in the four columns of the KWL chart by writing the answers to: What they already know; What they think they know; What they think they will learn and What they have learned. • Student will create a paragraph frame that can either be a process or a contrast paragraph. The process or contrast paragraph has sentence starters that correspond to the topic being read.

Comprehension Tier 3	Comprehension Tier 3
• Students will engage in "pair up" activity. A better reader (reads) will collaborate with a poorer reader (retells). • Teacher will identify a central word from the reading. Student will write all their associations for that word and write a sentence depicting what those associations mean. • Teacher will design a situation similar to the text being read. The students will work in groups and discuss possible solutions to the problematic situations. • Teacher will model each of the following reciprocal skills: summarizing, questioning, clarifying, and predicting to improve comprehension. Groups will be formed and students will participate in one of the four skills. • Student will survey the text ; develop questions; read the passage; answer their questions; retell what they have read; create graphic organizer and write a summary at the end of the SQ3R method. • Teacher will use a semantic map organizer and write the key concept word on the board from the text. Lines are projected out from the word that have the following categories: (1) Where; (2) How; (3) What it looks like; (4) Features of the concept; and (5) How the features are used in the semantic map organizer. • Teacher will read a story that contains visual imagery details. As the story is read, students will be asked to answer the following questions: What does it look like? What does it smell like? What does it feel like? What does it taste like?	• As the teacher reads a text, the student will fill out a visual framework organizer. • Teacher will model her thinking process by saying her thoughts out loud. Student will practice think-alouds with other students in class. • Teacher will select one important concept and develops questions on all three levels of questioning (literal, interpretive & applied). Student will answer the questions developed by the teacher on a reflection question chain. • Student will generate the QAR (Question-Answer Relationships) questions from the following questions: (1) Right There questions (literal level); (2) Think and Search questions (relationship of information relating to each other); (3) Author and You (inferential questions); and On My Own (background knowledge of student not from the text). • Teacher will read different versions of the same story. Student will collaborate with fellow classmates to discuss possible solutions to the problems that are central to the plot. • Teacher will read a visual story. Students will draw what they imagined during the reading.

Programs & Products for Reading (See Appendix C for web sites)

Product	Publisher	Tier	Type	Phonemic Awareness	Phonics	Word Study	Fluency	Vocabulary	Compre-hension
10th Planet:Vowels	Sunburst	1,2,3	Software	x	x				
10th Planet-Word Parts	Sunburst	1	Software		x	x			
10thPlanet:Letter sounds.	Sunburst	1,2,3	Software	x	x				
Accelerated Reader	Renaissance	1,2	Software			x	x	x	x
Alligator to Zucchini	Great Source	2,3	Supplemental	x	x		x	x	x
Alphabet Sounds. Set	Data Command	1,2,3	Software	x	x				
Basic Word Concepts	Sunburst	1,2,3	Software					x	
Bookroom Collection	Benchmark	2	Supplemental						x
Breaking the Code	SRA	3	Supplemental	x					
Breakthrough to Literacy	Wright Group	2,3	Supplemental	x					
Build a Word	Steck Vaughn	2	Supplemental		x				
Build Up Kit	Benchmark	2	Supplemental	x	x				
Building Vocabulary from Wood Roots	Teacher Created Materials	1	Supplemental					x	
Chall-Popp Phonics	Continental Press	1	Supplemental		x				
Charlesbridge Reading Fluency	Charlesbridge	2	Software			x	x	x	
Chicka Chicka Boom Boom	Davidson Assoc.	1,2,3	Software	x	x				
Collaborative Strategic Reading	Sopris West	2	Supplemental						x
Comprehension Plus	Pearson	2,3	Supplemental						x
Comprehension Strategies/ Activities Intervention	Success for All	2,3	Supplemental						x
Corrective Reading	SRA	2,3	CORE	x	x	x	x	x	x
Corrective Reading		3	Supplemental	x	x	x	x	x	x
Curious George	Great Source	2	Supplemental		x			x	
Daily Vocabulary	Great Source	2	sup					x	
Daisy Quest	Great Wave	1,2,3	Software	x	x				

Programs & Products for Reading (See Appendix C for web sites)

Product	Publisher	Tier	Type	Phonemic Awareness	Phonics	Word Study	Fluency	Vocabulary	Compre-hension
Daisy's Castle	Adventure Learning	1,2,3	Software	X	X				
Destination Read	Riverdeep	2,3	Software	X	X	X	X	X	X
Diminie Collection of Myths & Legends	Pearson	2	Supplemental						X
Discover Intensive Phonics	HEC	2	Software	X	X	X	X	X	
Dominie Collection of Aesop's Fables	Pearson	2	Supplemental						X
Dominie Collections of Traditional Tales	Pearson	2	Supplemental						X
Dominie Vocabulary Builders	Pearson	2	Supplemental					X	
Dominie World	Rigby	2	Supplemental						X
Early Intervention in Reading	SRA	2.3	Supplemental	X					
Early Reading Intervention	Wright Group	2,3	Supplemental	X					
Early Reading Intervention	Scott Foresman	3	Supplemental	X					
Early Reading Intervention	Scott Foresman	2	Supplemental	X	X	X	X	X	
Early Reading Tutor	SRA	2,3	Supplemental	X					
Early Success	Houghton Mifflin	3	Supplemental		X	X	X		
Early Vocabulary	Sopris West	2,3	Supplemental					X	
Earobics	Cognitive Concepts	1,2,3	Software	X	X	X	X	X	X
Easy as ABC	Queue	1,2,3	Supplemental	X	X				
Emergent Reader	Sunburst	1	Software					X	
Exploring Nonfiction	Teachers Created Materials	1,2,3	Supplemental			X	X	X	X
Factivity Series	Pearson	3							X
Failure Free Reading		3	Supplemental	X	X	X	X	X	X

Programs & Products for Reading (See Appendix C for web sites)

Product	Publisher	Tier	Type	Phonemic Awareness	Phonics	Word Study	Fluency	Vocabulary	Compre-hension
Fast for Word: Reading 1,2,3,4,5	Scientific Learning	1,2,3	Software			x	x	x	x
Fast for Word: Reading Assistant	Scientific Learning	1,2	Software			x	x	x	x
Fast for Word: Language & Language to Reading	Scientific Learning	2,3	Software	x	x				
Fast Track Phonics	Success for All	2,3	Supplemental		x				
Fast Track Reading	Wright Group	2,3	Supplemental	x		x	x		x
First Stories	Pacific Learning	2	Supplemental	x	x		x	x	x
Fluency Kit	Benchmark	2	Software			x	x		x
Fluency Kit for Independent Practice	Benchmark	2	Supplemental			x	x		
Fluent Reader	Renaissance	1,2	Supplemental			x	x		
Fluent Reader Made	Renaissance	2,3	Supplemental			x	x		
Focus Reading and Language Program	Plato	2,3	Software	x	x	x	x	x	x
Foundations	Wilson	2,3	Supplemental	x	x				
Foundations	Wright Group	3	Supplemental			x	x		
Fundations	Wilson Language Training	3	Supplemental	x	x	x	x	x	
Great Leaps	Diarmuid	2,3	Supplemental			x	x		
Guided Reading: Sunshine	Wright Group	2	Supplemental			x	x		x
Guilded Reading: Storybook	Wright Group								x
Headsprout	Yriondo Educational	1,2	Software	x	x	x	x	x	x
Herman Method	Sopris West	3	Supplemental	x	x	x	x	x	x
High Frequency Word Vocabulary	Benchmark	2	Supplemental					x	
Horizons	SRA	2.3	CORE	x	x	x	x	x	x

Programs & Products for Reading (See Appendix C for web sites)

Product	Publisher	Tier	Type	Phonemic Awareness	Phonics	Word Study	Fluency	Vocabulary	Compre-hension
Houghton Mifflin Reading	Houghton Mifflin	1	CORE	x	x	x	x	x	x
Images Theme Books.	Great Source	2	Supplemental			x	x	x	x
Imagine It	SRA	1	Supplemental	x					
Island Reading Journal	Sunburst	2,3	Supplemental					x	
Joseph's Readers Talking	Failure Free Reading	2	Software					x	
Journey Into Reading	Continental Press	1	Supplemental					x	
Kaleidoscope	SRA	3	CORE		x				X
Key Skills for Reading: Letters and Words	Sunburst	1,2,3	Software	x	x				
Key Skills Phonic Master	Sunburst	2,3	Software		x			x	
Key Skills Phonics Solution	Sunburst	2,3	Software		x			x	
Key Three Routine	Sopris West	2	Supplemental						x
Kid Centered Learning	Dominie	3				x			
Kid Phonics	Great Source	1,2,3	Supplemental	x	x			x	
Kid Phonics	Davidson	1,2,3	Supplemental		x				
Knock Knock	Sunburst	1,2,3	Software	x	x				
Ladder to Literacy	Paul Brooks Pub.	2	Supplemental	x					
Language for Learning	SRA	2,3	Supplemental					x	x
Language for Thinking	SRA	2,3	Supplemental					x	x
Language!	Sopris West	2,3	CORE	x	x	x	x	x	x
Leapfrog	Schoolhouse	2	Software	x	x				
Learn About ABC/Letter Sounds	Sunburst	1,2,3	Software	x	x				
Let's Make a Word	Creative Wonders	1,2,3	Supplemental	x	x				
Lexia	Lexia Learning	2,3	Software	x	x	x	x	x	x
Literacy by Design	Rigby	1	CORE	x	x	x	x	x	x
Little Readers	Great Source	2	Supplemental			x	x	x	x

Programs & Products for Reading (See Appendix C for web sites)

Product	Publisher	Tier	Type	Phonemic Awareness	Phonics	Word Study	Fluency	Vocabulary	Compre-hension
Matchword	Wright Group	2	Supplemental	x	x			x	
Measuring Up	Peoples Education	1,	Supplemental					x	
Measuring Up	Peoples Education	1	Supplemental						x
Multiple Meaning Vocabulary	Sopris West	2	Supplemental					x	
Multisensory Reading	Rogercenter	1,2,3	Supplemental		x				
Muppet Word Book	Sunburst	1,2,3	Software		x				
Next Steps	Great Source	2	Supplemental			x	x	x	x
Odyssey Reading	Compass Learning	2,3	Software		x	x	x	x	x
Open Court	SRA	1,2,3	CORE	x	x	x	x	x	x
Open Court	SRA	1	CORE	x	x	x	x	x	x
Open Court Phonic Kit	SRA	2,3	Supplemental	x	x	x	x		
Orbit Collections	Pacific Learning	2	Supplemental					x	x
Pacific Literacy Guided Reading	Pacific Learning	2	Supplemental			x	x	x	
Pacific Literacy Shared Reading	Pacific Learning	2	Supplemental						x
PALS	Sopris West	2,3	Supplemental	x	x	x	x	x	x
Phonemic Awareness	SRA	2							
Phonemic Awareness	SRA	2	Supplemental	x					
Phonic Funnies	Sopris West	1,2	Supplemental		x				
Phonic Solution Plus	Sunburst	1,2,3	Software					x	
Phonics 1a/2a	Sunburst	1,2,3	Software	x	x				
Phonics 2c	Sunburst	1	Software					x	
Phonics Based Learning	Lexia Learning	1,2,3	Software		x				
Phonics for the Real World	Rosen Publishing	2	Software	x	x	x			
Phonics Mart	Steck-Vaughn	1,2,3	Supplemental		x				
Phonics Master	Cambridge Lab Inc.	1,2,3	Supplemental		x				
Phonics Q	Phonic Q	2	Supplemental	x	x				

Programs & Products for Reading (See Appendix C for web sites)

Product	Publisher	Tier	Type	Phonemic Awareness	Phonics	Word Study	Fluency	Vocabulary	Compre-hension
Phono Graphix	Read America	2	Supplemental	X	X				
PM Plus Readers	Rigby	2	Supplemental			X	X	X	
Preventing Academic Failure	EPS	2,3	Supplemental	X	X	X	X	X	X
Primary Phonics	EPS	1,2	Supplemental		X	X			
Python Path	Sunburst	1,2,3	Software	X	X				
Quick Reads & Quick Read	Pearson	2,3	Software			X	X		X
Read 180		1,2	Software			X	X	X	X
Read Naturally	Read Naturally	2,3	Software			X	X		
Read Naturally	Read Naturally	2,3	Software				X		X
Read Well	Sopris West	1,2,3	CORE	X	X	X	X	X	X
Read Write and Type Learning System	Riverdeep	2,3	Software	X	X	X			
Reader's Theater Kit	Benchmark	2	Supplemental						X
Readers Theater	Benchmark	2	Supplemental			X	X		
Reading and Phonics	Brighter Child	1,2,3	Software	X	X				
Reading and Phonics	Brighter Child	2,3	Supplemental		X				
Reading Blaster	Davidson	1,2,3	Supplemental		X				
Reading Blaster	Sunburst	1,2,3	Software					X	X
Reading Comprehension & Critical Thinking	Sunburst	1	Software						X
Reading Explorers Pathfinders	Benchmark	2,3	Supplemental	X	X	X	X	X	X
Reading Horizon	HEC Software	1,2,3	Software		X				
Reading Intervention Tool Kit	Peoples Education	2	Supplemental					X	X
Reading Machine	SWEPS Educational	1,2,3	Supplemental		X				
Reading Master	SRA	2,3	Supplemental	X					X
Reading Mastery Signature	SRA	1,2	CORE	X	X	X	X	X	X

Programs & Products for Reading (See Appendix C for web sites)

Product	Publisher	Tier	Type	Phonemic Awareness	Phonics	Word Study	Fluency	Vocabulary	Compre-hension
Reading Maze	Great Wave	1,2,3	Software		x				
Reading Recovery	Reading Recovery	2,3	Supplemental			x			
Reading Street	Pearson	1	CORE	x	x	x	x	x	x
Reading Street	Scott Foresman	1	CORE	x	x	x	x	x	x
Reading Who?	Sunburst	1,2,3	Software		x				
Reading Wings	Success for All	2,3	Supplemental						x
Recipe for Reading	EPS	1,2,3	Supplemental	x	x	x	x		
Rewards	Sopris West	2	CORE	x	x	x	x	x	x
Rigby Focus	Rigby	2	Supplemental			x	x	x	
Road to the Code	Paul Brooks	3	Supplemental	x					
Sails Literacy Series	Rigby	2	Supplemental			x	x		x
Shutterbug Books	Steck Vaughn	2	Supplemental					x	x
Simon Sounds It Out	Don Johnson	1,2,3	Supplemental	x	x				
Six-Minute Solution	Sopris West	1,2	Supplemental			x	x		
Soar to Success	Houghton Mifflin	3	Software		x	x		x	x
Sound Partners	Sopris West	2,3	Supplemental	x	x				
Spell Read PAT		2	Supplemental	x	x	x	x	x	x
SPIRE	EPS	2,3	Supplemental	x	x	x	x	x	x
Start Up Phonics	Benchmark	2	Supplemental	x	x				
Step Up to Success	Peoples Education	2	Supplemental					x	x
Stepping Stones to Literacy	Sopris West	2,3	Supplemental	x	x	x	x		
Storyteller Guided Reading	Wright Group	2	Supplemental			x	x	x	x
Storytown	Harcourt	1	CORE	x	x	x	x	x	x
Success for All		3	Supplemental	x	x	x	x	x	x
Success Maker	Pearson	2,3	Supplemental						x
Sugar & Snails	Entrex	1,2,3	Supplemental		x				

Programs & Products for Reading (See Appendix C for web sites)

Product	Publisher	Tier	Type	Phonemic Awareness	Phonics	Word Study	Fluency	Vocabulary	Compre-hension
Super QAR	Wright Group	2	Supplemental						x
SuperSonic Phonics	Curriculum Assoc.	1,2,3	Supplemental		x				
TIME for Kids Exploring Nonfiction Reading	Teacher Created Materials	1,2	Supplemental			x	x	x	x
Touch Phonics	EPS	2,3	Supplemental	x	x				
Treasures	Macmillan	1	CORE	x	x	x	x	x	x
Treasures	Macmillan/McGraw	1	CORE	x	x	x	x	x	x
Triumphs	Macmillan	1	CORE	x	x	x	x	x	x
Trophies	Harcourt	1	CORE	x	x	x	x	x	x
Ultra Phonics Tutor	ProLexia	1,2,3	Software	x	x				
Universal Literacy	Voyager	1	CORE	x	x	x	x	x	x
Vocabulary Companion	Sunburst	1,2,3	Software					x	
Vocabulary Development	Sunburst	1,2,3	Software					x	
Vocabulary for Achievement	Great Source	2	Supplemental					x	
Voices Reading	Zaner-Bloser	2	CORE	x	x	x	x	x	x
Voyager Extended	Voyager Expanded	2	Supplemental	x	x	x	x	x	x
Voyager Passport	Voyager Expanded	2,3	CORE	x	x	x	x	x	x
Voyager Ticket to Read	Voyager	1	Supplemental			x	x		
Voyager Ticket to Read	Voyager	1	Supplemental					x	x
Waterford Early Rdg.	Addison Wesley	1,2,3	Software	x	x	x	x	x	x
Wilson	Wilson	2,3	Supplemental	x	x	x	x		
Wilson Reading System		3	Supplemental	x	x	x	x	x	x
Word Crunch	Teacher Support	2,3	Software			x	x		
Word Crunch: Common Words	Teacher Support	1	Software			x	x		
Word Explorer	Peoples Education	2	Supplemental					x	
Word Family	Wright Group	2,3	Supplemental		x	x			

Programs & Products for Reading (See Appendix C for web sites)

Product	Publisher	Tier	Type	Phonemic Awareness	Phonics	Word Study	Fluency	Vocabulary	Compre-hension
Word Family	Wright Group	2,3	Supplemental					x	
Word Magic	Mindplay	1,2,3	Supplemental		x				
Word Munchers	Cambridge Dev. Lab	1,2,3	Supplemental		x				
Word Munches	Riverdeep	2,3	Software					x	x
Words at Work	Pacific Learning	2	Supplemental	x	x				
Words at Work	Pacific Learning	2	Supplemental					x	
Words for Academic Writing	Sopris West	2	Supplemental					x	
Wright Skills	Wright Group	2	Supplemental	x	x				

Chapter 3

What is Spelling?

Spelling is a skill that is intimately related to reading and the relationship of letters to sounds. Direct spelling instruction usually begins mid first-grade with teaching the sound that corresponds to the letter. This is the opposite of reading. Spelling instruction follows a logical sequence that begins with phonemic awareness and then sound-symbol association skills. Through proper spelling instruction, a student learns that there are rules for spelling and these rules govern how regular phonemic words are spelled. There are also irregular spelling words (sight words) that do not follow any rules. These words must be memorized through reading and direct instruction.

There is a range of competencies that students must be proficient in if they are to spell correctly. These include:

- **Phonological Encoding:** Phonemic Awareness, Auditory Memory, Auditory Discrimination and Auditory Synthesis are the basis of this skill. The student must be able to attach the sound to the written letter.
- **Grapheme Memory:** Visual Memory, Visual Discrimination, Visual Spatial and Visual Closure are the basis of this skill. The student must be able to attach the visual symbol of the letter to the sound of the letter.
- **Segmentation:** Phonemic Awareness and Phonics are the basis of this skill, which includes all the areas of Auditory and Visual Processing discussed in Phonological Encoding and Grapheme Memory. A student must be able to take words apart sound by sound and syllable by syllable. The student must also be able to blend words together from their separate sounds and syllables.
- **Syllabication Rules and Spelling Generalization Rules:** Phonics and Word Study are the basis of this skill. The student must be able to remember the rules that are associated with syllabication and apply them to spelling. The student must also apply the letter/sound combinations to spelling.
- **Attention to the details of the spelling words:** Automaticity in the knowledge of Phonemic Awareness, Phonics, and Word Study are the basis of this skill. The student must be sufficiently comfortable with his or her knowledge base to pay attention to the spelling word and the rules that apply to it.
- **Semantic and morphological knowledge:** Language skills are an important component to spelling. The student must be able to conceptualize and formulate ideas about words that explain objects, events and relationships.
- **Memory:** Auditory, Auditory Sequential, Visual and Visual Sequential Memory are the basis for this skill. The student must be able to remember and recall the letter sounds, letter symbols and the rules that govern spelling automatically and with speed.
- **Reading:** All the skills used in reading such as Visual Processing, Auditory Processing, Language Processing and the five components of reading effect spelling. The more that a student reads, the better he becomes in spelling.

Underpinnings of Spelling disorders:

In order to remediate spelling errors, the lack of skills that caused the spelling problems in the first place should be addressed. The following sections with their Tier 1, Tier 2 and Tier 3 interventions should, therefore, be considered: (See Table of Contents for location of these strategies/activities.)

- **Auditory Processing**
  - —Auditory Memory
  - —Auditory Discrimination
  - —Auditory Synthesis
- **Visual Processing**
  - —Visual Discrimination
  - —Visual Spatial Processing
  - —Visual and Visual Sequential Memory
  - —Visual Closure
- **Language**
  - —Syntactic Processing
- **Reading**
  - —Phonemic Awareness
  - —Phonics
    - Letter Naming Skills
    - Letter-Sounds Associative Skills
  - —Word Study

Characteristics of poor spelling skills with <u>auditory processing weaknesses</u>:

- Difficulty discriminating between individual sounds in the beginning, middle and end of words
- Difficulty processing rapid auditory input so that consonant sounds that cannot be sustained are not perceived
- Poor ability remembering and analyzing the sequence of individual sounds and sequences of sounds (syllables) in words
- Difficulty blending individual sounds into words
- Difficulty listening to words and omitting one sound and substituting another
- Difficulty remembering the sounds that individual letter and phonetically regular/ irregular letter combinations represent
- Difficulty rapidly retrieving letter sounds while analyzing words, so that the beginning of the word is forgotten by the time the last sound of the word is heard
- Difficulty with vowel sounds
- Substituting of words that are conceptually related but not phonetically related
- Difficulty with sight vocabulary and memorization
- Guessing at unfamiliar words rather than using word analysis skills
- Spelling below reading level by two years
- Correct spelling based on redundancy rather than knowledge
- Bizarre spellings with no specific error pattern
- Spelling word is visually close to being spelled correctly but is phonetically incorrect
- Spelling word is phonetically spelled correctly but is visually incorrect
- Spelling correct in isolation but not transferable into sentence or paragraph form
- Words are spelled with omissions, insertions, transposition or reversals of letters
- Spelling homonyms incorrectly even when the homonyms are in sentences that give the student the meaning of the word
- Spelling errors more evident in written language

Characteristics of poor spelling skills with visual processing weaknesses:

- Confusion with letters that differ in orientation (e.g., b-d, m-w, p-q, t-f)
- Confusion with words that can be reversed (e.g., saw-was)
- Very limited sight vocabulary
- Losing one's place while reading
- Omitting letters and words because they are not visually noted
- Omitting letters within words
- Difficulty learning irregular words that cannot be sounded out
- Difficulty with rapid retrieval of words due to visual memory problems
- Confusion with visual stimuli in reading
- Difficulty sounding out phonetically regular words even up to grade level
- Difficulty recalling the shape of letter when writing
- Spelling phonetically without specific error pattern
- Correctly spelling difficult phonetic words but not simple irregular words
- Spelling correctly in isolation but not transferring into sentence or paragraph form
- Spelling words incorrectly many different ways
- Spelling words with omissions, insertions, transposition or reversals of letter within those words
- Spelling homonyms incorrectly even when they are in sentences that give the student the meaning of the word
- Spelling errors more evident in written language

Spelling	Spelling Tier 1
Spelling is a skill that is intimately related to reading and the relationship of letter to sounds. Spelling instruction follows a logical sequence that begins with phonemic awareness and then adds sound-symbol association skills. A student learns that there are rules for spelling and these rules govern how regular phonemic words are spelled. There are also irregular spelling words (sight words) that do not follow any rules. Unfortunately these words must be memorized through reading and direct instruction. **Modifications and accommodations for spelling:** • Create spelling word bank • Do not count spelling in grading • Use a computer dictionary • Use a computer and spell check	**Suggested Interventionist: General Education Teacher with consultation from the Special Education teacher/Occupational Therapist/Speech Pathologist** **Suggested Session: Small group, explicit instruction within the CORE reading/spelling program 2x a week within the classroom.** **Strategies/Activities for Spelling Skills:** • Teacher will use programs that enhance the acquisition of sound-symbol association. • Student will be taught to use spelling recognition memory. • Student will be taught alternative spellings and asked to pick out the right spelling for the word. • Student will be taught targeted letter combinations for spelling. • Student will be taught specific spelling rules and asked to look at words and pick out the spelling rule that applies. • Student will be given a word bank of correctly spelled words to use in sentences. • Teacher will teach prefixes, suffixes and roots of words.

Spelling Tier 2	Spelling Tier 2
Suggested Interventionist: Reading Teacher; Speech Pathologist; Occupational Therapist, Special Education Teacher **Suggested Session: 30 minutes 2 to 3x a week in a small group or individual inside the classroom.** **Underpinnings Strategies for Spelling Skills (refer to those chapters):** • **Auditory Processing Skills (Tier 2):** —Auditory Memory —Auditory Discrimination —Auditory Synthesis • **Visual Processing Skills (Tier 2):** —Visual Discrimination —Visual Spatial Processing —Visual and Visual Sequential Memory —Visual Closure • **Language Processing Skills (Tier 2):** —Syntactic Processing • **Reading Skills (Tier 2):** —Phonemic Awareness —Phonics • Letter Naming Skills • Letter-Sounds Associative Skills —Word Study	**Strategies/Activities for Spelling Skills:** • Student will be taught all of the sounds for the consonants, blends and vowels. • Student will be taught the six types of syllables: —**Closed Syllable:** The vowel in a syllable will be followed by a consonant. This consonant "closes in" the vowel and causes the vowel to have a short sound. —**Silent /e/ Syllable:** A syllable that has a consonant-vowel-consonant or vowel-consonant configuration will be considered a closed syllable. When an /e/ is added to these combinations, the /e/ is silent but changes the vowel from a "short " sound to a "long" sound. The long sound of the vowel makes the vowel say the name of the vowel. —**Controlled /r/ Syllable:** When the five vowels are followed by the letter /r/, /er/, /ir/, /ur/, /or/, /ar/, the /r/ is said to control the sound of the vowels. The vowels are neither "short" nor "long" but have a different sound. The sounds for /er/, /ir/, /ur/, /ar/, /or/ all have the sound of /er/ as in the examples of: her, bird, turn, collar, actor. The /ar/ has the second sound of /r/, as in star and the /or/ has the sound of /or/ as in horn.

Spelling	Tier 2	Spelling	Tier 2
	—**Consonant /le/ Syllable:** The consonant /le/ always stays together at the end of a word. It will either be the second syllable in a two-syllable word or the third syllable in a three-syllable word. The endings are: /ble/, /zle/, /tle/, /dle/, /gle/, /ple/, /kle/, /cle/ and /fle/. When saying the ending it always sounds as though there is a /ul/ sound as in table, puzzle, little, people, ankle, ruffle, etc. —**Vowel-Vowel Team:** This rule consists of all vowel combinations of two or three vowels, known as vowel diphthongs and vowel digraphs. These combinations of vowels appear together in a syllable and make one sound. —**Open Syllable:** This syllable is different than the closed syllable. It always has a single vowel at the end of the syllable which will be a "long" vowel sound. It is always followed by a single consonant which is part of the next syllable. **Spelling Generalizations Rules:** • **1+1+1 Rule or the Doubling Rule:** In a one-syllable word that has one ending consonant and one vowel before the consonant, the consonant is doubled when an ending beginning with a vowel is added (e.g. gag = gagging). If the ending begins with a consonant, the ending consonant is not doubled (e.g., sad=sadly). Remember, there must be only one syllable, only one consonant at the end and only one vowel preceding the ending consonant.		• **Silent /e/ Rule:** A one-syllable word that ends in /e/ drops the /e/ when an ending that begins with a vowel is added (e.g., blame= blaming). The /e/ is not dropped when adding an ending beginning with a consonant (e.g., like=likely). • **-ful and –ly Rule:** These common suffixes beginning with consonants are added to the base word as they stand. If the base word ends with a silent /e/, the /e/ will not be dropped (e.g., surely). If the base word ends in /l/, the /l/ will not be dropped (e.g., legally). However, if the ending of the word is /le/, the /le/ is dropped and the /ly/ is added (ex: simple= simply). • **The "Y" Rule:** There are two groups of /y/ as an ending. The first group are those ending in /y/ preceded by a consonant. If the word ends in /y/ and is preceded by a consonant, change the /y/ to /i/ when adding a suffix that begins with a vowel (e.g., tries). However, if the suffix begins with an /i/, keep the /y/ and add the suffix (e.g., typist). The second group are words that end in /y/ but are preceded by a vowel. The /y/ is not dropped and the ending is added (e.g., playing).

Spelling Tier 3	Spelling Tier 3
Suggested Interventionist: Special Education Teacher, Reading Teacher; Speech Pathologist; Occupational Therapist **Suggested Session: 60 minutes 5X a week in a small group or individual basis in addition to the CORE spelling program outside of the classroom** **Underpinnings strategies for Spelling Skills (refer to those chapters):** • **Auditory Processing Skills (Tier 3):** —Auditory Memory —Auditory Discrimination —Auditory Synthesis • **Visual Processing Skills (Tier 3):** —Visual Discrimination —Visual Spatial Processing —Visual and Visual Sequential Memory —Visual Closure • **Language Processing Skills (Tier 3):** —Syntactic Processing • **Reading Skills (Tier 3):** —Phonemic Awareness —Phonics • Letter Naming Skills • Letter-Sounds Associative Skills —Word Study	**Strategies/Activities to Develop Letter-Sound Correspondence:** • **Visual Sound Presentation:** Teacher will present sound cards visually for the student to recognize and say. Sounds will be presented individually and the teacher follows a prescribed sequence of sounds. • **Auditory/Kinesthetic Presentation:** Teacher will present sounds. The student will repeat the sound and then write the sound. • **Sounds are taught within a sequence and one at a time.** When each sound is taught, it will be added to the previous sounds and will be reviewed together during the next Visual Sound Presentation. • **Visual Word Presentation:** Word cards that follow the sequence of sounds will be presented visually and the student will be asked to read each word. These words have only one new sound and include a review of the previous sounds taught. • **Auditory/Kinesthetic Word Presentation:** Words that are presented visually will be presented for dictation by the teacher. The student will repeat the words and write them down. • **Visual Presentation of Phrases:** Phrases will be presented visually by the teacher for the student to read. • **Auditory/Kinesthetic Presentation of Phrases:** Phrases will be presented to the student. The student will repeat the phrase and then write it down. • **Visual Presentation of Sentences:** Sentences will be visually presented to the student and the student will read the sentences out loud.

Spelling Tier 3	Spelling Tier 3
• **Auditory/Kinesthetic Presentation of sentences:** Sentences will be presented for dictation to the student. The student will repeat the sentence and write it down. • All sounds will be presented in the above sequence until all consonants, short vowels, blends, diphthongs, digraphs, controlled /r/ sounds and double vowel teams are learned. **Students practice Strategies/Activities with Words:** • **Segmentation**—Teacher will say a one-syllable word (cvc) and will repeat the same word saying the individual sounds of that word. Teacher will show the letter that corresponds to the sound. Student will repeat the individual sounds while pointing to the corresponding letters. • **Blending Sounds**—Teacher will show letters to the student and ask the student to say each individual corresponding sound of the letters shown. The letters spell out a one-syllable word. Student will be asked to look at the letters that spell the word and say the sounds quickly together to blend the word. • **Manipulating Phonemes by Adding a Letter**—Teacher will spell a word. Student and teacher will read the word together. Teacher will add a letter (either in the beginning or end of the word). Student will reread the new word with the additional letter. • **Deleting Letter/Sounds**—Teacher will spell a one-syllable word. Student and teacher will read it together. Teacher will eliminate a letter (from the beginning, end or middle of the word). Student will read the new word.	• **Substituting Letter/Sound**—Teacher will spell a new one-syllable word. Teacher will change a letter to spell a new word. Student will sound out the new word and will read each word quickly. • **Rearranging Letter/Sound**—Teacher will show some letters. Student will tell the teacher the sound corresponding with each independent letter. Teacher will arrange the letters into a word. Student will read the word. Teacher will rearrange the letters to form another word. Student will read the new word. **Strategies/Activities to Develop Word Study:** • Teacher will teach different kinds of commonly occurring letter chunks and spelling patterns, such as: /et/, /ake/; endings /s/, /ed/, /ing/, /er/, /est/; suffixes, prefixes and root words. • Teacher will introduce words that have the same visual configuration as other words for memorization. • Teacher will introduce sight words on 3x5 colored cards repeatedly several times a day. Student will write his own colored cards and will write the sight words on different surfaces to help memory. • Teacher will create a Word Wall with different word families written on the charts. • Teacher will create a Word Wall with contractions, spelling demons, homophones. Teacher will include pictures of the words next to the words. • After words are visually introduced to the student, sentences will be written in different format on the subsequent days for the student to reread.

Spelling Tier 3	Spelling Tier 3
• Student will be given a combination of letters to create the words to which he has been introduced. • Student will sort words by vowel teams and will say the words while sorting them. • Student will play word games with different word families or familiar "chunks" of words. • Student will create new words from root words by adding prefixes and suffixes. • Student will be asked to create his own word list with designated spelling patterns. • Teacher will use pocket charts to model words that turn into contractions. • Teacher will play concentration with syllables that make up two-syllable compound words. • Teacher will create Word Walls with words that have silent letters in them. • Teacher will use K-W-L Chart using words from core subject areas such as social studies and science. • Teacher will use Language Experience Chart. • Teacher will use literacy centers for word sorts, rereading books, writing responses to stories.	**Student is taught the six types of syllables:** • **Closed Syllable:** The vowel in a syllable will be followed by a consonant. This consonant "closes in" the vowel and causes the vowel to have a short sound. • **Silent /e/ Syllable:** A syllable that has a consonant-vowel-consonant or vowel-consonant configuration will be considered a closed syllable. When an /e/ is added to these combinations, the /e/ is silent but changes the vowel from a "short " sound to a "long" sound. The long sound of the vowel makes the vowel say the name of the vowel. • **Controlled /r/ Syllable:** When the five vowels are followed by the letter /r/ /er/, /ir/, /ur/, /or/, /ar/, the /r/ is said to control the sound of the vowels. The vowels are neither "short" nor "long," but have a different sound. The sounds for /er/, /ir/, /ur/, /ar/, /or/ all have the sound of /er/, as in the examples of: her, bird, turn, collar, actor. The /ar/ has the second sound of /r/, as in star, and the /or/ has the sound of /or/, as in horn . • **Consonant /le/ Syllable:** The consonant /le/ always stays together at the end of a word. It will either be the second syllable in a two-syllable word or the third syllable in a three-syllable word. The endings are: /ble/, /zle/, /tle/, /dle/, /gle/, /ple/, /kle/, /cle/ and /fle/. When saying the ending it always sounds as though there is a /ul/ sound, as in table, puzzle, little, people, ankle, ruffle, etc.

Spelling Tier 3	Spelling Tier 3
• **Vowel-Vowel Team:** This rule consists of all vowel combinations of two or three vowels, known as vowel diphthongs and vowel digraphs. These combinations of vowels appear together in a syllable and make one sound. • **Open Syllable:** This syllable is different than the closed syllable. It always has a single vowel at the end of the syllable which will be a "long" vowel sound. It is always followed by a single consonant which is part of the next syllable. **Spelling Generalizations Rules:** • **1+1+1 Rule, or the Doubling Rule:** In a one-syllable word that has one ending consonant and one vowel before the consonant, the consonant is doubled when an ending beginning with a vowel is added (e.g., gag = gagging). If the ending begins with a consonant, the ending consonant is not doubled (e.g., sad = sadly). Remember: there must be only one syllable, only one consonant at the end and only one vowel preceding the ending consonant. • **Silent /e/ Rule:** A one-syllable word that ends in /e/ drops the /e/ when an ending that begins with a vowel is added (e.g., blame = blaming). The /e/ is not dropped when adding an ending beginning with a consonant (e.g., like = likely). • **-ful and –ly Rule:** These common suffixes beginning with consonants are added to the base word as they stand. If the base word ends with a silent /e/, the /e/ will not be dropped (e.g., surely). If the base word ends in /l/, the /l/ will not be dropped (e.g., legally). However, if the ending of the word is /le/, the /le/ is dropped and the /ly/ is added (e.g., simple = simply).	• **The "Y" Rule:** There are two groups of /y/ as an ending. The first group are those ending in /y/ preceded by a consonant. If the word ends in /y/ and is preceded by a consonant, change the /y/ to /i/ when adding a suffix that begins with a vowel (e.g., tries). However, if the suffix begins with an /i/, keep the /y/ and add the suffix (e.g., typist). The second group are words that end in /y/ but are preceded by a vowel. The /y/ is not dropped and the ending is added (e.g., playing).

Programs & Products for Spelling/Written Expression (See Appendix C for web sites) pg. 1 of 3

Product	Publisher	Tier	Type	Spelling	Writing	Grammar	PA/Phonics	Word Study
Basic Grammar Series	PCI	1,2,3	Supplemental			X		
Basic Writing Series	PCI	1,2,3	Supplemental		X	X		
Basic Writing Skills	Sopris West	2,3	Supplemental		X			
Draftbuilder	Don Johnson	2,3	Software		X			
Editor in Chief	Critical Thinking	1,2,	Supplemental		X	X		
EZ Stroywriter	PCI	1,2,3	Software		X	X		
Find the Errors	PCI	1,2,3	Supplemental	X	X	X		
Got Grammar	PCI	1,2,3	Supplemental			X		
Grammar Fun	PCI	1,2	Supplemental			X		
High Noon Spelling	Academic Therapy	2,3	Supplemental	X				
High Performance Writing	SRA	2,3	Supplemental		X	X		
Key Skills for Reading & Spelling	Sunburst	2,3	Software	X			X	
Key Skills for Reading: Letters & Sounds	Sunburst	2,3	Software	X			X	
Key Skills Phonics Solution	Sunburst	2,3	Software	X			X	
Kids Works Deluxe	SunBurst	2,3	Software		X			
LA Warm UP	PCI	1,2,3	Supplemental	X	X	X		
Language Concepts Bundle	SunBurst	2,3	Software		X			
Language Concepts—	SunBurst	2,3	Software		X			
Parts of Speech								
Language Concepts—Writing	Sun-burst	2,3	Software		X			
Language Mechanics	Critical Thinking	1,2	Supplemental		X	X		
Language Smarts	Critical Thinking	2,3	Supplemental	X	X	X		
Letter Tiles for Spelling	Sopris West	1,2,3	Supplemental	X			X	
Letters & Numbers	Sunburst	2,3	Software	X			X	X
Missing Links	Sunburst	2,3	Software	X	X		X	X

Programs & Products for Spelling/Written Expression (See Appendix C for web sites) pg. 2 of 3

Product	Publisher	Tier	Type	Spelling	Writing	Grammar	PA/Phonics	Word Study
Paragraph Editing	PCI	1,2,3	Supplemental	x	x	x		
Paragraph Practice Series	PCI	1,2,3	Supplemental	x	x	x		
Phonics3a-Adverbs.	Sun-burst	2,3	Software	x				
Phonics 1a,1b,2a:Vowel Sounds	Sunburst	2,3	Software	x			x	
Phonics 3b-Adverbs	Sunburst	2,3	Software	x				x
Prescriptive Spelling	SRA	2,3	Supplemental	x	x	x		
Proofreading Curriculum	PCI	1,2,3	Supplemental	x	x	x		
Punctuation Puzzle	Critical Thinking	1,2	Supplemental		x	x		
Reading for Meaning	Sunburst	2,3	Software		x			
Real Word Writing	PCI	1,2,3	Supplemental	x	x	x		
Sentence Factory	PCI	1,2,3	Supplemental	x	x	x		
Sentence Fun	PCI	1,2,3	Supplemental		x	x		
Sentence Master	Laureate	2,3	Software		x	x		
Sound Partners	Sopris West	1,2,3	Supplemental	x			x	
Spell Doctor	Sopris West	1,2	Supplemental	x				
Spell That Right	PCI	1,2	Supplemental	x				
Spelling Blaster	Sun-burst	2,3	Software	x				
Spelling DooRiddles	Critical Thinking	1,2	Supplemental					
Spelling Through Morphographs	SRA	2,3	Supplemental	x				
Spellography	Sopris West	1,2,3	Supplemental	x				
Spotlight on Writing	SRA	1,2,3	Supplemental		x	x		
SRA Spelling	SRA	2,3	Supplemental	x				
Step Up to Writing	Sopris West	2,3	Supplemental		x			
Step Up to Writing in Math	Sopris West	2,3	Supplemental		x			
Storybook Weaver Deluxe	Sunburst	2,3	Software		x			
Swim,Swam,Swum	Laureate	2,3	Software		x	x		x
Teach It, Write It, Test It	PCI	1,2,3	Supplemental		x	x		

Programs & Products for Spelling/Written Expression (See Appendix C for web sites)

Product	Publisher	Tier	Type	Spelling	Writing	Grammar	PA/Phonics	Word Study
Tracking Down Parts of Speech	PCI	1,2,3	Software			x		
Twenty Categories	Laureate	2,3	Software		x	x		
Types of Writing	PCI	1,2,3	Supplemental		x	x		
Word Roots	Critical Thinking	2,3	Supplemental	x				
Write Outloud	Don Johnson	2,3	Software		x			
Writers Block	SunBurst	2,3	Software		x			
Writing Basics	PCI	1,2,3	Supplemental		x	x		
Writing Process Series	SunBurst	2,3	Software		x			
Writing Trek Series	PCI	1,2,3	Software		x	x		

CHAPTER 4

What is Written Expression?

Written expression is the ability to write one's thoughts in sentences and paragraphs with the correct use of grammar, spelling and sequence of thought.

Different Written Language Areas

1. Visual Spatial Difficulties—problems forming letter shapes, and upper and lower case letters. Difficulty maintaining consistent spacing between letters and words and staying on a line or within margins. (Strategies/activities for these difficulties are not included in this edition.)

2. Language Processing Difficulties—problems organizing thoughts on paper, involving deficits in skills such as spelling, vocabulary, grammar, syntax and organization.

Key Characteristics of written language problems:

- Difficulty expressing thoughts in writing; avoidance of writing tasks
- Difficulty in spelling, grammar skills, punctuation
- Unfinished words or letters, or omitted words in writing samples
- Writing content which does not reflect the student's spoken language
- Talking to self while writing
- Writing does not make sense; run on sentences; sentence fragments
- Difficulty with syntax
- Difficulty organizing thoughts on paper
- Difficulty keeping track of thoughts already written down
- Large gap between written ideas and ideas spoken aloud
- Extreme slowness and little output when writing and putting thoughts on paper
- Difficulty copying from the board
- Difficulty taking notes
- Difficulty with print or cursive writing
- Difficulty thinking of words to write

Written Expression: Vocabulary

Vocabulary	Vocabulary Tier 1
Vocabulary—adequate vocabulary development is necessary for competent writing. Examples of academic problems in this area: • Vocabulary below age level • Difficulty understanding vocabulary words • Difficulty generating antonyms, synonyms, homonyms • Difficulty retrieving words • Difficulty generating homophones and homographs • Difficulty using adjectives and adverbs correctly • Difficulty using vocabulary words correctly **Accommodations and Modifications:** • Preferential seating • Oral directions and written directions • Note taker buddy • Teacher's copy of lecture outline • VAKT information presented together • Tape recorders to supplement note taking • Tape recording important assignments • Partially completed outline so student can fill in details with one or two words • Use of a spell checker • Allow abbreviations in some writing (i.e., b/c for because) • Do not count spelling on rough drafts • Decreased quantity of written work to be produced • Decreased complexity of the writing task • Decreased rate of producing written work • Additional time for writing tasks including note taking and copying • Use of writing computer programs	**Suggested Interventionist: General Education Teacher with consultation from the Speech Pathologist/Special Education Teacher/ Reading Teacher** **Suggested Session: Small group, explicit instruction within the CORE program 2x a week within the classroom** **Strategies/Activities for Vocabulary Development:** • Student will identify the parts of a dictionary entry and demonstrate understanding of each part. • Student will demonstrate appropriate use of a dictionary. • Student will keep vocabulary notebooks or vocabulary word boxes. • Student will draw representations of new vocabulary words and their associated concepts. • Student will give appropriate definitions for words that have more than one definition. • Student will use new vocabulary in sentences. • Student will work with two or three other students when learning new vocabulary words and their definitions. • Teacher will list vocabulary words from content area subjects on the board and develop their definitions with student. • Teacher will give examples of how to use new vocabulary words in sentences. • Teacher will provide student with lists of homonyms explaining differences in meaning; student will use the homonyms in sentences.

Vocabulary Tier 2	Vocabulary Tier 3
Suggested Interventionist: Reading Teacher; Speech Pathologist; Special Education Teacher	**Suggested Interventionist: Special Education Teacher, Reading Teacher; Speech Pathologist**
Suggested Session: 30 minutes 2 to 3x a week in a small group or individual in addition to the CORE writing program inside the classroom.	**Suggested Session: 60 minutes 5X a week in a small group or individual basis in addition to the CORE writing program outside of the classroom**
Strategies for Vocabulary Development: • Student will learn to correctly pronounce new words by utilizing online dictionary sound files. • Student will frequently review new vocabulary. • Student will develop semantic maps for new vocabulary words. • Student will organize vocabulary words according to categories. • Student will break down new vocabulary words into useful chunks (For example: the vocabulary word is "chariot." The student will answer the questions "What is it?" "What category does it belong to?" "When was it used?" "Where was it used?" "What does it look like?"). • Student will play games of matching vocabulary words with their definitions. • Teacher will point out new definitions for previously learned words. • Teacher will provide positive feedback when new vocabulary words are used. • Teacher will give the student a topic of conversation, such as transportation, and ask the student to discuss the topic for two minutes using new and known vocabulary words in their conversation.	**Strategies for Vocabulary Development:** • Student will identify the parts of a dictionary entry and demonstrate understanding of each. • Student will demonstrate appropriate use of a dictionary. • Student will keep vocabulary notebooks or vocabulary word boxes. • Student will draw representations of new vocabulary words and their associated concepts. • Student will give appropriate definitions for words that have more than one definition. • Student will use new vocabulary in sentences. • Student will work with two or three other students when learning new vocabulary words and their definitions. • Teacher will provide the student with lists of homophones explaining meanings and will ask student to use the homonyms in sentences. • Teacher will provide the student with lists of homographs explaining meanings and will ask the student to use the homographs in sentences. • Teacher will provide the student with a list of words containing homonyms, homographs and homophones and will ask the students to separate the words according to type (homonyms, homographs, homophones).

Written Expression: Sentence Writing

<table>
<tr><th>Sentence Writing</th><th>Sentence Writing Tier 1</th></tr>
<tr><td>

Sentence Writing—involves the ability to generate sentences that are governed by English syntax and English grammar rules. Examples of academic problems in this area:

- Difficulty with sentence structure
- Sentence fragments
- Overuse of simple sentences
- Difficulty generating complex sentences

Accommodations and Modifications:

- Preferential seating
- Oral directions and written directions
- Note taker buddy
- Teacher's copy of lecture outline
- VAKT information presented together
- Tape recorders to supplement note taking
- Tape recording important assignments
- Partially completed outline so student can fill in details with one or two words
- Use of a spell checker
- Allow abbreviations in some writing (e.g., b/c for because)
- Do not count spelling on rough drafts
- Decreased quantity of written work to be produced
- Decreased complexity of the writing task
- Decreased rate of producing written work
- Additional time for writing tasks including note taking and copying
- Use of writing computer programs

</td><td>

Interventionist: General Education Teacher with consultation from the Speech Pathologist/Special Education Teacher/Reading Specialist

Session: Small group, explicit instruction within the CORE program 2x a week within the classroom

Strategies/activities for Sentence Writing:

- Teacher will explain that a sentence is a complete thought with a subject and a verb.
- Student will read sentences and identify the subject and the verb of each sentence.
- Teacher will explain what a sentence fragment is: a phrase or group of words that are related but do not make a complete thought, with a subject and a verb.
- Student will change sentence fragments into complete sentences.
- Teacher will teach the student to improve simple sentences by using stronger action verbs. Teacher and student will develop lists of strong action verbs.
- Teacher will teach the student to improve simple sentences by using better descriptor words such as adjectives and adverbs. The teacher and student will develop lists of adjectives and adverbs.
- Teacher will identify the four types of sentences (declarative, interrogative, imperative and exclamatory) and will give the student lists of sentences that must be categorized according to the sentence types.

</td></tr>
</table>

Sentence Writing Tier 1	Sentence Writing Tier 2
• Student will practice writing the four types of sentences using the same topic. • Student will change declarative sentences to interrogative, exclamatory or imperative sentences. • Teacher will provide the student with lists of subordinate conjunctions. • Teacher will demonstrate how to use each subordinate conjunction in a sentence. • Student will generate sentences which incorporate subordinate conjunctions using the complex sentences structure. • Teacher will ask student to revise sentences using stronger word pictures. • Teacher will bring in comic strips and will ask student to write a sentence under each picture in the comic strip. • Teacher will exchange student sentences from the above strategy and will ask student to identify the vivid descriptive words. • Teacher will discuss/define a complete sentence, a sentence fragment and a run-on sentence. Student will identify each of the three types of sentences from a group of thirty sentences. • Student will practice writing sentences using "time" words, such as final, last, next, before, after, during. • Student will write a "how to" paragraph using the above "time" words.	**Suggested Interventionist: Reading Teacher; Speech Pathologist; Special Education Teacher** **Suggested Session: 30 minutes 2 to 3x a week in a small group or individual in addition to the CORE writing program inside the classroom.** **Strategies/activities for Sentence Writing:** • Student will chunk sentences into a "who" section, an "action" section, a "what" section, and a "when" section. Student will be shown how to fold paper into four columns and write the appropriate word in each column. • Teacher will show the student sentence patterns such as "who," "action," "what," "where," etc., and ask the student to create his own sentences. • Student will find sentences from magazines and newspapers and categorize the sentences according to learned sentence patterns. • Teacher will show student how to answer a question with a declarative sentence by using part of the question in the sentence. • Teacher will discuss the three basic sentence structures: simple, compound and complex. Examples of all three structures are kept on the blackboard, or on a transparency or in a "Sentence Box," which is a 4" x 7" box for storing note cards. • Teacher will identify a topic and student will create sentences for each sentence structure. Student will work with a partner for this activity.

Sentence Writing Tier 2	Sentence Writing Tier 2
• Teacher will have student write one sentence for each sentence structure. Student will then exchange sentences with a partner who will try to write a better sentence. • Student will change declarative sentences to interrogative, exclamatory or imperative sentences. • Teacher will provide the student with lists of subordinate conjunctions. • Teacher will demonstrate how to use each subordinate conjunction in a sentence. • Student will generate sentences incorporating subordinate conjunctions using the complex sentence structure. • Teacher will provide student with pictures and photographs of people engaged in action activities and ask the student to write a sentence describing the action using one adverb. Teacher will ask student to share his sentences with other students in their group. • Teacher will give student lists of words (adverbs) that convey a vivid "word picture" (e.g., nervously, laughingly, slowly, disgustedly). Teacher will then ask student to write sentences using these words. • Teacher will give student passages to read and ask him to highlight the "word picture." • Teacher will provide student with lists of sensory words, such as see, hear, taste, touch, and then ask student to develop semantic word maps that can describe the sensory words. • Teacher will ask student to write sentences using a sensory word description from their semantic word map. • Teacher will provide student with character cartoon pictures and ask student to write a sentence using descriptive words (adjectives, adverbs) to describe the cartoon character.	• Teacher will bring in comic strips and ask student to write a sentence under each picture in the comic strip. • Teacher will teach semantic mapping. (Student will work with four or five other students. One student will be the scribe. A concept to be studied is written on the middle of a large piece of paper. Each student identifies an associated concept or thought about the targeted word. The scribe writes down the students' thoughts on Post-it Notes, one thought per note. The Post-its are placed on the large paper. Then the student will categorize their ideas into four or five major ideas.) • Teacher will discuss/define a complete sentence, a sentence fragment and a run-on sentence. Student will identify from a group of thirty sentences each of the three types of sentences. • Student will change sentence fragments to complete sentences. • Student will practice writing sentences using "time" words, such as final, last, next, before, after, during. • Student will write a "how to" paragraph using the above "time" words.

Sentence Writing Tier 3	Sentence Writing Tier 3
Suggested Interventionist: Special Education Teacher, Reading Teacher; Speech Pathologist **Suggested Session: 60 minutes 5x a week in a small group or individual basis in addition to the CORE writing program outside of the classroom** **Strategies/Activities for Sentence Writing:** • Teacher will have student read an article or story and then ask student questions about the story and have him write short responses (a couple of words or phrases) on a sheet of paper. • Teacher will teach brainstorming by selecting a topic and asking the student to give ideas about the topic. Teacher will write the ideas on the board so student can see all the ideas. This provides visual reminders of what has been said and facilitates connections between various concepts.) • Teacher will have student practice answering question words such as "who," "what," "why," "when," "where," "how." • Student will write dictated messages providing information on "who," "what," "when," "where," "why." • Teacher will discuss/define a complete sentence, a sentence fragment and a run-on sentence. Student will identify from a group of thirty sentences each of the three types of sentences. • Student will change sentence fragments to complete sentences.	• Student will change run-on sentences to complete sentences. • Student will combine two simple sentences into a single sentence using "but." • Student will write a "how to" paragraph using the above "time" words. • Student will change declarative sentences to interrogative, exclamatory or imperative sentences. • Teacher will provide lists of subordinate conjunctions and demonstrate how to use each one in a sentence. • Student will generate sentences incorporating subordinate conjunctions using the complex sentence structure. • Teacher will provide student with pictures and photographs of people engaged in action activities and ask student to write a sentence describing the action using one adverb. Teacher will ask student to share his sentences with other students in a group. • Teacher will teach semantic mapping. (Student will work in groups of four or five. One student will be the scribe. A concept to be studied is written on the middle of a large piece of paper. Each student identifies an associated concept or thought about the targeted word. The scribe writes down the students' thoughts on Post-it Notes, one thought per note. The Post-its are placed on the large paper. Then the students will categorize their ideas into four or five major ideas.)

Written Expression: Developing Written Expression

Developing Written Expression	Developing Written Expression Tier 1
Writing Paragraphs—this skill requires students to engage in pre-writing exercises such as reading, brainstorming, discussing; developing outlines; organizing facts, details, etc; using transitions; writing conclusions; revising; proofreading. **Accommodations and Modifications:** • Preferential seating • Oral directions and written directions • Note taker buddy • Teacher's copy of lecture outline • VAKT information presented together • Tape recorders to supplement note taking • Tape recording important assignments • Partially completed outline so student can fill in details with one or two words • Use of a spell checker • Allow abbreviations in some writing (i.e., b/c for because) • Do not count spelling on rough drafts • Decreased quantity of written work to be produced • Decreased complexity of the writing task • Decreased rate of producing written work • Additional time for writing tasks including note taking and copying • Use of writing computer programs	**Interventionist: General Education Teacher with consultation from the Speech Pathologist/Special Education Teacher/ Reading Teacher** **Session: Small group, explicit instruction within the CORE program 2x within the classroom** **Strategies/activities for Prewriting:** • Student will identify a topic or area of interest. Student will read and gather information about the topic and then write important or interesting facts learned about the topic. • Teacher will demonstrate how to brainstorm. (Teacher will introduce a topic and ask students to give their ideas about the topic. Teacher will write down all the ideas on the board and give student cues that are associated with the topic. For example: Topic—Pollution. Student will brainstorm on what is in the environment, what is useful to the environment, what is harmful to the environment.) • Student will review and discuss his writing with other students in the classroom. • Student will record questions or ideas that were generated during group discussion. • Teacher will introduce the brainstorming activity called Semantic Mapping. (Students will work in groups of four or five. One student is designated as scribe and writes down brainstormed words, ideas, phrases.)

Developing Written Expression Tier 1	Developing Written Expression Tier 1
• Teacher will demonstrate how to write an introductory paragraph which introduces the main idea of an essay. • Student will write introductory paragraphs after having been given main idea prompts such as, "My favorite sport is…" • Teacher will demonstrate how to write a concluding paragraph of an essay after presenting an essay which lacks the concluding paragraph. • Student will practice writing concluding paragraphs after studying several essays lacking concluding paragraphs. • Teacher will show student how to write an informal outline using overhead transparencies. (The informal outline will consist of topic, key ideas about the topic, and examples or explanations of the key ideas.) • Teacher will use the informal outline to write several paragraphs. Student will attempt to write paragraph from the informal outline. **Strategies/Activities for Writing Paragraphs:** • Student will generate ideas and words associated with an assigned topic. • Student will write a paragraph from a basic outline for several paragraphs. • Teacher will explain how to free-write. (After reading and brain-storming, the student will write one page about the topic, using his semantic maps or self-questions, but he must write continually for ten minutes.)	• Teacher will give the student familiar topics, such as favorite restaurant or favorite TV show, about which to free-write. • Student will write in his journal every day, choosing his own topics. • Teacher will have an index card box with topics and associated questions to help provide suggestions for journaling. • Teacher will use Venn diagrams to help student write, compare and contrast paragraphs. • Teacher will use sequential chain graphic organizers to show cause and effect. • Teacher will use circular graphic organizer to show cycles. • Teacher will teach the student to outline before writing. • Teacher will tell student to draw a picture of a thought for a paragraph he intends to write. • Student will dictate ideas for a paragraph into a tape recorder and then listen to them later write them down. • Student will use a computer to organize information and check spelling. • Student will outline thoughts for paragraphs by writing one key word or phrase for each paragraph, and then return later to write the sentences for the paragraph. • Student will try quietly talking to self while writing. This may provide useful auditory feedback.

Developing Written Expression Tier 2	Developing Written Expression Tier 2
Suggested Interventionist: Reading Teacher; Speech Pathologist; Special Education Teacher **Suggested Session: 30 minutes 2 to 3x a week in a small group or individual in addition to the CORE writing program inside the classroom.** **Strategies/Activities for Prewriting:** • Teacher will demonstrate how to brainstorm. (Teacher will introduce a topic and ask the student to give ideas about the topic. Teacher will write down all the ideas on the board. Teacher will give cues that are associated with the topic For example: Topic—Pollution. Teacher will ask the student to brainstorm on what is in the environment, what is useful to the environment, what is harmful to the environment.) • Teacher will give the student examples of how to answer "why" questions. (e.g., "Why is it a good idea to rake leaves in the fall?" —because you can fall on wet leaves, —because they blow on everyone else's lawn, —because they cover the grass and freeze over the grass.) • Teacher will pose several "why" questions and ask student to answer each question with several "because" answers. Then the student will arrange "because" answers into a paragraph. • Teacher will demonstrate how to write an introductory paragraph which introduces the main idea of an essay. • Student will write introductory paragraphs after being given main idea prompts such as, "My favorite sport is…"	• Teacher will demonstrate how to write a concluding paragraph of an essay after presenting the student with an essay which lacks the concluding paragraph. • Student will practice writing concluding paragraphs after having been given several essays without concluding paragraphs. • Teacher will show student how to write an informal outline using overhead transparencies. (The informal outline will consist of topic, key ideas about the topic, and examples or explanations of the key ideas. **Strategies/Activities for Writing Paragraphs:** • The teacher will assign a topic and the student will generate ideas and words associated with the topic. • Teacher will teach independent brainstorming. Teacher will give the student a topic and ask the student to list what he knows about the topic. • Teacher will teach self-questioning or question asking. Teacher will provide model questions to use: What do I know about this topic? What am I writing about it? Can I connect this topic to anything else? How can I group my ideas? • Teacher will explain how to free-write. After reading and brainstorming, the student will write one page about the topic. Student will use semantic maps or self-questions, but must write continually for ten minutes.

Developing Written Expression Tier 2	Developing Written Expression Tier 2
• Teacher will give student familiar topics, such as favorite restaurant, or favorite TV show, about which to free-write. • Student will write in his journal every day. Student will choose his own topics. Teacher will have an index card box with topics and associated questions to help student write in his journal if the student asks for suggestions. • Teacher will ask the student to free-write on a topic, but emphasize the senses when writing about the topic. (Example: the topic is butterflies and student must free-write only about what the sense of sight tells us about butterflies.) • Teacher will ask student to free-write about his bedroom or a familiar place and describe the place using all five senses. • Teacher will teach student to use graphic organizers when preparing to write a paragraph. The graphic organizer is a visual representation of information. • Teacher will illustrate how to use a Venn diagram when writing compare-and-contrast paragraphs. • Teacher will illustrate how to use a sequential chain graphic organizer when writing a cause-and-effect paragraph. • Teacher will draw a circular graphic organizer when writing about cycles. • Teacher will demonstrate how to outline a topic before writing the paragraph.	**Strategies/Activities for Proofreading:** • Teacher will teach student to use the COPS* acronym developed by Schumacher, Nolan, and Deshler **C** — Capitalization **O** — Oral Reading **P** — Punctuation **S** — Spelling • Teacher will give student sentences to read and correct, using the COPS strategy. • Teacher will display COPS acronym available on the bulletin board. • Teacher will ask student to exchange his written paragraphs or essays with a fellow student and make corrections if necessary.

Developing Written Expression Tier 3	Developing Written Expression Tier 3
Suggested Interventionist: Special Education Teacher, Reading Teacher; Speech Pathologist **Suggested Session: 60 minutes 5x a week in a small group or individual basis in addition to the CORE writing program outside of the classroom** **Strategies/Activities for Prewriting:** • Teacher will demonstrate how to write an introductory paragraph which introduces the main idea of an essay. • Teacher will demonstrate how to write a concluding paragraph of an essay after presenting student with an essay which lacks the concluding paragraph. • Teacher will read a story to the class and ask the student if the story makes him think of something. He can stop listening and write down what he is are thinking about. • Student will keep all written work in a classroom notebook or folder. • Teacher will show student how to write an informal outline using overhead transparencies. (The informal outline will consist of topic, key ideas about the topic, and examples or explanations of the key ideas).	Strategies/Activities for Writing Paragraphs: • Teacher will assign a topic and the student will generate ideas and words associated with the topic. • Teacher will give student familiar topics, such as favorite restaurant, or favorite TV show, about which to free-write. • Student will write in his journal every day, choosing his own topics. Teacher will have an index card box with topics and associated questions to help student if he asks for suggestions. • Teacher will ask the student to free-write on a topic, but emphasize the senses when writing about the topic. For example: the topic is butterflies and student must free-write only about what the sense of sight tells us about butterflies. • Teacher will ask student to free-write about his bedroom or a familiar place and describe the place using all five senses. • Teacher will teach student to use graphic organizers when preparing to write a paragraph. The graphic organizer is a visual representation of information. • Teacher will use Venn diagrams to help the student write, compare and contrast paragraphs. • Teacher will use sequential chain graphic organizers to show cause and effect.

Developing Written Expression Tier 3	
• Teacher will use circular graphic organizer to show cycles. • Teacher will teach outlining before writing. Strategies/Activities for Proofreading: • Teacher will teach student to use the COPS* acronym developed by Schumacher, Nolan, and Deshler **C** — Capitalization **O** — Oral Reading **P** — Punctuation **S** — Spelling • Teacher will give the student a checklist to use consistently after writing. The checklist will be more specific than COPS. • Teacher will provide student with an extensive checklist to use for proofreading. The checklist will include reminders that sentences are complete thoughts.	

Written Expression: Paragraph Frames

<table>
<tr><th>Paragraph Frames</th><th>Paragraph Frames Tier 1</th></tr>
<tr><td>

Paragraph Frames—Paragraph Frames help students organize when they are writing multiple paragraphs. Expository paragraph frames provide a structure for retelling information presented in expository text. There are five basic ways to organize information in expository text:

- Description—topic introduced and followed by attributes;
- Sequence—topic introduced and details presented in order;
- Cause/effect—event introduced and its effects described;
- Compare/contrast—similarities and differences in two or more things are presented;
- Problem/solution—a problem is presented and student fills in details with one or two words.

Accommodations and Modifications:

- Encourage use of a spell checker
- Allow abbreviations in some writing (i.e., b/c for because)
- Do not grade spelling on rough drafts
- Decrease the volume of written work to be produced
- Decrease the complexity of the writing task
- Decrease the rate of producing written work
- Allow more time for writing tasks including note taking and copying
- Allow the use of computer writing programs

</td><td>

Interventionist: General Education Teacher with consultation from the Speech Pathologist/Special Education Teacher

Session: Small group, explicit instruction within the CORE program 2x within the classroom

Strategies/Activities for Paragraph Frames:

- Teacher will provide student with outlines or paragraph frames for writing. (Paragraph frames ensure that students use sentences in a paragraph that follow logically and develop an idea. In the paragraph frame the first sentence is the topic sentence which is followed by details to support the topic sentence. The last sentence is a conclusion sentence. The frame takes the form of topic sentence, supporting details, conclusion.)
- Teacher will define a topic sentence, detail sentence, concluding sentence.
- Teacher will give student paragraphs to read and ask him to identify the topic sentence, supporting details and concluding sentence.
- Teacher will give student a topic sentence and ask him to write two more sentences that support the topic.
- Teacher will provide student with the following frame for a five-sentence paragraph:

Topic Sentence ____________________
Detail 1 ____________________
Detail 2 ____________________
Detail 3 ____________________
Concluding Sentence ____________________

</td></tr>
</table>

Paragraph Frames Tier 1	Paragraph Frames Tier 2
• Teacher will ask student to write two paragraphs using the above frame twice. Teacher will give student the lead topic sentence: "There are three reasons I like the autumn and there are three reasons I dislike autumn." • Student will use graphic organizers to help write paragraphs. • Teacher will introduce the following paragraph frame that gives more support to the problem writer. • Example: All living things are made of cells. For example, ______________, __________________, ______________, and ______________ are all made of cells. Cells vary in size from____________ to______________. All cells have three parts ____________, ____________ and ____________. Every cell's DNA has 2 functions:____________, and ____________. The cell is the fundamental structural unit of all living organisms. • Teacher will give student a list of transitional words to use when connecting details in a paragraph. • Student will use graphic organizers to help write paragraphs.	**Suggested Interventionist: Reading Teacher; Speech Pathologist; Special Education Teacher** **Suggested Session: 30 minutes 2 to 3x a week in a small group or individual in addition to the CORE writing program inside the classroom.** **Strategies/Activities for Paragraph Frames:** • Teacher will provide the student with outlines or paragraph frames for writing. (Paragraph frames ensure that students use sentences in a paragraph that follow logically and develop an idea. In the paragraph frame the first sentence is the topic sentence which is followed by details to support the topic sentence. The last sentence is a conclusion sentence. The frame takes the form of topic sentence, supporting details, conclusion.) • Teacher will give the student a topic sentence and ask him to write two more sentences that support the topic. • Teacher will provide student with paragraphs that have no conclusion and ask student to write a concluding sentence. • Teacher will give student a cartoon strip of five pictures/cartoons and ask student to write a topic sentence for the first cartoon, three supporting sentences for the next three cartoons, and a concluding sentence for the last cartoon. • Teacher will give student a list of transitional words and phrases, such as "however," "on the other hand," "in contrast," to use when introducing the second paragraph of a two paragraph essay.

Paragraph Frames Tier 3	Paragraph Frames Tier 3
Suggested Interventionist: Special Education Teacher, Reading Teacher; Speech Pathologist **Suggested Session: 60 minutes 5x a week in a small group or individual basis in addition to the CORE writing program outside of the classroom** **Strategies/Activities for Paragraph Frames:** • Teacher will provide student with outlines or paragraph frames for writing. Paragraph frames ensure that students use sentences in a paragraph that follow logically and develop an idea. In the paragraph frame the first sentence is the topic sentence which is followed by details to support the topic sentence. The last sentence is a conclusion sentence. The frame takes the form of topic sentence, supporting details, conclusion. • Teacher will provide student with paragraphs that have no conclusion and ask the student to write a concluding sentence. • Teacher will give student a cartoon strip of five pictures/cartoons and ask student to write a topic sentence for the first cartoon, three supporting sentences for the next three cartoons, and a concluding sentence for the last cartoon. • Teacher will give student a list of transitional words and phrases, such as "however," "on the other hand," "in contrast," to use when introducing the second paragraph of a two-paragraph essay. • Teacher will give student a list of transitional words to use when connecting details in a paragraph.	• Teacher will ask student to write two paragraphs using the above frame twice. Teacher will give student the lead topic sentence: "There are three reasons I like the autumn and there are three reasons I dislike autumn." • Student will use graphic organizers to help write paragraphs. • Teacher will illustrate the following paragraph frame that gives more support to the problem writer. • Example: All living things are made of cells. For example, ____________, ____________, ____________, and ____________ are all made of cells. Cells vary in size from____________ to____________. All cells have three parts ____________, ____________ and ____________. Every cell's DNA has 2 functions:____________, and ____________. The cell is the fundamental structural unit of all living organisms. • Teacher will give student a list of transitional words to use when connecting details in a paragraph. • Student will use graphic organizers to help write paragraphs.
	For *Programs & Products for Written Expression*, see end of Chapter 3 (Spelling Section).

Chapter 5

Math

The National Council of Teachers of Mathematics, the world's largest organization devoted to improving mathematics education, has developed a set of mathematical concepts, or standards, that are important for teaching and learning mathematics. There are two categories of standards: thinking math standards and content math standards. The thinking standards focus on the nature of mathematical reasoning, and include problem solving, communication, reasoning, and connections. The content standards are specific to math topics and include estimation, number sense, geometry and spatial sense, measurement, statistics and probability, fractions and decimals, and patterns and relationships.

Achieving math concepts or standards requires that a student develop critical factors that affect math learning. These factors include a student's cognitive ability of awareness of the knowledge that must be learned as well as the ability to process information both as a quantitative learner who breaks down math problems into pieces, being very methodological and sequential as well as a qualitative learner who approaches math holistically and intuitively, reasoning by verbalizing through questions, associations and concrete examples. Students must be math ready with all the prerequisite skills necessary to learn mathematics and understand the "language" of mathematics.

Mastery in math requires progress in the six scaffolding levels of mathematics. They are as follows:

- Intuitive Connections: Student connects a new concept with prior experiences.
- Concrete Modeling: Student looks for concrete material to show an example of the concept.
- Pictorial: Student draws to illustrate the concept which helps with the concrete modeling of the concept.
- Abstract: Student illustrates the concept into mathematical notation, by using number symbols, operational signs, formula and equations.
- Application: Student applies the concept to word problems.
- Communication: Student can be tested on the concept or teach the concept successfully to others.

The Report from the National Mathematics Advisory Panel 2008, is being carefully scrutinized. One of its most significant recommendations that impacts RTI and this guide is the following: "Progress has been made in understanding the difficulties that children with learning disabilities have with the learning of concepts, procedures, and facts in some areas of arithmetic. However, little is known about the source of their difficulties in other core areas, including fractions and algebra. Preliminary research has identified some of the mechanisms that contribute to exceptional mathematics learning, but much remains to be discovered." The report continues to state: "Research is needed on the cognitive mechanisms that contribute to learning disabilities;

precocious learning in mathematical domains beyond whole number arithmetic is needed to better understand the sources of individual differences in children's mathematical learning."

In the spirit of this statement, the authors of this guide have structured the math section to help increase understanding of why a student has difficulty achieving in mathematics, and to provide strategies and activities that address the components of the difficulty. They present the question: What is dyscalculia?

Dyscalculia is a neurological learning disability that affects a person's ability to learn and do mathematics. People with dyscalculia are diverse; some are able to memorize basic facts and do simple operations but cannot understand higher-level concepts. Others quickly catch on to complex mathematics but cannot seem to master the basics. Dyscalculia may be complicated by other factors such as language processing, attention deficit, poor instruction, or lack of motivation. Dyscalculia is divided into six subtypes:

1) **Verbal Dyscalculia**—difficulty retrieving and naming math symbols, math terms, operations, and associating numerals to amounts of things.

2) **Practognostic Dyscalculia**—difficulty manipulating real or pictured items for mathematical purposes; may be able to read, write and imitate written numbers but cannot compare, comprehend, or describe part-whole relationships, spatial details, shapes and sizes.

3) **Lexical Dyscalculia**—difficulty reading serial numbers, digits, signs and symbols, and may transpose numbers, insert or omit digits.

4) **Graphical Dyscalculia**—difficulty in writing and/or copying math symbols; numbers may be mixed up or in opposite direction.

5) **Ideognostical Dyscalculia**—difficulty with comprehending quantitative concepts and calculating the easiest sums mentally or at age appropriate level.

6) **Operational Dyscalculia**—difficulty learning and applying the rules of math functions resulting in problems successfully performing math operations.

The strategies/activities that follow are divided into these six subtypes of dyscalculia as well as Tier 1, Tier 2 and Tier 3. Some of the strategies/activities are repeated across multiple tiers as well as across subtypes. This is done purposefully because sometimes the strategy fits a few subtypes, or the subtypes can overlap and the strategy becomes appropriate for more than one. Furthermore, it is recognized that many teachers have a limited comfort level with math instruction; therefore, some of the strategies are highly simplistic and discrete. It is important to note that there is never one cause or easy solution to mathematics difficulties.

Areas of Math: Verbal Dyscalculia

<table>
<tr><th>Math: Verbal Dyscalculia</th><th>Math: Verbal Dyscalculia Tier 1</th></tr>
<tr><td>

Verbal Dyscalculia—involves difficulty retrieving or naming the different math symbols, math terms, etc. Examples of academic problems in this area:

- Difficulty in verbally naming amounts of objects, numbers, terms, symbols and operations
- Difficulty associating numerals to amounts of objects
- Difficulty verbally counting patterns
- Difficulty writing numbers as they are literally pronounced

Accommodations and Modifications:

- Reduce difficulty of reading level for word problems
- Grade pass/fail or change the grading system
- Use of examples on tests
- Use of graph paper
- Folding paper in columns
- Flash cards/frequent repetition
- Use of symbols
- Use of problem solving sequence chart
- Verbalize steps
- Color code key operations symbols
- Color code columns and rows of math problems
- Use of computation aids
- Modify number of problems
- Use of manipulatives
- Seat student near the teacher giving the instruction

</td><td>

Suggested Interventionist: General Education Teacher with consultation from the Special Education teacher/Math Specialist

Suggested Session: Small group, 2x a week explicit instruction within the CORE math program within the classroom

Strategies/Activities for Verbal Dyscalculia:

- Teacher will use the four modalities of visual, auditory, tactile, and kinesthetic to introduce concepts (multisensory approach).
- Student will be allowed to sub-vocalize the steps in the math problem.
- Teacher will not use lengthy explanations or passive activities. This hinders attention, learning, and memory.
- Teacher will use mnemonics to aid memory in solving math problems.
- Teacher will post memory aides on the walls in the classroom (basic facts, counting chart, place value chart and multiplication facts).
- Teacher will use concrete examples to teach mathematical vocabulary.
- Teacher will use manipulatives to illustrate the meaning of math signs and symbols.
- Teacher will post sequential steps and procedures for math operations on a chart.

</td></tr>
</table>

Math: Verbal Dyscalculia Tier 1	Math: Verbal Dyscalculia Tier 1
• Student will verbally restate the steps as he works examples. • Student will read word problems several times aloud. • Student will memorize math language before he understands math language. • Teacher will read math problems aloud, if student cannot read. • Student will learn basic addition facts before learning subtraction facts. • Teacher will use multiple concrete objects to help student memorize the facts. • Teacher will encourage student to use his fingers to form addition and subtraction combinations. • Teacher will use daily drill activities to help the student memorize math facts (e.g., written problems, flash cards, etc.). • Teacher will use timed drills only to reinforce basic math facts already learned. • Student will use a number line attached to a desk to add and subtract. • Teacher will encourage the student to practice facts at home with flash cards, computer programs or games. • Student will play games or use computer programs in order to reinforce math facts.	• Teacher will choose a fact with which the student is unsuccessful and review it several times a day. • Student will use a calculator to check and correct the problems completed on a worksheet. • Student will work with a "math-fact buddy" each day on drill activities (e.g., flash cards, games). • Student will develop his own math-facts reference sheet for addition, subtraction, multiplication, or division to use when solving math problems. • Student will reinforce multiplication facts by practicing skip counting (e.g., 5's: 5, 10, 15, 20, 25, 30, etc.). • Student will complete a math-fact quiz sheet as an anchoring activity upon arrival each morning. • Teacher will allow the student to keep a chart of facts in his math notebook for reference if he continues to have difficulty with facts. • Student will sing along with music to learn math facts. • Student will use math-fact records and tapes for math-fact drill activities. • Student will build upon math facts he already knows, reinforcing facts he has mastered. Teacher will add one new fact at a time as the student demonstrates success.

Math: Verbal Dyscalculia Tier 2	Math: Verbal Dyscalculia Tier 2
Suggested Interventionist: Special Education Teacher, Math Specialist **Suggested Session: 30 minutes 2 to 3x a week in a small group or individual basis in addition to the CORE math program inside the classroom** **Strategies/Activities for Verbal Dyscalculia:** • Teacher will use mathematical vocabulary with concrete examples. • Student will explain procedures to the teacher when having a problem with the example. • Student will use mathematical language in informal conversation as often as possible. • Student will use a calculator to reinforce learning. • Student will use a calculator to solve several problems each day. The problems will be separated into steps. • Student will practice math facts using computer software programs that provide immediate feedback. • Teacher will introduce multiplication and division facts even though the student does not know the addition and subtraction facts. Student will use a calculator to compensate. • Student will use calculator on every math quiz in order to keep up with the class. • Student will use a calculator for drill activities of basic math facts.	• Teacher will create opportunities for the student to apply math facts to real-life situations (e.g., getting change in the cafeteria, going to a restaurant, etc.). • Students will practice and reinforce math facts using a computer with software programs that provide game-like activities. • Student will independently solve half of his math problems each day, using a calculator to complete the rest of the assignment. • Teacher will stress meaning rather than memorization of math language. • Teacher will use manipulative objects and pictures to teach the student basic math facts while providing a visual image. • Students will use rods of different lengths and colors to learn and memorize each addition and subtraction fact. • Teacher will discuss and teach all the math language used in addition such as: add, sum, digits, columns, etc. • Teacher will discuss and teach all the math language used in subtraction, such as: take away, minus, rows and columns. • Student will play math-fact games with other students.

Math: Verbal Dyscalculia **Tier 3**	**Math: Verbal Dyscalculia** **Tier 3**
Suggested Interventionist: Special Education Teacher, Math Specialist **Suggested Session: 60 minutes 5x a week in a small group or individual basis in addition to the CORE math program outside of the classroom** **Strategies/Activities for Addition Facts:** • Teacher will make rods of different sizes. The rods can be either three-dimensional or one-dimensional. The teacher can also use Cuisenaire rods, Stern rods or Unifex cubes. —Ten rod = 10 inches long —Nine rod = 9 inches long —Eight rod = 8 inches long —Seven rod = 7 inches long —Six rod = 6 inches long —Five rod = 5 inches long —Four rod = 4 inches long —Three rod = 3 inches long —Two rod = 2 inches long —One rod = 1 inch long	• Teacher will line up the rods of different sizes vertically and explain that every rod has a "buddy" that completes the addition fact. Each set of two rods will add up to the sum of 10. Student can visualize the different sizes that add up to the largest rod (10). They continue: — 10 rod = 1 rod + 9 rod — 10 rod = 2 rod + 8 rod — 10 rod = 3 rod + 7 rod — 10 rod = 4 rod + 6 rod — 10 rod = 5 rod + 5 rod 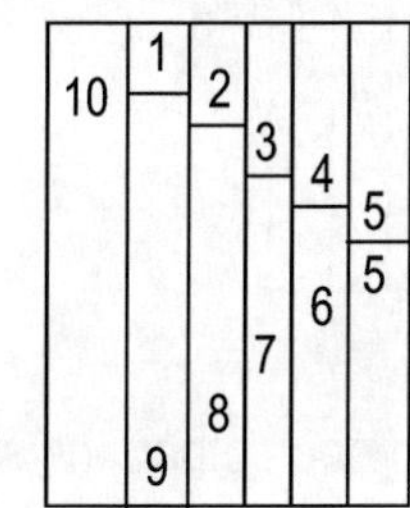 • After placing the vertical rods next to each other, the teacher will write the addition equations that correspond to the number rods vertically on graph paper. $\begin{array}{r}1\\+9\\\hline 10\end{array}\quad\begin{array}{r}2\\+8\\\hline 10\end{array}\quad\begin{array}{r}3\\+7\\\hline 10\end{array}\quad\begin{array}{r}4\\+6\\\hline 10\end{array}\quad\begin{array}{r}5\\+5\\\hline 10\end{array}$ • Student will write the equations on 3x5 index cards without the answer.

Math: Verbal Dyscalculia	**Tier 3**

- Student will again place the rods of different sizes vertically. However, the student now reverses the vertical order of the rods.
  - — 10 rod = 9 rod + 1 rod
  - — 10 rod = 8 rod + 2 rod
  - — 10 rod = 7 rod + 3 rod
  - — 10 rod = 6 rod + 4 rod
  - — 10 rod = 5 rod + 5 rod

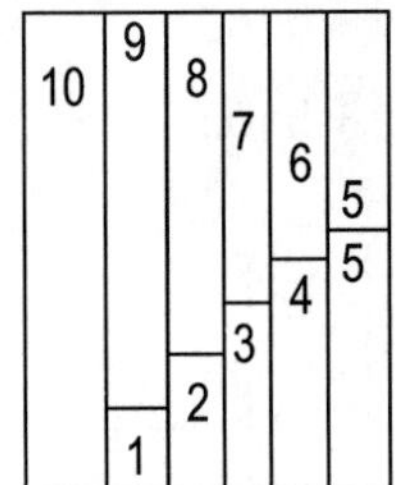

- After placing the rods next to each other, the student will write the addition equations that correspond to the number rods on graph paper.

$$\begin{array}{rrrrr} 9 & 8 & 7 & 6 & 5 \\ \underline{+1} & \underline{+2} & \underline{+3} & \underline{+4} & \underline{+5} \\ 10 & 10 & 10 & 10 & 10 \end{array}$$

- Student will write the equations on 3x5 index cards without the answer. There are now nine addition facts for the family of ten.

Math: Verbal Dyscalculia	**Tier 3**

- Student will place the rods of different sizes next to each other horizontally.
  - — 10 rod = 1 rod + 9 rod
  - — 10 rod = 2 rod + 8 rod
  - — 10 rod = 3 rod + 7 rod
  - — 10 rod = 4 rod + 6 rod
  - — 10 rod = 5 rod + 5 rod

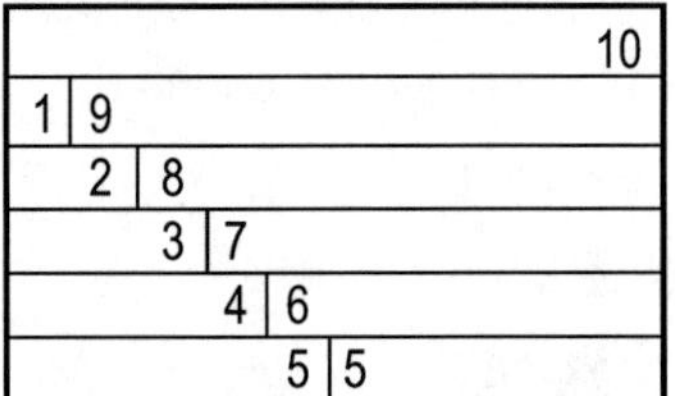

- After placing the rods horizontally, teacher will write the addition equations that correspond to the number rods on graph paper.
  - — 1 + 9 = 10
  - — 2 + 8 = 10
  - — 3 + 7 = 10
  - — 4 + 6 = 10
  - — 5 + 5 = 10
- Student will write the equations on 3x5 index cards without the answer.

Math: Verbal Dyscalculia Tier 3	Math: Verbal Dyscalculia Tier 3
• Student will place the rods once again horizontally. The student will reverse the order of the rods. — 10 rod = 9 rod + 1 rod — 10 rod = 8 rod + 2 rod — 10 rod = 7 rod + 3 rod — 10 rod = 6 rod + 4 rod — 10 rod = 5 rod + 5 rod 10 9 | 1 8 | 2 7 | 3 6 | 4 5 | 5 • After placing the rods horizontally, the student will write the addition equations on graph paper. — 9 + 1 = 10 8 + 2 = 10 7 + 3 = 10 — 6 + 4 = 10 5 + 5 = 10 • Student will write the equations on 3x5 index cards without the answers. There are now 18 addition facts for the family of ten. • Student will continue to create the different commutative functions of addition. Student will continue to write these equations on graph paper and 3x5 cards. • Student will continue to work concretely with the rods, graph paper and index cards for all of the addition families of 9, 8, 7, 6, 5, 4, 3, 2. • Teacher will continue to reinforce memory facts by giving mixed addition fact-sheet quizzes every day.	**Strategies/Activities for Subtraction Facts:** • Teacher will explain the language of subtraction. • Teacher will place the ten rod on top of a table. Teacher will put the one rod into the hand of the student. Teacher will hold the 1's partner (the nine rod that adds up to 10) under the table. • Student will be asked what is the "buddy" that, when added to the nine rod, equals 10. When the student answers 1, the teacher rephrases the question: if the one rod is "taken away" from the ten rod, what number would you have? Student will answer 9. • Student will be asked to write the equation on a piece of graph paper vertically and horizontally: 10 - 1 9 10 - 1 = 9 • Student will write the equation on a 3x5 card without the answer. • Teacher will start the next fact by placing the ten rod on top of the table and replacing the nine rod with the eight rod. • Teacher will give the student a two rod and ask the student what is the 2's "buddy" that adds up to 10. Student will answer 8. • Teacher will rephrase the question: If you "take away" the two rod from the ten rod what number rod would you have? Student will answer 8.

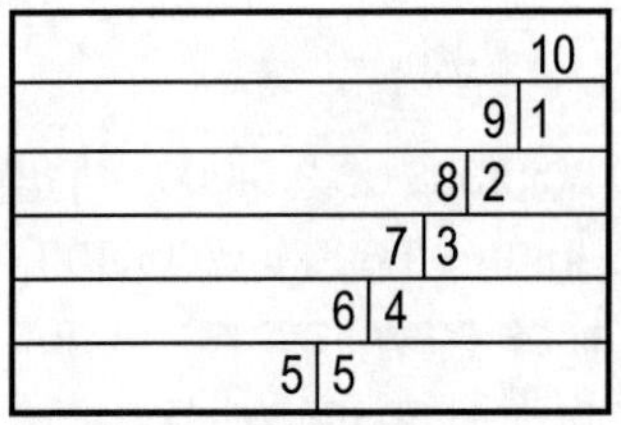

Math: Verbal Dyscalculia Tier 3	Math: Verbal Dyscalculia Tier 3
• Student will write the equation on a piece of graph paper both vertically and horizontally. $\begin{array}{r} 10 \\ -2 \\ \hline 8 \end{array}$ 10 - 2 = 8 • Student will write the equation on a 3x5 index card vertically and horizontally without the answers. • Teacher will continue to create the remainder of the equations using the "buddy" process. The following equations will be created: 10-3=7; 10-4=6; 10-5=5; 10-6=4; 10-7=3; 10-8=2; 10-9=1. • Student and teacher will continue through this process while discovering or creating the subtraction facts of the 10, 9, 8, 7, 6, 5, 4, 3, 2 families. • Teacher will continue to reinforce memory of the addition and subtraction facts by continuously giving the student fact-sheet quizzes after each new fact learned. **Strategies/Activities for Carrying and Borrowing in Addition and Subtraction:** **Visualizing the setting up of addition problems:** • Teacher will explain to the student that color-coding helps in addition. Student will be asked to get out a green, yellow and red highlighter. • When there is a two-column addition example, the student will highlight the column closest to his right hand with the green highlighter (green means start).	• Student will highlight the column closest to his left hand with a red highlighter (red means stop). • If there are columns in between the green and red colors, the student will highlight those columns in yellow (yellow means slow down). **Strategies/Activities for carrying in addition:** • Teacher will write a two-column addition example on the board. The example is: = ___ $\begin{array}{r} 55 \\ +46 \\ \hline \end{array}$ • Teacher will draw two columns on a piece of paper. The column on the right is highlighted in green and the column on the left is highlighted in red. A line will be drawn across the top of the page about two inches from the top. This space will be used to carry numbers in addition. • Teacher will explain that the colors represent place value and the green column is always the 1's column and the red column (in two-column addition) will always be the 10's column. • Teacher will explain that as the numbers are added, the numbers being carried are written in the color of the column being added. • Student will use rods to arrive at the answer. • Student will retrieve the five rod and the six rod. Student will place the two rods vertically, beside the written example. • Student will place the number ten rod next to the rods representing the numbers in that column. • Student will explain that the five rod plus the six rod add up to more than the ten rod. The two rods when added together are 11.

Math: Verbal Dyscalculia **Tier 3**

- Student will trade in the five and six rods for the ten rod and one rod. Teacher shows how to represent 11.

1	
5	5
- 4	6
	1

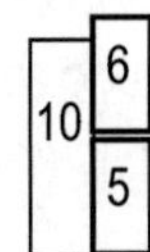

- Student writes 1 (in green pen) over the red column and the 1 under the green column, as the first part of the answer.
- The second column (red) has the number 1 in the space provided on the top of the column. Student will take another five rod plus the four rod representing the numbers in the second column (highlighted in red).
- Student will place the two rods vertically next to the ten rod.

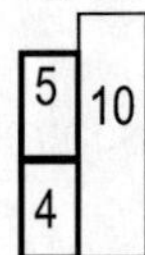

- Student will be able to see that the five rod and the four rod add up to 9 (which is less than 10). However, he must add the number from the top of the red column which is 1. All three numbers add up to 10.
- Student will place a 0 under the second (red) column and a 1 to the left of it. The answer is 101.
- Teacher will continue teaching carrying by introducing three-column addition. A three-column example is written with the column closest to the student's right hand highlighted in green, middle column highlighted in yellow and the column to the left highlighted in red.

Math: Verbal Dyscalculia **Tier 3**

- Teacher will write another example on the board.

$$\begin{array}{r} 179 \\ \underline{+\ 53} \end{array}$$

- Student will place the three rod and the nine 9 rod above each other next to the ten rod. Student adds the value of the rods and sees that the sum is more than the ten rod. The student trades in the nine rod and three rod for a ten rod and a two rod. The sum of the ten rod and the two rod = 12.
- Teacher will show how to represent the 12 by placing the 10 over the yellow column and the 2 under the green column. Student will change the ten rod to a written number 1 over the yellow column and the number 2 stays under the green column.

$$\begin{array}{r} (1) \\ 179 \\ \underline{+\ \ 53} \\ 2 \end{array}$$

- Student will represent the numbers in the second column with the corresponding rods. Student will place the seven rod plus the five rod plus the one rod that was carried vertically next to the ten rod. The sum is 13.

1 / 7 / 5 | 10 = 3 / 10

- Teacher will point out that the sum of 13 is more than the ten rod.
- Student will trade the seven rod, the five rod and the one rod (that was carried) for a ten rod and a three rod. The 3 is placed under the yellow column and the ten rod is placed on the top of the red column. Ten rod is replaced by the number 1 on the top of the third red column (written in red pen).

Math: Verbal Dyscalculia Tier 3	Math: Verbal Dyscalculia Tier 3
• Student will add the 1 that represents the ten rod and the 1 that is in the example. The sum is 2 and this number is placed under the third column (the red column). The answer to the example is 232. • Student will continue this process until all carrying facts are understood. **Strategies/Activities in Visualizing Subtraction:** • Teacher will explain that color-coding helps in math. When a student looks at a two- or three-column subtraction problem, he will use his green and red highlighters. • In a subtraction problem, student will highlight the bottom row with a green highlighter and the top row with a red highlighter. • The green highlighter means that the student starts from the green row (symbolizes start) and ends at the red row (symbolizes stop). **Strategies/Activities for Borrowing in Subtraction:** • Teacher will write a two-column subtraction example on the board and on graph paper. 84 - 53 • Teacher will explain that color-coding is used in subtraction as well as in addition. • All subtraction will start with the bottom number (green) being subtracted from the top number (red). • Teacher will use an envelope with pennies in it to represent the numbers on the top row.	• Teacher will explain that the number 3 (green) must be subtracted from the number 4 (red). • Teacher will place on top of the first column an envelope with four pennies in it representing the number 4. Teacher will ask the student to subtract the lower number 3 from the top number which is 4. • Student will take the three pennies from the envelope and say how many pennies are left. Student will say the number 1 and place the 1 under the first column. • Teacher will put eight pennies in the envelope. The student will subtract the number 5 from the eight pennies and will place a 3 under the second column. The answer to the non-borrowing problem equals 31. • Teacher will give the student worksheets with math subtraction examples without borrowing. • Teacher will continue teaching subtraction using the "envelope" process. • The next problem will be an example of borrowing in subtraction. The problem is 854 - 395 • Color-coding will continue in three-digit subtraction with the top numbers colored with red highlighter and the bottom numbers colored with green highlighter. • Student will write the problem on graph paper with each number in its own box. Student will color-code the rows.

Math: Verbal Dyscalculia — Tier 3

- Teacher will place the envelope with four pennies on the top of the first row on the right.
- Student will try to take five pennies out of the envelope. When this is not possible, the teacher will explain that the student must borrow more money to be able to subtract.
- Student will borrow ten pennies from the next column.
- Student will add ten pennies to the four pennies and the answer will be fourteen pennies.
- In order to borrow the ten pennies, the student must cross out the number 5 from the top row of the middle column and subtract 1 from it and write the number 4 on top of that row.
- Student will take five pennies from the fourteen pennies (in the envelope) and have nine pennies left. Student will write the number 9 under the first column.
- The envelope with four pennies in it will be placed above the second column.
- Student will subtract the number 9 in the second column from the envelope that has only four pennies in it. The student will now have to borrow ten pennies from the third column.
- When the student borrows ten pennies from the third row, he crosses out the number 8 and replaces it with the number 7.Ten pennies are added to the envelope. The envelope that is placed above the second column now has fourteen pennies in it. Student removes nine pennies and has five pennies left and places that number 5 under the second column.
- Student will continue to subtract in the third column. Envelope with seven will be placed above the third column. Student will take away three pennies from the seven pennies and have four pennies left.

Math: Verbal Dyscalculia — Tier 3

- Student will place the 4 under the third column. The answer equals 459.
- Teacher will complete the example on the board using graph chalk lines.

```
  74
 8̸5̸4
-395
----
 459
```

Strategies/Activities for Multiplication Facts:

- Teacher will review, illustrate and explain all the vocabulary words that are used in the multiplication process.
- Teacher will use a number line and the rods.
- Student will be instructed to make multiple rods of each number to illustrate the process called multiplication.
- Teacher will create a number line that matches the sizes of the rods (inch rods, Cuisenaire rods, Stern rods, Unifex cube rods).
- Teacher will illustrate how to use the number line.
- Teacher will take 3 seven inch rods and place them on a comparable number line; the number rods add up to 21.
- Teacher will explain that multiplication is addition.
- Teacher will write on the board. 7 + 7 + 7 = 21 or 3 x 7=21.
- Teacher will explain that instead of adding the seven rods three times, there is an easier way of doing this: it is called multiplication. Teacher will explain that the symbol (x) means multiplication.

Math: Verbal Dyscalculia **Tier 3**

- The following multiplication sequence will be followed while creating each multiplication table. The sequence is: 3 x table; nine x table; 5 x table; 2 x table; 10 x table; 4 x table; 6 x table; 7 x table; 8 x table.
- Student will create a multiplication chart using graph paper with 12 squares by 12 squares. Horizontally across the top, the student writes the multiplication numbers 1x, 2x, 3x, 4x, 5x, 6x, 7x, 8x, 9x, 10x. In a vertical direction, student writes the same numbers down the left side of the chart.
- As the student "discovers" each of the multiplication facts, he places that equation on the chart in two ways. For example, 3 x 1 is placed under the 3x table heading as 3 x 1 = 3 and then in the third box vertically next to the number three under the 1 x table column. That number reads 1 x 3 = 3.

	1 x	2 x	3 x	4 x	5 x	6 x	7 x	8 x	9 x	10 x
1 x			3x1							
2 x										
3 x	1x3									
4 x										
5 x										
6 x										
7 x										
8 x										
9 x										
10 x										

Math: Verbal Dyscalculia **Tier 3**

- By putting the equations on the chart two ways (3 x 1 and 1 x 3) the student will see that when he learns one fact he is actually learning two facts. He visually sees how the chart fills in with two facts for two different tables.
- Student will not only write these tables on his chart two ways but write them on cards, two ways horizontally and two ways vertically.

3 x 1 = 3
1 x 3 = 3

3 x 1 = 3; 1 x 3 = 3

- Teacher will explain that no matter how the fact is written, it is still the same fact and has the same answer.
- Student will be given worksheets to reflect all multiplication tables written in each of the four forms. The multiplication fact worksheet reflects each new table as it is learned.
- Teacher will include at least one of every type of addition and subtraction fact learned as well. The multiplication facts will be reviewed by playing the following games: Concentration and War using the index cards.

Math: Verbal Dyscalculia Tier 3	Math: Verbal Dyscalculia Tier 3

Math: Verbal Dyscalculia — **Tier 3**

Strategies/Activities for Long Multiplication:

- Teacher will explain that color-coding will again be used.
- Student will color-code the problems by highlighting in green the first bottom number in the right column and the second bottom number in red. If there are three numbers, the middle number is highlighted in yellow. The concept of green = start, yellow = slow and red = stop is reinforced.
- Teacher will write the example on graph paper so that there are additional squares on top of the columns to write the number being carried.
- Teacher will use an example that multiplies a two digit number by a one digit number.
- Teacher will ask how much is 2 x 4.Student will answer 8 and write 8 under the first column in green pen.
- Teacher will ask how much is 2 x 5.Student will answer 10 and places the 10 in green under the second and third column so that each number has its own space.

$$\begin{array}{r} 54 \\ \underline{\times\ 2} \\ 108 \end{array}$$

- After the student understands the concept, the teacher will choose an example with carrying, such as:

$$\begin{array}{r} 66 \\ \underline{\times\ 7} \end{array}$$

Math: Verbal Dyscalculia — **Tier 3**

- Teacher will ask the student how much is 7 x 6, and the student answers 42.
- Student will be directed to place the 4 above the second column in green pen and the 2 under the first column in green pen.
- Teacher will ask the student how much is 7 x 6. Student answers 42; however there is a number already placed above the second column.
- Student will be directed to add this number to the 42 because that number has been waiting (or carried over) to be added to the next number. Student will say that the numbers written under the second and third column will be 46. The answer to the problem equals 462.

$$\begin{array}{r} (4) \\ 66 \\ \underline{\times\ 7} \\ 462 \end{array}$$

- Teacher will continue to give the student these examples on graph paper until they become automatic.
- Teacher will write a two-digit times two-digit example on the board within a graph paper illustration.
- The problem is 28 x 24. Remember to write the first bottom number in green and the second bottom number in red.
- Teacher will ask the student how much is 4 x 8. Student will answer 32 and then place the 3 in the graph square above the second column and the 2 under the first column in green.

Math: Verbal Dyscalculia **Tier 3**

- Teacher will ask the student how much is 4 x 2. Student will answer 8; however, there is a number that has been waiting to be carried or added to the number 8. Student will add 8 + 3. The number is 11 and the student will place that number under the second and third columns in green.
- Student will be directed to use the red pencil because he will be multiplying by the second (red) number. Student will be directed to place a red 0, to be used as a spacer, to the right under the 2 of the first column.
- Teacher will ask the student how much is 2 X 8. The answer is 16 and the student now places the one above the second column in red. Student is told to only pay attention to the red number and ignore the green numbers. The red 6 is placed under the second column.
- Teacher will ask the student how much is 2 x 2. Student will answer 4 and is reminded that there is a 1 waiting to be added to the number 4. One (1) + 4 = 5 and the red 5 is placed under the third column.
- Student will be directed to draw a line under the entire example and place an addition symbol in the space to the left of the last number.
- Student will add the numbers starting with the right column. The answer = 672. The bottom numbers are not color coded but are written in black.

```
 (1)
 (3)
  28
x 24
 112
 560
 672
```

Math: Verbal Dyscalculia **Tier 3**

- This procedure will be continued with three-digit times three-digit problems; four-digit times four-digit problems, etc.
- Remember, the answers to the multiplication example will be color-coded. The first row is in green, the second yellow and the third red. These colors correspond with the colors of the multipliers: first multiplier is green, the second multiplier is yellow and the third multiplier is in red.

Division Strategy for Division Facts:

- Teacher will illustrate and explain the different vocabulary and symbols used in division. Teacher will explain that to divide means to make numbers smaller by seeing how many of a smaller number is in the bigger number.
- Teacher will use the following materials to illustrate the division facts. The teacher will need 18 tokens.
- Teacher will put eighteen tokens in a box. Teacher will choose a number such as 6 and ask the student to see how many sets of 6 there are in the box with eighteen tokens.
- Student will retrieve three sets of 6 and respond with the number 3. There are three sets of 6. Teacher will write the division example on the board and explain the positioning of the numbers.
- The larger number 18 will be placed inside the division symbol. Outside of the division symbol, to the left is placed the number 6. The number 3 is placed on the top as that is the answer when 18 is divided by 6.

```
    3
6 / 18
```

Math: Verbal Dyscalculia Tier 3	
• Teacher will use all the different kinds of phrases common in division such as: how many 6s are there in 18; 6 goes into 18 how many times? • Student will be asked to use a number line and see how many 9s are in 18. Student will find out that there are two 9s in 18. • Student will continue using the number line and will write the answer on graph paper and on the board using division symbols. • After this process, teacher will explain that division is the reverse operation of multiplication. If the student knows the multiplication facts, he will know the division facts. If he knows that 6 x 3 = 18, he knows that 18 divided by 3 = 6. If he knows that 3 x 6 =18, he knows that 18 divided by 6 =3. • Division facts will be taught by reversing the process of multiplication. • Each division fact will be written on 3 x 5 index cards. • Student will reinforce division facts by playing games such as Concentration or War.	

Area of Math: Practognostic Dyscalculia

<table>
<tr><th>Math: Practognostic Dyscalculia</th><th>Math: Practognostic Dyscalculia Tier 1</th></tr>
<tr><td>

Practognostic Dyscalculia—refers to difficulty in applying math concepts when using pictures and/or manipulatives. Examples of academic problems in this area:

- Difficulty visualizing math concepts
- Difficulty in manipulating, adding, comparing, or estimating quantity of pictured items
- Difficulty comparing, comprehending or describing part-whole relationships, spatial details, shapes and size.
- Difficulty performing perceptual skills
- Difficulty recognizing objects by touching
- Difficulty with rote counting

Accommodations and Modifications:

- Use of examples on tests/modify number of problems
- Use of graph paper/fold paper in columns
- Flash cards/frequent repetition
- Use of symbols/manipulative
- Use of problem solving sequence chart
- Verbalize steps
- Color code key operations symbols
- Color code columns and rows
- Use of computation aids

</td><td>

Suggested Interventionist: General Education Teacher with consultation from the Special Education teacher/Math Specialist

Suggested Session: Small group 2x a week, explicit instruction within the CORE math program within the classroom

Strategies/Activities for Practognostic Dyscalculia:

Student will use manipulatives (concrete objects) to demonstrate mathematical concepts and procedures. These may include, but are not limited to:

- tokens (poker chips, buttons, etc.)
- colored rods
- number line
- geometric shapes (three dimensional)
- inch cubes
- Cuisenaire rods
- play money and cash register
- base-ten charts and sticks
- attribute blocks
- scales
- linear measuring tools (yardstick, ruler)
- volume measuring tools (cups, quarts, liters)

</td></tr>
</table>

Math: Practognostic Dyscalculia Tier 2	Math: Practognostic Dyscalculia Tier 2
Suggested Interventionist: Special Education Teacher, Math Specialist **Suggested Session: 30 minutes 2 to 3x a week in a small group or individual basis in addition to the CORE math program inside the classroom** **Strategies/Activities for Practognostic Dyscalculia:** • Teacher will illustrate Visual Clustering by displaying numbers in conjunction with familiar dot patterns. Student will use patterns on dice, playing cards, dominoes or any other familiar pattern. Student will begin to associate the quantity 4 with the number 4. • Teacher will use familiar objects within a student's environment as the concrete representations of numbers. For example, use packs of gum while teaching the concept of subtraction. The pack has ten sticks of gum. If you subtract three sticks from ten, the student would "take away" three sticks. The remainder of the ten sticks would be seven sticks of gum. • Teacher will use mnemonics to help the student memorize steps in solving math problems. • Teacher will post memory aides on the walls in the classroom (basic facts, counting chart, place value chart and multiplication facts). • Teacher will create opportunities for the student to apply math facts to real-life situations (e.g., getting change in the cafeteria, going to a store to buy something, etc.). • Student will practice and reinforce math facts using software programs that provide game-like activities.	• Student will complete a math-fact quiz sheet for a daily drill as an anchoring activity each morning. • Student will keep a chart of facts he is having difficulty memorizing in his math notebook. • Student will sort numbers from a bag of different numbers with eyes closed. • Student will play computer games requiring sorting or matching. • Teacher will create number cubes out of blank face dice. On each side of the dice a fraction or decimal is written. Student will throw two dice and determine which of the dice has the greater value. • Teacher will adapt graphic organizers to support/reinforce math concepts, math processes and math steps. • Student will highlight common patterns in math word problems (e.g., how many, add or subtract, etc.). • Teacher will create a deck of cards of paired math facts. Each fact should have the corresponding visual cluster of dots. The cards will be used for a game such as Concentration.

Math: Practognostic Dyscalculia Tier 3	Math: Practognostic Dyscalculia Tier 3
Suggested Interventionist: Special Education Teacher, Math Specialist **Suggested Session: 60 minutes 5x a week in a small group or individual basis in addition to the CORE math program outside of the classroom** **Strategies/Activities for Addition Facts:** • Teacher will make rods of different sizes. The rods can be either three-dimensional or one-dimensional. The teacher can also use Cuisenaire rods, Stern rods or Unifex cubes. —Ten rod = 10 inches long —Nine rod = 9 inches long —Eight rod = 8 inches long —Seven rod = 7 inches long —Six rod = 6 inches long —Five rod = 5 inches long —Four rod = 4 inches long —Three rod = 3 inches long —Two rod = 2 inches long —One rod = 1 inch long	• Teacher will line up the rods of different sizes vertically and explain that every rod has a "buddy" that completes the addition fact. Each set of two rods will add up to the sum of 10. Student can visualize the different sizes that add up to the largest rod (10). They continue: — 10 rod = 1 rod + 9 rod — 10 rod = 2 rod + 8 rod — 10 rod = 3 rod + 7 rod — 10 rod = 4 rod + 6 rod — 10 rod = 5 rod + 5 rod 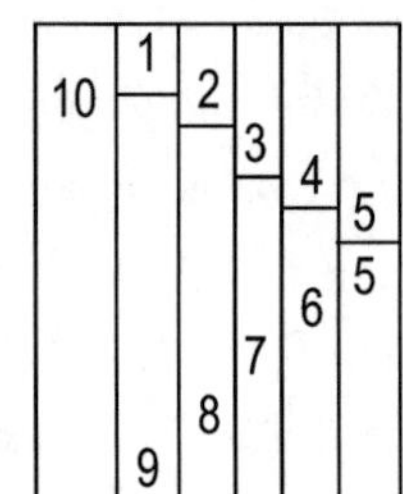 • After placing the vertical rods next to each other, the teacher will write the addition equations that correspond to the number rods vertically on graph paper. $\begin{array}{r}1\\+9\\\hline10\end{array}$ $\begin{array}{r}2\\+8\\\hline10\end{array}$ $\begin{array}{r}3\\+7\\\hline10\end{array}$ $\begin{array}{r}4\\+6\\\hline10\end{array}$ $\begin{array}{r}5\\+5\\\hline10\end{array}$ • Student will write the equations on 3x5 index cards without the answer.

Math: Practognostic Dyscalculia Tier 3	Math: Practognostic Dyscalculia Tier 3
• Student will again place the rods of different sizes vertically. However, the student now reverses the vertical order of the rods. — 10 rod = 9 rod + 1 rod — 10 rod = 8 rod + 2 rod — 10 rod = 7 rod + 3 rod — 10 rod = 6 rod + 4 rod — 10 rod = 5 rod + 5 rod 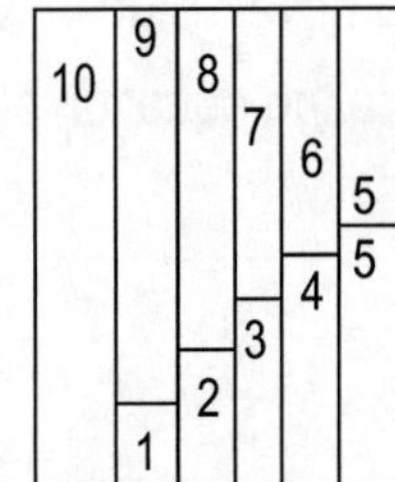 • After placing the rods next to each other, the student will write the addition equations that correspond to the number rods on graph paper. $\begin{array}{r}9\\+1\\\hline 10\end{array}$ $\begin{array}{r}8\\+2\\\hline 10\end{array}$ $\begin{array}{r}7\\+3\\\hline 10\end{array}$ $\begin{array}{r}6\\+4\\\hline 10\end{array}$ $\begin{array}{r}5\\+5\\\hline 10\end{array}$ • Student will write the equations on 3x5 index cards without the answer. There are now nine addition facts for the family of ten.	• Student will place the rods of different sizes next to each other horizontally. — 10 rod = 1 rod + 9 rod — 10 rod = 2 rod + 8 rod — 10 rod = 3 rod + 7 rod — 10 rod = 4 rod + 6 rod — 10 rod = 5 rod + 5 rod 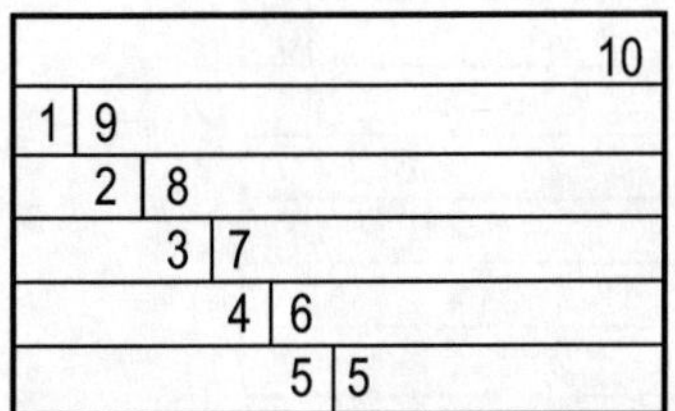 • After placing the rods horizontally, teacher will write the addition equations that correspond to the number rods on graph paper. — 1 + 9 = 10 — 2 + 8 = 10 — 3 + 7 = 10 — 4 + 6 = 10 — 5 + 5 = 10 • Student will write the equations on 3x5 index cards without the answer.

Math: Practognostic Dyscalculia — Tier 3

- Student will place the rods once again horizontally. The student will reverse the order of the rods.
  - 10 rod = 9 rod + 1 rod
  - 10 rod = 8 rod + 2 rod
  - 10 rod = 7 rod + 3 rod
  - 10 rod = 6 rod + 4 rod
  - 10 rod = 5 rod + 5 rod

10	
9	1
8	2
7	3
6	4
5	5

- After placing the rods horizontally, the student will write the addition equations on graph paper.
  - 9 + 1 = 10 8 + 2 = 10 7 + 3 = 10
  - 6 + 4 = 10 5 + 5 = 10
- Student will write the equations on 3x5 index cards without the answers. There are now 18 addition facts for the family of ten.
- Student will continue to create the different commutative functions of addition. Student will continue to write these equations on graph paper and 3x5 cards.
- Student will continue to work concretely with the rods, graph paper and index cards for all of the addition families of 9, 8, 7, 6, 5, 4, 3, 2.
- Teacher will continue to reinforce memory facts by giving mixed addition fact-sheet quizzes every day.

Math: Practognostic Dyscalculia — Tier 3

Strategies/Activities for Subtraction Facts:

- Teacher will explain the language of subtraction.
- Teacher will place the ten rod on top of a table. Teacher will put the one rod into the hand of the student. Teacher will hold the 1's partner (the nine rod that adds up to 10) under the table.
- Student will be asked what is the "buddy" that, when added to the nine rod, equals 10. When the student answers 1, the teacher rephrases the question: if the one rod is "taken away" from the ten rod, what number would you have? Student will answer 9.
- Student will be asked to write the equation on a piece of graph paper vertically and horizontally:

$$\begin{array}{r} 10 \\ \underline{-\,1} \\ 9 \end{array} \qquad 10 - 1 = 9$$

- Student will write the equation on a 3x5 card without the answer.
- Teacher will start the next fact by placing the ten rod on top of the table and replacing the nine rod with the eight rod.
- Teacher will give the student a two rod and ask the student what is the 2's "buddy" that adds up to 10. Student will answer 8.
- Teacher will rephrase the question: If you "take away" the two rod from the ten rod what number rod would you have? Student will answer 8.

Math: Practognostic Dyscalculia Tier 3	Math: Practognostic Dyscalculia Tier 3
• Student will write the equation on a piece of graph paper both vertically and horizontally. 10 / - 2 / 8 10 - 2 = 8 • Student will write the equation on a 3x5 index card vertically and horizontally without the answers. • Teacher will continue to create the remainder of the equations using the "buddy" process. The following equations will be created: 10-3=7; 10-4=6; 10-5=5; 10-6=4; 10-7=3; 10-8=2; 10-9=1. • Student and teacher will continue through this process while discovering or creating the subtraction facts of the 10, 9, 8, 7, 6, 5, 4, 3, 2 families. • Teacher will continue to reinforce memory of the addition and subtraction facts by continuously giving the student fact-sheet quizzes after each new fact learned. **Strategies/Activities for Carrying and Borrowing in Addition and Subtraction:** **Visualizing the setting up of addition problems:** • Teacher will explain to the student that color-coding helps in addition. Student will be asked to get out a green, yellow and red highlighter. • When there is a two-column addition example, the student will highlight the column closest to his right hand with the green highlighter (green means start).	• Student will highlight the column closest to his left hand with a red highlighter (red means stop). • If there are columns in between the green and red colors, the student will highlight those columns in yellow (yellow means slow down). **Strategies/Activities for carrying in addition:** • Teacher will write a two-column addition example on the board. The example is: = ___ 55 / + 46 • Teacher will draw two columns on a piece of paper. The column on the right is highlighted in green and the column on the left is highlighted in red. A line will be drawn across the top of the page about two inches from the top. This space will be used to carry numbers in addition. • Teacher will explain that the colors represent place value and the green column is always the 1's column and the red column (in two-column addition) will always be the 10's column. • Teacher will explain that as the numbers are added, the numbers being carried are written in the color of the column being added. • Student will use rods to arrive at the answer. • Student will retrieve the five rod and the six rod. Student will place the two rods vertically, beside the written example. • Student will place the number ten rod next to the rods representing the numbers in that column. • Student will explain that the five rod plus the six rod add up to more than the ten rod. The two rods when added together are 11.

Math: Practognostic Dyscalculia **Tier 3**

- Student will trade in the five and six rods for the ten rod and one rod. Teacher shows how to represent 11.

	1	
	5	5
-	4	6
		1

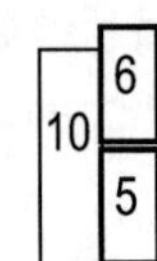

- Student writes 1 (in green pen) over the red column and the 1 under the green column, as the first part of the answer.
- The second column (red) has the number 1 in the space provided on the top of the column. Student will take another five rod plus the four rod representing the numbers in the second column (highlighted in red).
- Student will place the two rods vertically next to the ten rod.

5 | 10
4 |

- Student will be able to see that the five rod and the four rod add up to 9 (which is less than 10). However, he must add the number from the top of the red column which is 1. All three numbers add up to 10.
- Student will place a 0 under the second (red) column and a 1 to the left of it. The answer is 101.
- Teacher will continue teaching carrying by introducing three-column addition. A three-column example is written with the column closest to the student's right hand highlighted in green, middle column highlighted in yellow and the column to the left highlighted in red.

Math: Practognostic Dyscalculia **Tier 3**

- Teacher will write another example on the board.

$$\begin{array}{r} 179 \\ \underline{+\ 53} \end{array}$$

- Student will place the three rod and the nine 9 rod above each other next to the ten rod. Student adds the value of the rods and sees that the sum is more than the ten rod. The student trades in the nine rods and three rod for a ten rod and a two rod. The sum of the ten rod and the two rod = 12.
- Teacher will show how to represent the 12 by placing the 10 over the yellow column and the 2 under the green column. Student will change the ten rod to a written number 1 over the yellow column and the number 2 stays under the green column.

$$\begin{array}{r} (1) \\ 179 \\ \underline{+\ \ 53} \\ 2 \end{array}$$

- Student will represent the numbers in the second column with the corresponding rods. Student will place the seven rod plus the five rod plus the one rod that was carried vertically next to the ten rod. The sum is 13.

1 / 7 / 5 | 10 = 3 / 10

- Teacher will point out that the sum of 13 is more than the ten rod.
- Student will trade the seven rod, the five rod and the one rod (that was carried) for a ten rod and a three rod. The 3 is placed under the yellow column and the ten rod is placed on the top of the red column. Ten rod is replaced by the number 1 on the top of the third red column (written in red pen).

Math: Practognostic Dyscalculia Tier 3
• Student will add the 1 that represents the ten rod and the 1 that is in the example. The sum is 2 and this number is placed under the third column (the red column). The answer to the example is 232. • Student will continue this process until all carrying facts are understood. **Strategies/Activities in Visualizing Subtraction:** • Teacher will explain that color-coding helps in math. When a student looks at a two- or three-column subtraction problem, he will use his green and red highlighters. • In a subtraction problem, student will highlight the bottom row with a green highlighter and the top row with a red highlighter. • The green highlighter means that the student starts from the green row (symbolizes start) and ends at the red row (symbolizes stop). **Strategies/Activities for Borrowing in Subtraction:** • Teacher will write a two-column subtraction example on the board and on graph paper. 84 <u>- 53</u> • Teacher will explain that color-coding is used in subtraction as well as in addition. • All subtraction will start with the bottom number (green) being subtracted from the top number (red). • Teacher will use an envelope with pennies in it to represent the numbers on the top row.

Math: Practognostic Dyscalculia Tier 3
• Teacher will explain that the number 3 (green) must be subtracted from the number 4 (red). • Teacher will place on top of the first column an envelope with four pennies in it representing the number 4. Teacher will ask the student to subtract the lower number 3 from the top number which is 4. • Student will take the three pennies from the envelope and say how many pennies are left. Student will say the number 1 and place the 1 under the first column. • Teacher will put eight pennies in the envelope. The student will subtract the number 5 from the eight pennies and will place a 3 under the second column. The answer to the non-borrowing problem equals 31. • Teacher will give the student worksheets with math subtraction examples without borrowing. • Teacher will continue teaching subtraction using the "envelope" process. • The next problem will be an example of borrowing in subtraction. The problem is 854 <u>- 395</u> • Color-coding will continue in three-digit subtraction with the top numbers colored with red highlighter and the bottom numbers colored with green highlighter. • Student will write the problem on graph paper with each number in its own box. Student will color-code the rows.

Math: Practognostic Dyscalculia Tier 3

- Teacher will place the envelope with four pennies on the top of the first row on the right.
- Student will try to take five pennies out of the envelope. When this is not possible, the teacher will explain that the student must borrow more money to be able to subtract.
- Student will borrow ten pennies from the next column.
- Student will add ten pennies to the four pennies and the answer will be fourteen pennies.
- In order to borrow the ten pennies, the student must cross out the number 5 from the top row of the middle column and subtract 1 from it and write the number 4 on top of that row.
- Student will take five pennies from the fourteen pennies (in the envelope) and have nine pennies left. Student will write the number 9 under the first column.
- The envelope with four pennies in it will be placed above the second column.
- Student will subtract the number 9 in the second column from the envelope that has only four pennies in it. The student will now have to borrow ten pennies from the third column.
- When the student borrows ten pennies from the third row, he crosses out the number 8 and replaces it with the number 7. Ten pennies are added to the envelope. The envelope that is placed above the second column now has fourteen pennies in it. Student removes nine pennies and has five pennies left and places that number 5 under the second column.
- Student will continue to subtract in the third column. Envelope with seven will be placed above the third column. Student will take away three pennies from the seven pennies and have four pennies left.

Math: Practognostic Dyscalculia Tier 3

- Student will place the 4 under the third column. The answer equals 459.
- Teacher will complete the example on the board using graph chalk lines.

```
  74
 ~~85~~4
- 395
  459
```

Strategies/Activities for Multiplication Facts:

- Teacher will review, illustrate and explain all the vocabulary words that are used in the multiplication process.
- Teacher will use a number line and the rods.
- Student will be instructed to make multiple rods of each number to illustrate the process called multiplication.
- Teacher will create a number line that matches the sizes of the rods (inch rods, Cuisenaire rods, Stern rods, Unifex cube rods).
- Teacher will illustrate how to use the number line.
- Teacher will take 3 seven inch rods and place them on a comparable number line; the number rods add up to 21.
- Teacher will explain that multiplication is addition.
- Teacher will write on the board. 7 + 7 + 7 = 21 or 3 x 7=21.
- Teacher will explain that instead of adding the seven rods three times, there is an easier way of doing this: it is called multiplication. Teacher will explain that the symbol (x) means multiplication.

Math: Practognostic Dyscalculia Tier 3	**Math: Practognostic Dyscalculia** Tier 3
• The following multiplication sequence will be followed while creating each multiplication table. The sequence is: 3 x table; nine x table; 5 x table; 2 x table; 10 x table; 4 x table; 6 x table; 7 x table; 8 x table. • Student will create a multiplication chart using graph paper with 12 squares by 12 squares. Horizontally across the top, the student writes the multiplication numbers 1x, 2x, 3x, 4x, 5x, 6x, 7x, 8x, 9x, 10x. In a vertical direction, student writes the same numbers down the left side of the chart. • As the student "discovers" each of the multiplication facts, he places that equation on the chart in two ways. For example, 3 x 1 is placed under the 3x table heading as 3 x 1 = 3 and then in the third box vertically next to the number three under the 1 x table column. That number reads 1 x 3 = 3.	• By putting the equations on the chart two ways (3 x 1 and 1 x 3) the student will see that when he learns one fact he is actually learning two facts. He visually sees how the chart fills in with two facts for two different tables. • Student will not only write these tables on his chart two ways but write them on cards, two ways horizontally and two ways vertically. 3 x 1 = 3 3 x 1 = 3; 1 x 3 = 3 1 x 3 = 3 • Teacher will explain that no matter how the fact is written, it is still the same fact and has the same answer. • Student will be given worksheets to reflect all multiplication tables written in each of the four forms. The multiplication fact worksheet reflects each new table as it is learned. • Teacher will include at least one of every type of addition and subtraction fact learned as well. The multiplication facts will be reviewed by playing the following games: Concentration and War using the index cards.

	1 x	2 x	3 x	4 x	5 x	6 x	7 x	8 x	9 x	10 x
1 x			3x1							
2 x										
3 x	1x3									
4 x										
5 x										
6 x										
7 x										
8 x										
9 x										
10 x										

Math: Practognostic Dyscalculia Tier 3	Math: Practognostic Dyscalculia Tier 3
Strategies/Activities for Long Multiplication: • Teacher will explain that color-coding will again be used. • Student will color-code the problems by highlighting in green the first bottom number in the right column and the second bottom number in red. If there are three numbers, the middle number is highlighted in yellow. The concept of green = start, yellow = slow and red = stop is reinforced. • Teacher will write the example on graph paper so that there are additional squares on top of the columns to write the number being carried. • Teacher will use an example that multiplies a two digit number by a one digit number. • Teacher will ask how much is 2 x 4. Student will answer 8 and write 8 under the first column in green pen. • Teacher will ask how much is 2 x 5. Student will answer 10 and places the 10 in green under the second and third column so that each number has its own space. 54 x 2 108 • After the student understands the concept, the teacher will choose an example with carrying, such as: 66 x 7	• Teacher will ask the student how much is 7 x 6, and the student answers 42. • Student will be directed to place the 4 above the second column in green pen and the 2 under the first column in green pen. • Teacher will ask the student how much is 7 x 6. Student answers 42; however there is a number already placed above the second column. • Student will be directed to add this number to the 42 because that number has been waiting (or carried over) to be added to the next number. Student will say that the numbers written under the second and third column will be 46. The answer to the problem equals 462. (4) 66 x 7 462 • Teacher will continue to give the student these examples on graph paper until they become automatic. • Teacher will write a two-digit times two-digit example on the board within a graph paper illustration. • The problem is 28 x 24. Remember to write the first bottom number in green and the second bottom number in red. • Teacher will ask the student how much is 4 x 8. Student will answer 32 and then place the 3 in the graph square above the second column and the 2 under the first column in green.

Math: Practognostic Dyscalculia Tier 3	Math: Practognostic Dyscalculia Tier 3
• Teacher will ask the student how much is 4 x 2. Student will answer 8; however, there is a number that has been waiting to be carried or added to the number 8. Student will add 8 + 3. The number is 11 and the student will place that number under the second and third columns in green. • Student will be directed to use the red pencil because he will be multiplying by the second (red) number. Student will be directed to place a red 0, to be used as a spacer, to the right under the 2 of the first column. • Teacher will ask the student how much is 2 X 8. The answer is 16 and the student now places the one above the second column in red. Student is told to only pay attention to the red number and ignore the green numbers. The red 6 is placed under the second column. • Teacher will ask the student how much is 2 x 2. Student will answer 4 and is reminded that there is a 1 waiting to be added to the number 4. One (1) + 4 = 5 and the red 5 is placed under the third column. • Student will be directed to draw a line under the entire example and place an addition symbol in the space to the left of the last number. • Student will add the numbers starting with the right column. The answer = 672. The bottom numbers are not color coded but are written in black. (1) ~~(3)~~ 28 x 24 112 560 **672**	• This procedure will be continued with three-digit times three-digit problems; four-digit times four-digit problems, etc. • Remember, the answers to the multiplication example will be color-coded. The first row is in green, the second yellow and the third red. These colors correspond with the colors of the multipliers: first multiplier is green, the second multiplier is yellow and the third multiplier is in red. **Division Strategy for Division Facts:** • Teacher will illustrate and explain the different vocabulary and symbols used in division. Teacher will explain that to divide means to make numbers smaller by seeing how many of a smaller number is in the bigger number. • Teacher will use the following materials to illustrate the division facts. The teacher will need 18 tokens. • Teacher will put eighteen tokens in a box. Teacher will choose a number such as 6 and ask the student to see how many sets of 6 there are in the box with eighteen tokens. • Student will retrieve three sets of 6 and respond with the number 3. There are three sets of 6. Teacher will write the division example on the board and explain the positioning of the numbers. • The larger number 18 will be placed inside the division symbol. Outside of the division symbol, to the left is placed the number 6. The number 3 is placed on the top as that is the answer when 18 is divided by 6. 3 6 / 18

Math: Practognostic Dyscalculia Tier 3	
• Teacher will use all the different kinds of phrases common in division such as: how many 6s are there in 18; 6 goes into 18 how many times? • Student will be asked to use a number line and see how many 9s are in 18. Student will find out that there are two 9s in 18. • Student will continue using the number line and will write the answer on graph paper and on the board using division symbols. • After this process, teacher will explain that division is the reverse operation of multiplication. If the student knows the multiplication facts, he will know the division facts. If he knows that 6 x 3 = 18, he knows that 18 divided by 3 = 6. If he knows that 3 x 6 =18, he knows that 18 divided by 6 =3. • Division facts will be taught by reversing the process of multiplication. • Each division fact will be written on 3 x 5 index cards. • Student will reinforce division facts by playing games such as Concentration or War.	

Area of Math: Lexical Dyscalculia

Math: Lexical Dyscalculia	Math: Lexical Dyscalculia Tier 1
Lexical Dyscalculia—relates to the impaired reading of math vocabulary and symbols, and knowing what they represent in math problems Examples of academic problems in this area: • Difficulty with or inability in reading serial numbers, digits, place value, operational signs, math symbols, fractions, squares, roots, decimals and the language of math • Directional confusion • Difficulty with transposing numbers; interchanging similar digits and inappropriately inserting or omitting digits, words and signs • Difficulty with place value • Difficulty writing numbers because of inefficient coordination of visual perception skills and fine motor skills **Accommodations and Modifications:** • Reduce difficulty of reading level for word problems • Use of examples on tests • Use of graph paper or folding paper in columns • Use of color-coded operations symbols • Use of problem solving sequence chart/verbalize steps • Color code columns and rows of math problems • Use of computation aids • Modify number of problems • Use of manipulatives and calculator • Teach the language of math; underline answer words • Provide reference cards/charts to explain essential math vocabulary • Rewrite problem to simplify vocabulary • Use pictures to describe word problem • Have students restate word problem in their own words	**Suggested Interventionist: General Education Teacher with consultation from the Special Education teacher/Math Specialist** **Suggested Session: Small group 2x a week, explicit instruction within the CORE math program within the classroom** **Strategies/Activities for Lexical Dyscalculia:** • Student will write and solve his own math word problems using real-life experiences, and solve. • Student will identify key words in problems by highlighting needed information, crossing out extra information, and by creating a box around the question. • Teacher will illustrate a simple way to solve word problems including the following steps: —Understanding the problem by knowing what the problem is asking; —Devising a plan that addresses strategies to try, operations to use, ways to check work, etc.; —Carrying out the plan; —Reviewing to determine if answers are logical, accurate, and understandable. • Teacher will instruct student on how to plan strategies for solving problems. • Student will learn to illustrate a picture by creating a visual image or creating a model.

Math: Lexical Dyscalculia Tier 1	Math: Lexical Dyscalculia Tier 1
• Teacher will restate math problems in different ways by breaking complex problems into simpler ones. • Teacher will illustrate a chart of all the steps of the problem. • Teacher will describe a similar problem that has already been solved. • Student will read math problems aloud while identifying the mathematical operation required. • Teacher will use simple math language when teaching how to solve word problems. • Student will write a number sentence from the problem after reading a math word problem. • Teacher will create word problems for number sentences. Teacher will place sentences on the board. • Student will restate math word problems in his own words to promote understanding. • Teacher will illustrate how to break down each math word problem into sequential steps. • Student will make notes on setting up the math problem as he reads it. • Teacher will provide a list of sequential steps to follow in solving word problems. • Teacher will illustrate the first few problems of the math assignment for the student. • Student will highlight common patterns in math word problems (e.g., how many, add or subtract, etc.). • Teacher will provide a list of words/phrases which indicates an addition, subtraction, and multiplication or division operation.	• Teacher will provide relevant vocabulary found in math word problems and show concrete examples of those words. • Teacher will combine word problems with calculation math problems to introduce the solving of word problems. Teacher gradually changes the problems to total word problems. • Teacher will present phrases translated into numbers (e.g., four less than ten equals 10-4). • Teacher will illustrate number problems written four different ways but are the same number problem. 2+3= 5; 3+2=5 (vertically and horizontally.). • Teacher will correlate word problems with computation procedures. • Student will practice matching math operation symbols to the word identifying the operation by using flash cards (e.g., +, -, x,): add, subtract, multiply and divide in a concentration game, concentration, etc. • Student will talks through math word problems • Student will show the concepts of more than, less than, equal to, and zero using concrete objects. • Students will practice recognizing operational symbols which can be color-coded: addition in red, subtraction in orange, multiplication in purple and divisions in pink. • Student will use color-coded symbols within math problems. • Student will use a separate color paper for each type of math problem. Gradually different types of math problems will be introduced on the same page. However, each math problem should be color-coded like the math sheets.

Math: Lexical Dyscalculia Tier 2	Math: Lexical Dyscalculia Tier 2
Suggested Interventionist: Special Education Teacher, Math Specialist **Suggested Session: 30 minutes 2 to 3x a week in a small group or individual basis in addition to the CORE math program inside the classroom** **Strategies/Activities for Lexical Dyscalculia:** • Student will learn how to catch his own mistakes and explain the errors using a calculator. • Teacher will use cooperative groups to facilitate problem solving. • Student will verbally analyze the steps that are required to solve word problems (e.g., "What information is given?" "What is asked?" "What operations is used?" etc.). • Teacher will represent the numerical amounts, in concrete forms, that are presented in the word problems (e.g., problems involving money use real or play money). • Teacher will ask the student to identify the primary question that must be answered to solve a given word problem. In more difficult word problems the student might be asked for two or more questions. • Student will make up word problems for other students in the classroom to solve. • Teacher will break down each math word problem into specific steps.	• Student will learn why he needs to know a math concept. • Teacher will provide real-life concrete examples and opportunities for the student to apply those concepts to. • Student will make notes to "set the problem up" in written form as the math word problem is read. • Student will simulate situations which relate to math word problems (e.g., trading, selling, buying, etc.). • Student will solve math word problems by manipulating objects and by stating the process used. • Teacher will discuss and provide a list of words/phrases which usually indicate an addition, subtraction, and multiplication and division operation. • Student will check answers to word problems using a calculator. The calculator can also be used to reinforce the learning of math facts. • Student will practice solving math word problems by using a computer software program that gives immediate feedback. • Student will practice recognizing operational symbols by using different color flash cards for each math symbol. • Teacher will illustrate how to convert words into their numerical equivalents to solve word problems (e.g., three weeks = 21 days, one third = 1/3, one year = 12 months, two quarters = 50 cents, one yard = 36 inches, etc.). • Teacher will present relevant vocabulary often found in math word problems.

Math: Lexical Dyscalculia **Tier 2**

- Teacher will present phrases to be translated into numbers and then word problems.
- Teacher will reduce the number of problems assigned to the student at one time.
- Teacher will demonstrate how to solve math word problems by reading the problem and solving the problem on paper step-by-step.
- Teacher will provide concrete examples to apply these concepts in real-life situations, using computer software that addresses those situations.
- Teacher will use cooperative groups to facilitate problem solving by verbally analyzing those steps necessary to complete the problem. Teacher will be the group facilitator.
- Teacher will provide practice in solving math word problems by using a computer software program that gives immediate feedback.
- Student will manipulate objects as the teacher describes the operation.

Math: Lexical Dyscalculia **Tier 3**

Suggested Interventionist: Special Education Teacher, Math Specialist

Suggested Session: 60 minutes 5x a week in a small group or individual basis in addition to the CORE math program outside of the classroom

Strategies/Activities for Lexical Dyscalculia:

- Student will identify common concept relationships that exists among math terms presented. The math concept will be placed on the top of the page. A circle is drawn and divided into four sections. Student will place the different attributes or example problems that belong to the concept within the four sections of the circle.
- Student will describe within the concept definition map what the concept is, make comparisons to other concepts, tell what properties it has and cite examples of it.
- Student will use a Frayer model diagram to discover what the math concept is and what it is not. The math word will be written in the middle of the diagram. Student will label each quarter of the diagram with: the Definition of the concept; Characteristics of the concept; Examples of the concept; and Non-examples of the concept.

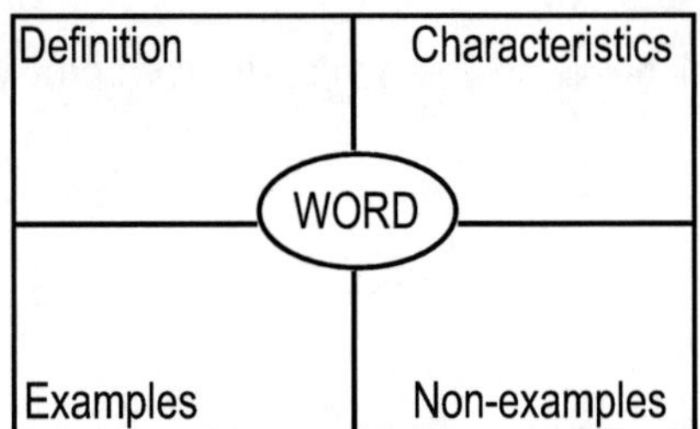

Math: Lexical Dyscalculia Tier 3	Math: Lexical Dyscalculia Tier 3
• Student will generate lists of words that belong to a particular concept being taught. These categories will identify significant relationships among the terms of the concept. • Student will create a matrix. Along the left side of the matrix key terms are listed. Across the top of the matrix features will be written that the key terms and concept might share. Student will place an x to indicate when a property applies to the term. • Student will take a piece of paper and divide it into four sections. One section has the vocabulary concept written down. The second section has the definition of that concept. The third section has a visual representation drawn describing the concept and the fourth section has a personal association drawn or written down. • Student will place words with math concepts on 3x5 cards and will sort these words into math categories. There must be relationships between words. Student will explain the relationship and identify one term that is not related. • Teacher will create a deck of cards of paired math facts or equations or any other category in math. These paired concept cards will be used for a game such as Concentration. • Student will match mathematical equations to the equivalent language used to read them. Each student shall have set of eight cards. Each card has a mathematical statement given in symbols. Teacher will verbally say a mathematical statement. Student who has its equivalent in number form claims the two cards. Winner has the most cards.	• Teacher will create number cubes out of blank face dice. On each side of the dice a fraction or decimals are written. Student will throw two dice and has to determine which of the dice has the greater value. (ex. ½ is greater than 3). • Teacher will use graphic organizers to teach math concepts, teach math processes and teach math steps. • Teacher will introduce a four column organizer. The headings for the columns are: K-What facts do I KNOW from the information in the problem; N-Which information do I not need; W-What does the problem ask; and S-What Strategy /operation/tools will I use to solve the problem. Student will read a word problem and fill in the four columns with information. • Student will act out word problems using concrete forms (money) that represent the word problem. • Students will use a calculator when solving word problems.

Area of Math: Graphical Dyscalculia

Math: Graphical Dyscalculia	Math: Graphical Dyscalculia Tier 1
Graphical Dyscalculia—relates to difficulty writing math symbols, math terms without reversing them. Examples of academic problems in this area: • Difficulty with writing math symbols • Difficulty forming individual digits or copying them • Difficulty encoding numbers correctly • Mixing up order or direction of numbers • Difficulty writing numbers because of inefficient fine motor/ coordination of visual perceptual skills **Accommodations and Modifications:** • Use of graph paper • Folding paper in columns • Use of symbols • Use of problem solving sequence chart • Color code key operations symbols • Color code columns and rows of math problems • Use of computation aids • Modify number of problems • Use of manipulatives • Scan worksheet into a computer and have the student finish the worksheet using the keyboard • Reduce the number of problems assigned and leave enough space on the page for the student to compute the problem • Reduce the amount of copying (if at all) • Provide large work space on tests	**Suggested Interventionist: General Education Teacher with consultation from the Special Education teacher/Math Specialist/OT** **Suggested Session: Small group 2x a week, explicit instruction within the CORE math program within the classroom** **Strategies/Activities for Graphical Dyscalculia:** • Student will use graph paper with of different size boxes to line up numbers in order to solve calculation problems. • Student will turn lined paper sideways (vertically) in order to line up numerals when solving problems. • Student will write directly in workbooks. • Student will practice writing numerals and math symbols. • Teacher will provide visual clues, such as colored lines, to indicate where the student begins to work math problems (e.g., right to left). • Teacher will give color-coded directions of where math problems begin on a page. • Teacher will reduce the amount of writing in math problems on a page. • Teacher will provide a lot of visual space for students to use in completing math problems.

Math: Graphical Dyscalculia Tier 2	Math: Graphical Dyscalculia Tier 2
Suggested Interventionist: Special Education Teacher, Math Specialist, Occupational Therapist **Suggested Session: 30 minutes 2 to 3x a week in a small group or individual basis in addition to the CORE math program inside the classroom** **Strategies/Activities for Graphical Dyscalculia:** • Student will use post-it notes beside word problems in the math text to show his work. • Student will use a calculator to solve math problems. • Student will be provided with practice in math by using a computer software program that gives immediate feedback. • Teacher will reduce the amount of information on a page if it is causing visual distractions. • Student will check math assignments using a calculator. **Visual Discrimination Math Activities:** • Teacher will prepare a sheet consisting of a set of numbers. One number in each group will be different. Student will circle the number that is different. • Teacher will designate a number that the student is to find in the magazine. Student will circle as many different sizes or style number as possible. • Student will play matching games with numbers. • Student will recognize numbers and shapes by touch alone.	• Student will be given a piece of newspaper. Student will circle designated numbers from the newspaper. • Student will be given various size and color numbers on various papers. Student will sort the numbers according to size and color. • Teacher has a range of numbers patterns that the student will copy. **Visual Motor Math Activities:** • Student will have a reduced amount of required copying from the chalkboard. • Teacher will write large numbers on the chalkboard with space between the lines. • Teacher will reduce amount of work required for completion of an assignment. • Student will use graph paper for all math problems. • Teacher will color code numbers that are in the one's, ten's column, etc. • Teacher will provide dot-to-dot pictures of numbers to student. • Teacher will utilize Legos to make three-dimensional buildings. • Teacher will ask the student to draw different shapes on top of other shapes.

Math: Graphical Dyscalculia Tier 2	Math: Graphical Dyscalculia Tier 2
Visual Coordination Math Activities: • Student will copy and use geo boards. • Student will use visual tracking worksheets. • Student will use fine motor workbooks. • Student will use pattern reproduction worksheets such as dot-to-dot. • Student will complete mazes. • Student will copy from the board. • Student will catch balls of different sizes. • Student will trace numbers in print and script. • Student will trace objects, geometric forms, numbers and faces. **Visual Figure Ground Math Activities:** • Student will complete number searches. • Student will complete activity workbooks with activities of spotting the difference in numbers. • Student will solve jigsaws and paint by numbers. • Student will circle the same number in a text. • Student will find hidden numbers on an activity sheet. • Student will sort numbers from a bag of different numbers with his eyes closed. • Student will play computer games requiring sorting or matching. • Teacher will provide a worksheet containing multiple replicas of numbers. Student will color only a specified portion of a number.	**Visual Memory Math Activities:** • Student will play concentration with number facts. • Student will participate in times exercises copying from the board to paper. • Student will be shown numbers on the overhead projector. A number will be removed and the student will reproduce the missing number. • Student will be encouraged to visualize and verbalize what he has seen. • Student will complete matching numbers worksheets. Numbers will be written backwards, forwards, upside down and inverted. • Student will reproduce templates or parquetry blocks from memory after the template is shown. • Student will pick out patterns and groups when remembering a sequence. Student will be shown a series of numbers. The numbers are mixed up and the student puts the numbers back in the original series. **Visual Closure Math Activities:** • Student will complete jigsaws/puzzles. • Student will complete dot-to-dots. • Student will color in pictures. • Student will complete number searches. • Student will write in sand. • Student will fill in the missing number in an ordered sequence.

Math: Graphical Dyscalculia Tier 2	Math: Graphical Dyscalculia Tier 3
• Student will match complete and incomplete shapes. • Student will use stencils. • Student will engage in model making. • Student will build three-dimensional models. **Visual Form Constancy Math Activities:** • Student will touch, feel and talk about three-dimensional numbers when their size and orientation may alter. • Student will color three-dimensional drawings and models of numbers. • Student will make models. • Student will compare and contrast the size and shape of numbers. • Student will outline jigsaws to see how individual parts fit together to make a whole. • Student will identify shapes, numbers and objects when a portion is missing. • Student will look at a design made from parquetry blocks with one piece missing. Student will find the appropriate block to complete the pattern.	**Suggested Interventionist: Special Education Teacher, Math Specialist, Occupational Therapist** **Suggested Session: 60 minutes 5x a week in a small group or individual basis in addition to the CORE math program outside of the classroom** **Strategies/Activities for Graphical Dyscalculia:** • Student will use post-it notes beside word problems in the math text to show his work. • Student will use a calculator to solve math problems. • Teacher will provide practice in math by using a computer software program that gives immediate feedback. • Teacher will reduce the amount of information on a page if it is causing visual distractions. • Student will check math assignments using a calculator. **Visual Discrimination Math Activities:** • Teacher will prepare a sheet consisting of a set of numbers. One number in each group will be different. Student will circle the number that is different. • Teacher will designate a number that the student is to find in the magazine. Student will circle as many different sizes or style number as possible.

Math: Graphical Dyscalculia Tier 3	Math: Graphical Dyscalculia Tier 3
• Student will play matching games with numbers. • Student will recognize numbers and shapes by touch alone. • Student will circle designated numbers from the newspaper. • Student will be given various size and color numbers on various papers. Student will sort the numbers according to size and color. • Teacher will have a range of numbers patterns which the student will copy. **Visual Motor in Math Activities:** • Student will have a reduced amount of required copying from the chalkboard. • Teacher will write large numbers on the chalkboard with space between the lines. • Teacher will reduce amount of work required for completion of an assignment. • Student will use graph paper for all math problems. • Teacher will color code numbers that are in the one's, ten's column, etc. • Teacher will provide dot-to-dot pictures of numbers. • Student will be asked to make collages. • Teacher will utilize Legos to make three-dimensional buildings. • Teacher will ask the student to draw different shapes on top of other shapes.	**Visual Coordination Math Activities:** • Student will copy and use geo boards. • Student will use visual tracking worksheets. • Student will use fine motor workbooks. • Student will use pattern reproduction worksheets such as dot-to-dot. • Student will complete mazes. • Student will copy from the board. • Student will catch balls of different sizes. • Student will trace numbers in print and script. • Student will trace objects, geometric forms, numbers and faces. **Visual Figure Ground Math Activities:** • Student will complete number searches. • Student will complete activities of spotting the difference in numbers. • Student will solve jigsaws and paint by numbers. • Student will circle the same number in a text. • Students will find hidden numbers on an activity sheet. • Student will sort numbers from a bag of different numbers with his eyes closed. • Student will play computer games requiring sorting or matching. • Teacher will provide a worksheet containing multiple replicas of numbers. Student will color only a specified portion of a number.

Math: Graphical Dyscalculia **Tier 3**

Visual Memory Math Activities:

- Student will play concentration with number facts.
- Student will participate in timed exercises copying from the board to paper.
- Student will be shown numbers on the overhead projector. The number will be removed and the student will reproduce the missing number.
- Student will be encouraged to visualize and verbalize what he has seen.
- Student will complete matching numbers worksheets. Numbers are written backwards, forwards, upside down and inverted.
- Student will reproduce templates or parquetry blocks from memory.
- Student will pick out patterns and groups when remembering a sequence.

Visual Closure Math Activities:

- Student will complete jigsaws/puzzles.
- Student will complete dot-to-dots.
- Student will color in pictures.
- Student will complete number searches.
- Student will write or draws in sand.
- Student will fill in the missing number in an ordered sequence.
- Student will match complete and incomplete shapes.

Math: Graphical Dyscalculia **Tier 3**

- Student will engage in construction games.
- Student will use stencils.
- Student will engage in model making.
- Student will build three-dimensional models.

Visual Form Constancy Math Activities:

- Student will touch, feel and talk about three-dimensional numbers when their size and orientation may alter.
- Student will color three-dimensional drawings and models of numbers.
- Student will make models.
- Student will compare and contrast the size and shape of numbers.
- Student will outline jigsaw puzzles to see how individual parts fit together to make a whole.
- Student will identify shapes, numbers and objects when a portion is missing.
- Student will look at a design made from parquetry blocks where one piece is missing. Student will find the appropriate block to complete the pattern.

Area of Math: Ideognostical Dyscalculia

Math: Ideognostical Dyscalculia	Math: Ideognostic Dyscalculia Tier 1
Ideognostical Dyscalculia—relates to difficulty conceptualizing math concepts, terms and steps. Examples of academic problems in this area: • Difficulty with mental comprehension of quantitative concepts • Difficulty distinguishing colors of objects, or objects from a competing background • Difficulty doing mental math • Difficulty expressing meaningful verbal identification of math symbols • Difficulty forming or assigning numbers and symbols meaning **Accommodations and Modifications:** • Reduce difficulty of reading level for word problems • Use of examples on tests • Use of graph paper • Folding paper in columns • Flash cards/frequent repetition • Use of symbols • Use of problem solving sequence chart • Verbalize steps • Color code key operations symbols • Color code columns and rows of math problems • Use of computation aids • Modify number of problems • Use of manipulatives	**Suggested Interventionist: General Education Teacher with consultation from the Special Education teacher/Math Specialist** **Suggested Session: Small group 2x a week, explicit instruction within the CORE math program within the classroom** **Strategies/Activities for Ideognostic Dyscalculia:** **Word Problems** • Student will use manipulative objects to illustrate place value by providing a visual image. • Teacher will illustrate the concepts and terminology necessary to learn place value. • Teacher will provide the student with concrete learning experiences in grouping manipulative objects into groups of ones, tens, hundreds, etc. Student label the column with number representations. • Student will understand the zero concept in place value by using real money concepts. • Teacher will use decimals while teaching money concepts in order to teach place value by association (e.g., $2.28 is the same as eight pennies or eight ones, two dimes or two tens, two dollars or two hundred). • Student will use the vertical lines on graph paper in order to visualize the concept of columns. • Student will visualize the concept of filling each column from right to left while moving on the next column from ones to tens, to hundreds, to thousands, etc

Math: Ideognostic Dyscalculia Tier 1	Math: Ideognostic Dyscalculia Tier 1
• Teacher will provide word problems that require a one-step process while teaching new concepts. • Teacher will write a number sentence after reading a math word problem. Student will follow the teacher's illustration in the assigned math problems. • Student will restate math word problems in his own words while breaking down each problem into sequential steps. • Students will use "sets" of objects from the environment while formulating math concepts to practice addition, subtraction, multiplication, and division problems. • Teacher will use concrete examples as associations while teaching math word problems. • Teacher will teach and reinforce shapes using common objects in the environment (round clocks, rectangle teacher desk, square tables, etc.). • Teacher will develop a measurement reference sheet to be used when solving math problems. • Teacher will reinforce the teaching of measurement concepts while using computer games. • Teacher will work the first couple of math problems of an math assignment with the student. • Student will use a calculator to reinforce learning math facts. • Student will practice a new skill individually, with an aide or teacher before the entire class attempts the activity • Teacher will provide practice of place value by using appropriate software programs.	• Teacher will supply watches for use while student is learning to tell time. • Student will use computer software programs to reinforce time concepts. • Teacher will create a marked-column format organizer on a master to be copied for the student to use in solving all assigned place value math problems. • Teacher will color-code all different place value columns so student uses columns accurately and continues to visualize the concept. • Teacher will use a digital clock to facilitate the telling time process. • Teacher will illustrate how a digital clock and a watch both tell the same time. • Teacher will make certain the student has mastery of math concepts with a calculator. • Teacher will prepare student on a math problem before he is called on to share with the class. • Student will know the basic concepts of fractions concretely and conceptually before being required to solve problems involving measurement (e.g., ¼ inch, 1 ½ feet, etc.). • Teacher will teach measurement problems concretely by using a recipe or building a model, etc. • Teacher will review, on a daily basis, those skills, concepts, tasks, etc., which have been taught. This should be used as an anchoring activity.

Math: Ideognostic Dyscalculia Tier 2	Math: Ideognostic Dyscalculia Tier 2
Suggested Interventionist: Special Education Teacher, Math Specialist **Suggested Session: 30 minutes 2 to 3x a week in a small group or individual basis in addition to the CORE math program inside the classroom** **Strategies/Activities for Ideognostic Dyscalculia:** • Teacher will use manipulative objects to teach place value by providing a visual image. • Student will use a calculator to solve math problems involving the use of columns. • Teacher will provide word problems that require a one-step process, making certain that the sentences are short and simple. • Teacher will illustrate and discuss words/phrases which usually indicate a specific operation like addition, subtraction, multiplication and division. • Student will practice the concept of regrouping by "borrowing" and "carrying" from objects in columns set up like math problems. • Student will use "sets" of objects from the environment to practice number operations. • Teacher will find opportunities for the student to apply measurement facts and use everyday measurement tools to real-life situations (e.g., cooking, measuring the lengths of objects, etc.). • Student will solve math word problems by manipulating objects. • Student will restate word problems in own words.	• Teacher will provide color-coded columns to help the student understand math concepts. • Teacher will teach the student to look for "clue" words that indicate the mathematical operation in a word problem. • Student will verbally analyze the steps that are required to solve word problems. • Teacher will represent numerical amounts in word problems in concrete forms (e.g., problems involving money use with real or play money). • Student will identify the primary question that must be answered to solve a given word problem. • Teacher will place the number sentences on the board and student will tell or write word problems that could be solved by the number sentences. • Student will practice using columns when solving math problems by using a computer program which automatically chooses the correct column. • Teacher will make certain math problems have concrete examples of concepts being taught. • Teacher will provide repeated physical demonstrations of abstract concepts. • Student will use a calculator to solve measurement problems and check the accuracy of problems. • Student will write notes to set the problem up in written form as he reads the math word problem. • Student will simulate situations which relate to math word problems (e.g., trading, selling, buying, etc.).

Math: Ideognostic Dyscalculia Tier 3	Math: Ideognostic Dyscalculia Tier 3
Suggested Interventionist: Special Education Teacher, Math Specialist **Suggested Session: 60 minutes 5x a week in a small group or individual basis in addition to the CORE math program outside of the classroom** **Strategies/activities for Ideognostic Dyscalculion:** • Student will identify common concept relationships that exist among math terms being used. The math concept is placed on the top of the page. A circle is divided into four sections. Student will place the different attributes or example problems that belong to the concept within the four sections of the divided circle. • Student will fill in the Concept Definition Map by describing what the concept is, make comparisons, tell what properties it has and cite examples of it. • Student will use a Frayer model diagram to discover what the math concept is and what it is not. The math word is written in the middle of the word Frayer diagram. Student will label each quarter of the diagram with: Definition of the concept; Characteristics of the concept; Examples of the concept; and Non-examples of the concept. (see page 192) • Student will generate lists of words that belong to a particular concept being taught. After the lists are generated, the student will sort words into categories. These categories should identify important relationships among the terms of the concept.	• Student will match mathematical equations to the equivalent language used to read them. • Teacher will create number cubes out of blank face dice. On each side of the dice a fraction or a decimals are written. Student will throw two dice and determine which of the dice has the greater value. (ex. ½ is greater than 3). • Teacher will use graphic organizers to teach math concepts, processes and math steps. Samples of graphic organizers are: Concept Definition Webs; Compare/Contrast; "Tree" Diagram. • Teacher will introduce the student to a four column organizer. The headings for the columns are: K-What facts do I KNOW from the information in the problem; N-Which information do I not need; W-What does the problem ask; and S-What Strategy/operation/tools will be used to solve the problem. Student will read a word problem and fills in the four columns with the information from the word problem. • Student will act out word problems using concrete forms that represent the word problem.

Math: Ideognostic Dyscalculia Tier 3
• Student will create a matrix. Along the left side of the matrix key terms are listed. Across the top of the matrix features are written the key terms that the concepts might share. Student will place an x to indicate when a property applies to the term. • Student will take a rectangle piece of paper and divide it into four sections. One section has the vocabulary concept written down. The second section has the definition of the concept written down. The third section has a visual representation drawn and the fourth section has a personal association drawn or written down. • Student will use 3x5 cards with math concepts to sort these words into math categories. Students will explain the relationship and identify one term that is unrelated to the others. • Teacher will create a deck of cards of paired math facts or equations or any other category in math and use for a game such as Concentration. • Student will make up their own word problems and give those problems to other students to solve. • Student will use a calculator when solving word problems.

Math: Ideognostic Dyscalculia Tier 3
• Teacher will provide practice in solving math word problems by using a computer software program that gives the student immediate feedback. • Three-Part Guide—This strategy/graphic organizer helps the student sort out the information in the word problem. The teacher will write a word problem at the top of the piece of paper. The paper is than divided into three parts. —The first part has four true and false statements about the word problem. The student writes whether they think any of the statements are true or false from their background knowledge. —The second part contains more math statements but these statements contain math ideas that are useful for solving the word problem. —The third part has calculations that help solve the word problem. Teacher models the Three-Part Guide and the student completes one in a group.

Area of Math: Operational Dyscalculia

Math: Operational Dyscalculia	Math: Operational Dyscalculia Tier 1
Operational Dyscalculia—relates to the ability to perform math operations such as addition, subtraction, multiplication, division, fractions, etc. Examples of academic problems in this area: • Difficult learning and applying the rules for addition, subtraction, multiplication and division • Difficulty changing operations • Inaccurate or over simplification of complex operations • Preference for written computation as opposed to mental computation **Accommodations and Modifications:** • Reduce difficulty of reading level for word problems • Grade pass/fail or change the grading scale • Use of examples on tests • Use of graph paper • Folding paper in columns • Flash cards/frequent repetition • Use of symbols • Use of problem solving sequence chart • Verbalize steps • Color code key operations symbols • Color code columns • And rows of math problems • Use of computation aids • Modify number of problems • Use of manipulatives	**Suggested Interventionist: General Education Teacher with consultation from the Math Specialist** **Suggested Session: small group 2x a week, explicit instruction within the Core math program within the classroom** **Strategies/Activities for Operational Dyscalculia:** • Student will be allowed to think critically and creatively by using calculators for everyday procedures as well as new concepts. • Teacher will illustrate how to use computers for mathematics, with emphasis on repeated opportunities for drill and practice, and encouragement of higher-level thinking. • Student will memorize basic math facts. • Student will chunk facts for memorization. • Student will be given extra time and practice. • Teacher will provide review of facts on a daily basis. • Teacher will provide multi-sensory (say, see, sing) activities as student writes facts. • Student will play computer math games that require recall of facts. • Teacher will teach memory tricks when teaching multiplication facts. • Teacher will emphasize reciprocal strategies such as turn-around facts (e.g., 3+6, 6+3; 8x5, 5x8), teaching all facts in horizontal and vertical forms. • Student will use calculators to move to higher level concepts such as fractions, decimals, algebra, etc. • Students will not be pressed for speed. Time drills produce anxiety.

Math: Operational Dyscalculia Tier 1	Math: Operational Dyscalculia Tier 1
• Student will solve addition, subtraction, multiplication and division problems by manipulating objects first and then using the calculator. • Teacher will illustrate and provide the student with a list of words/phrases which indicate addition, subtraction, multiplication and division operation in word problems. • Teacher will use daily drill as an anchoring activity to help the student memorize addition, subtraction, multiplication and division facts (e.g., written problems, flash cards, etc.). • Teacher will attach a number line to a student's desk in order to assist in the solving problems. • Teacher will create a math-facts reference sheet for addition, subtraction, multiplication and division facts for use when solving math problems. • Teacher will illustrate the concepts of more than, less than, equal, and zero using concrete objects. • Teacher will provide visual cues on paper when the student must change operations. • Teacher will use different color-coding for each operation symbol. Teacher will gradually reduce the use of colors when the student can complete the operations independently. • Student will recognize the concepts of all math operation symbols. • Teacher will make the math operation symbols extra large. • Student will highlight or underline the operations within the math problem before starting the problem. • Teacher will illustrate how to convert words into their numerical equivalents to solve word problems. • Teacher will illustrate concretely while teaching relevant vocabulary found in math.	• Teacher will illustrate the meaning of mathematical terms (e.g., sum, dividend, etc.). Student will review the terms and their meanings on daily drill sheets. • Teacher will provide a checklist to follow in solving math word problems. Student will check off each step as it is completed. • Teacher will provide practice in regrouping facts using a computer software program that is specific to the math problem. **Strategies/Activities for Regrouping:** • Teacher will provide daily drills as anchoring activities to help the student with regrouping (e.g., written problems, flash cards, etc.). • Teacher will use real life activities in applying regrouping skills. • Student will use a calculator to check answers. • Teacher will illustrate the proper sequence of steps when solving math problems on the overhead projector before the class begins a new assignment. (A copy of the overhead is given to the students who have problems in math.) • Student will use computer software programs that reinforce the proper sequence of steps in solving math problems. • Teacher will use consistent language to communicate regrouping (e.g., "borrow," "carry," etc.). • Student will practice the concept of regrouping by "borrowing" and "carrying" from objects in columns set up like math problems. • Teacher will require the student to check subtraction problems by adding the answer plus the subtrahend. • Teacher will use pennies and dimes to learn the concept of regrouping and borrowing while solving money math problems.

Math: Operational Dyscalculia Tier 1	Math: Operational Dyscalculia Tier 2
• Teacher will list the steps in solving math problems on the bulletin board so the student can use it as a reference. **Strategies/Activities for Fractions:** • Teacher will illustrate the concept of whole numbers in fractions by using concrete items such as a real pizza pie or a cup cake. • Student will solve math problems involving fractions and decimals using computer software. • Student will cut pieces of paper into equal numbers (e.g., thirds, eighths, tenths, etc.) and use these to learn more about fractions. • Student will solve fraction problems by using real-life measurement such as ounces, inches, pounds, etc., to determine weight, length, volume, etc. **Strategies/Activities for Decimals:** • Teacher will provide graph paper to solve decimal problems. Place numbers in different boxes. • Teacher will illustrate decimals by using money problems. • Student will solve math problems involving decimals by using concrete objects such as money. • Student will use a calculator when learning to solve problems involving decimals. • Teacher will provide the student with a daily shopping list of items with a corresponding list of the cost of each item (each involving a decimal point). Student will add up he spends. • Student will use menus, newspapers, and catalogues to illustrate adding numbers with decimals.	**Suggested Interventionist: Special Education Teacher, Math Specialist** **Suggested Session: 30 minutes 2 to 3x a week in a small group or individual basis in addition to the CORE math program inside the classroom** **Strategies/Activities for Operational Dyscalculia:** • Teacher will illustrate mathematical vocabulary with concrete examples. • Teacher will use mathematical language in informal conversation as often as possible. • Student will use a calculator to reinforce learning of the math facts. • Student will use a calculator to solve problems by separating each step of the problem. • Student will practice math facts using computer software programs. • Student will use a calculator to compensate. • Student will use a calculator for drill activities of basic math facts. • Teacher will create opportunities for the student to apply math facts to real-life situations (e.g., getting change in the cafeteria, going to a store, etc.).

Math: Operational Dyscalculia Tier 2	Math: Operational Dyscalculia Tier 2
• Student will play math fact games with other students. • Student will practice math facts using a computer with software programs that provide game-like activities in order to teach and reinforce facts. • Teacher will discuss and provide a list of words/phrases which indicate an addition, subtraction, and multiplication and division operation in word problems. • Teacher will provide the student with many concrete experiences to help him learn and remember math facts. • Student will use a calculator to reinforce learning addition, subtraction, multiplication and division. • Student will use a calculator for drill activities of basic addition, subtraction, multiplication and division facts. • Student will talk through the math problem as he solves it in order to identify errors he is making. • Student will estimate math solutions before solving as a tool for self-checking. • Student will verbally explain the problem to a teacher, or assistant before solving the problem. • Student will independently solve half of his/her addition, subtraction, multiplication and division facts/problems each day, using a calculator as reinforcement to solve the rest of the problems.	• Student will learn the concepts of: more than; less than; equal; and zero. • Student will be provided with enjoyable math activities during free time in the classroom (e.g., computer games, math games, manipulatives, etc.). • Student will perform alternative assignments when necessary. • Teacher will be consistent in the language used to communicate about addition, subtraction, multiplication and division. • Student will be provided with shorter math tasks, but given more of them throughout the day (e.g., four assignments of five problems each rather than one assignment of twenty problems). • Student will be taught to use resources in the environment to help him solve math problems.

Math: Operational Dyscalculia Tier 3	Math: Operational Dyscalculia Tier 3
Suggested Interventionist: Special Education Teacher, Math Specialist **Suggested Session: 60 minutes 5x a week in a small group or individual basis in addition to the CORE math program outside of the classroom** **Strategies/Activities for Addition Facts:** • Teacher will make rods of different sizes. The rods can be either three-dimensional or one-dimensional. The teacher can also use Cuisenaire rods, Stern rods or Unifex cubes. —Ten rod = 10 inches long —Nine rod = 9 inches long —Eight rod = 8 inches long —Seven rod = 7 inches long —Six rod = 6 inches long —Five rod = 5 inches long —Four rod = 4 inches long —Three rod = 3 inches long —Two rod = 2 inches long —One rod = 1 inch long	• Teacher will line up the rods of different sizes vertically and explain that every rod has a "buddy" that completes the addition fact. Each set of two rods will add up to the sum of 10. Student can visualize the different sizes that add up to the largest rod (10). They continue: — 10 rod = 1 rod + 9 rod — 10 rod = 2 rod + 8 rod — 10 rod = 3 rod + 7 rod — 10 rod = 4 rod + 6 rod — 10 rod = 5 rod + 5 rod 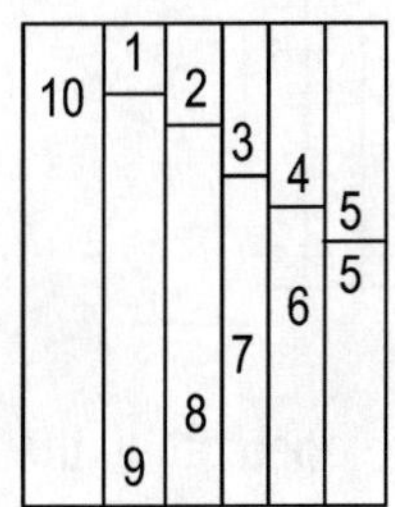 • After placing the vertical rods next to each other, the teacher will write the addition equations that correspond to the number rods vertically on graph paper. $\begin{array}{r}1\\+9\\\hline10\end{array}\quad\begin{array}{r}2\\+8\\\hline10\end{array}\quad\begin{array}{r}3\\+7\\\hline10\end{array}\quad\begin{array}{r}4\\+6\\\hline10\end{array}\quad\begin{array}{r}5\\+5\\\hline10\end{array}$ • Student will write the equations on 3x5 index cards without the answer.

Math: Operational Dyscalculia Tier 3	Math: Operational Dyscalculia Tier 3
• Student will again place the rods of different sizes vertically. However, the student now reverses the vertical order of the rods. — 10 rod = 9 rod + 1 rod — 10 rod = 8 rod + 2 rod — 10 rod = 7 rod + 3 rod — 10 rod = 6 rod + 4 rod — 10 rod = 5 rod + 5 rod 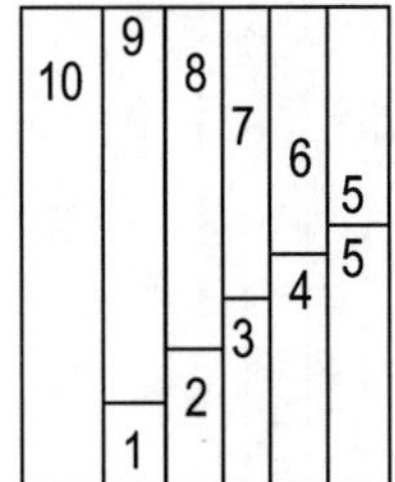 • After placing the rods next to each other, the student will write the addition equations that correspond to the number rods on graph paper. $\begin{array}{r}9\\+1\\\hline 10\end{array}$ $\begin{array}{r}8\\+2\\\hline 10\end{array}$ $\begin{array}{r}7\\+3\\\hline 10\end{array}$ $\begin{array}{r}6\\+4\\\hline 10\end{array}$ $\begin{array}{r}5\\+5\\\hline 10\end{array}$ • Student will write the equations on 3x5 index cards without the answer. There are now nine addition facts for the family of ten.	• Student will place the rods of different sizes next to each other horizontally. — 10 rod = 1 rod + 9 rod — 10 rod = 2 rod + 8 rod — 10 rod = 3 rod + 7 rod — 10 rod = 4 rod + 6 rod — 10 rod = 5 rod + 5 rod 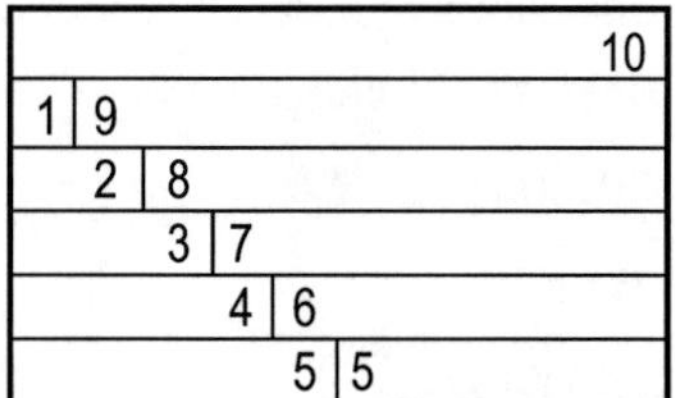 • After placing the rods horizontally, teacher will write the addition equations that correspond to the number rods on graph paper. — 1 + 9 = 10 — 2 + 8 = 10 — 3 + 7 = 10 — 4 + 6 = 10 — 5 + 5 = 10 • Student will write the equations on 3x5 index cards without the answer.

Math: Operational Dyscalculia Tier 3	Math: Operational Dyscalculia Tier 3

Math: Operational Dyscalculia — **Tier 3**

- Student will place the rods once again horizontally. The student will reverse the order of the rods.
  - — 10 rod = 9 rod + 1 rod
  - — 10 rod = 8 rod + 2 rod
  - — 10 rod = 7 rod + 3 rod
  - — 10 rod = 6 rod + 4 rod
  - — 10 rod = 5 rod + 5 rod

10	
9	1
8	2
7	3
6	4
5	5

- After placing the rods horizontally, the student will write the addition equations on graph paper.
  - — 9 + 1 = 10 8 + 2 = 10 7 + 3 = 10
  - — 6 + 4 = 10 5 + 5 = 10
- Student will write the equations on 3x5 index cards without the answers. There are now 18 addition facts for the family of ten.
- Student will continue to create the different commutative functions of addition. Student will continue to write these equations on graph paper and 3x5 cards.
- Student will continue to work concretely with the rods, graph paper and index cards for all of the addition families of 9, 8, 7, 6, 5, 4, 3, 2.
- Teacher will continue to reinforce memory facts by giving mixed addition fact-sheet quizzes every day.

Math: Operational Dyscalculia — **Tier 3**

Strategies/Activities for Subtraction Facts:

- Teacher will explain the language of subtraction.
- Teacher will place the ten rod on top of a table. Teacher will put the one rod into the hand of the student. Teacher will hold the 1's partner (the nine rod that adds up to 10) under the table.
- Student will be asked what is the "buddy" that, when added to the nine rod, equals 10. When the student answers 1, the teacher rephrases the question: if the one rod is "taken away" from the ten rod, what number would you have? Student will answer 9.
- Student will be asked to write the equation on a piece of graph paper vertically and horizontally:

$$\begin{array}{r} 10 \\ \underline{-1} \\ 9 \end{array} \qquad 10 - 1 = 9$$

- Student will write the equation on a 3x5 card without the answer.
- Teacher will start the next fact by placing the ten rod on top of the table and replacing the nine rod with the eight rod.
- Teacher will give the student a two rod and ask the student what is the 2's "buddy" that adds up to 10. Student will answer 8.
- Teacher will rephrase the question: If you "take away" the two rod from the ten rod what number rod would you have? Student will answer 8.

Math: Operational Dyscalculia Tier 3	Math: Operational Dyscalculia Tier 3

Math: Operational Dyscalculia — Tier 3

- Student will write the equation on a piece of graph paper both vertically and horizontally.

$$\begin{array}{r} 10 \\ \underline{-\ 2} \\ 8 \end{array} \qquad 10 - 2 = 8$$

- Student will write the equation on a 3x5 index card vertically and horizontally without the answers.
- Teacher will continue to create the remainder of the equations using the "buddy" process. The following equations will be created: 10-3=7; 10-4=6; 10-5=5; 10-6=4; 10-7=3; 10-8=2; 10-9=1.
- Student and teacher will continue through this process while discovering or creating the subtraction facts of the 10, 9, 8, 7, 6, 5, 4, 3, 2 families.
- Teacher will continue to reinforce memory of the addition and subtraction facts by continuously giving the student fact-sheet quizzes after each new fact learned.

Strategies/Activities for Carrying and Borrowing in Addition and Subtraction:

Visualizing the setting up of addition problems:

- Teacher will explain to the student that color-coding helps in addition. Student will be asked to get out a green, yellow and red highlighter.
- When there is a two-column addition example, the student will highlight the column closest to his right hand with the green highlighter (green means start).

Math: Operational Dyscalculia — Tier 3

- Student will highlight the column closest to his left hand with a red highlighter (red means stop).
- If there are columns in between the green and red colors, the student will highlight those columns in yellow (yellow means slow down).

Strategies/Activities for carrying in addition:

- Teacher will write a two-column addition example on the board. The example is: = ___ $\begin{array}{r} 55 \\ \underline{+\ 46} \end{array}$
- Teacher will draw two columns on a piece of paper. The column on the right is highlighted in green and the column on the left is highlighted in red. A line will be drawn across the top of the page about two inches from the top. This space will be used to carry numbers in addition.
- Teacher will explain that the colors represent place value and the green column is always the 1's column and the red column (in two-column addition) will always be the 10's column.
- Teacher will explain that as the numbers are added, the numbers being carried are written in the color of the column being added.
- Student will use rods to arrive at the answer.
- Student will retrieve the five rod and the six rod. Student will place the two rods vertically, beside the written example.
- Student will place the number ten rod next to the rods representing the numbers in that column.
- Student will explain that the five rod plus the six rod add up to more than the ten rod. The two rods when added together are 11.

Math: Operational Dyscalculia **Tier 3**

- Student will trade in the five and six rods for the ten rod and one rod. Teacher shows how to represent 11.

	1	
	5	5
	- 4	6
		1

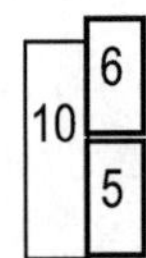

- Student writes 1 (in green pen) over the red column and the 1 under the green column, as the first part of the answer.
- The second column (red) has the number 1 in the space provided on the top of the column. Student will take another five rod plus the four rod representing the numbers in the second column (highlighted in red).
- Student will place the two rods vertically next to the ten rod.

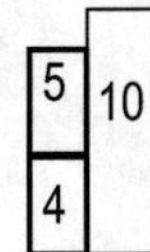

- Student will be able to see that the five rod and the four rod add up to 9 (which is less than 10). However, he must add the number from the top of the red column which is 1. All three numbers add up to 10.
- Student will place a 0 under the second (red) column and a 1 to the left of it. The answer is 101.
- Teacher will continue teaching carrying by introducing three-column addition. A three-column example is written with the column closest to the student's right hand highlighted in green, middle column highlighted in yellow and the column to the left highlighted in red.

Math: Operational Dyscalculia **Tier 3**

- Teacher will write another example on the board.

$$\begin{array}{r} 179 \\ \underline{+\ 53} \end{array}$$

- Student will place the three rod and the nine 9 rod above each other next to the ten rod. Student adds the value of the rods and sees that the sum is more than the ten rod. The student trades in the nine rods and three rod for a ten rod and a two rod. The sum of the ten rod and the two rod = 12.
- Teacher will show how to represent the 12 by placing the 10 over the yellow column and the 2 under the green column. Student will change the ten rod to a written number 1 over the yellow column and the number 2 stays under the green column.

$$\begin{array}{r} (1) \\ 179 \\ \underline{+\ \ 53} \\ 2 \end{array}$$

- Student will represent the numbers in the second column with the corresponding rods. Student will place the seven rod plus the five rod plus the one rod that was carried vertically next to the ten rod. The sum is 13.

1
7 10 = 3
5 10

- Teacher will point out that the sum of 13 is more than the ten rod.
- Student will trade the seven rod, the five rod and the one rod (that was carried) for a ten rod and a three rod. The 3 is placed under the yellow column and the ten rod is placed on the top of the red column. Ten rod is replaced by the number 1 on the top of the third red column (written in red pen).

Math: Operational Dyscalculia **Tier 3**

- Student will add the 1 that represents the ten rod and the 1 that is in the example. The sum is 2 and this number is placed under the third column (the red column). The answer to the example is 232.
- Student will continue this process until all carrying facts are understood.

Strategies/Activities in Visualizing Subtraction:

- Teacher will explain that color-coding helps in math. When a student looks at a two- or three-column subtraction problem, he will use his green and red highlighters.
- In a subtraction problem, student will highlight the bottom row with a green highlighter and the top row with a red highlighter.
- The green highlighter means that the student starts from the green row (symbolizes start) and ends at the red row (symbolizes stop).

Strategies/Activities for Borrowing in Subtraction:

- Teacher will write a two-column subtraction example on the board and on graph paper.

$$\begin{array}{r} 84 \\ \underline{-\ 53} \end{array}$$

- Teacher will explain that color-coding is used in subtraction as well as in addition.
- All subtraction will start with the bottom number (green) being subtracted from the top number (red).
- Teacher will use an envelope with pennies in it to represent the numbers on the top row.

Math: Operational Dyscalculia **Tier 3**

- Teacher will explain that the number 3 (green) must be subtracted from the number 4 (red).
- Teacher will place on top of the first column an envelope with four pennies in it representing the number 4. Teacher will ask the student to subtract the lower number 3 from the top number which is 4.
- Student will take the three pennies from the envelope and say how many pennies are left. Student will say the number 1 and place the 1 under the first column.
- Teacher will put eight pennies in the envelope. The student will subtract the number 5 from the eight pennies and will place a 3 under the second column. The answer to the non-borrowing problem equals 31.
- Teacher will give the student worksheets with math subtraction examples without borrowing.
- Teacher will continue teaching subtraction using the "envelope" process.
- The next problem will be an example of borrowing in subtraction. The problem is

$$\begin{array}{r} 854 \\ \underline{-\ 395} \end{array}$$

- Color-coding will continue in three-digit subtraction with the top numbers colored with red highlighter and the bottom numbers colored with green highlighter.
- Student will write the problem on graph paper with each number in its own box. Student will color-code the rows.

Math: Operational Dyscalculia **Tier 3**

- Teacher will place the envelope with four pennies on the top of the first row on the right.
- Student will try to take five pennies out of the envelope. When this is not possible, the teacher will explain that the student must borrow more money to be able to subtract.
- Student will borrow ten pennies from the next column.
- Student will add ten pennies to the four pennies and the answer will be fourteen pennies.
- In order to borrow the ten pennies, the student must cross out the number 5 from the top row of the middle column and subtract 1 from it and write the number 4 on top of that row.
- Student will take five pennies from the fourteen pennies (in the envelope) and have nine pennies left. Student will write the number 9 under the first column.
- The envelope with four pennies in it will be placed above the second column.
- Student will subtract the number 9 in the second column from the envelope that has only four pennies in it. The student will now have to borrow ten pennies from the third column.
- When the student borrows ten pennies from the third row, he crosses out the number 8 and replaces it with the number 7. Ten pennies are added to the envelope. The envelope that is placed above the second column now has fourteen pennies in it. Student removes nine pennies and has five pennies left and places that number 5 under the second column.
- Student will continue to subtract in the third column. Envelope with seven will be placed above the third column. Student will take away three pennies from the seven pennies and have four pennies left.

Math: Operational Dyscalculia **Tier 3**

- Student will place the 4 under the third column. The answer equals 459.
- Teacher will complete the example on the board using graph chalk lines.

$$\begin{array}{r} 74 \\ \not{8}\not{5}4 \\ \underline{-\,395} \\ 459 \end{array}$$

Strategies/Activities for Multiplication Facts:

- Teacher will review, illustrate and explain all the vocabulary words that are used in the multiplication process.
- Teacher will use a number line and the rods.
- Student will be instructed to make multiple rods of each number to illustrate the process called multiplication.
- Teacher will create a number line that matches the sizes of the rods (inch rods, Cuisenaire rods, Stern rods, Unifex cube rods).
- Teacher will illustrate how to use the number line.
- Teacher will take 3 seven inch rods and place them on a comparable number line; the number rods add up to 21.
- Teacher will explain that multiplication is addition.
- Teacher will write on the board. 7 + 7 + 7 = 21 or 3 x 7=21.
- Teacher will explain that instead of adding the seven rods three times, there is an easier way of doing this: it is called multiplication. Teacher will explain that the symbol (x) means multiplication.

Math: Operational Dyscalculia **Tier 3**

- The following multiplication sequence will be followed while creating each multiplication table. The sequence is: 3 x table; nine x table; 5 x table; 2 x table; 10 x table; 4 x table; 6 x table; 7 x table; 8 x table.
- Student will create a multiplication chart using graph paper with 12 squares by 12 squares. Horizontally across the top, the student writes the multiplication numbers 1x, 2x, 3x, 4x, 5x, 6x, 7x, 8x, 9x, 10x. In a vertical direction, student writes the same numbers down the left side of the chart.
- As the student "discovers" each of the multiplication facts, he places that equation on the chart in two ways. For example, 3 x 1 is placed under the 3x table heading as 3 x 1 = 3 and then in the third box vertically next to the number three under the 1 x table column. That number reads 1 x 3 = 3.

	1 x	2 x	3 x	4 x	5 x	6 x	7 x	8 x	9 x	10 x
1 x			3x1							
2 x										
3 x	1x3									
4 x										
5 x										
6 x										
7 x										
8 x										
9 x										
10 x										

Math: Operational Dyscalculia **Tier 3**

- By putting the equations on the chart two ways (3 x 1 and 1 x 3) the student will see that when he learns one fact he is actually learning two facts. He visually sees how the chart fills in with two facts for two different tables.
- Student will not only write these tables on his chart two ways but write them on cards, two ways horizontally and two ways vertically.

3 x 1 = 3　　　　3 x 1 = 3; 1 x 3 = 3
1 x 3 = 3

- Teacher will explain that no matter how the fact is written, it is still the same fact and has the same answer.
- Student will be given worksheets to reflect all multiplication tables written in each of the four forms. The multiplication fact worksheet reflects each new table as it is learned.
- Teacher will include at least one of every type of addition and subtraction fact learned as well. The multiplication facts will be reviewed by playing the following games: Concentration and War using the index cards.

Math: Operational Dyscalculia Tier 3	Math: Operational Dyscalculia Tier 3
Strategies/Activities for Long Multiplication: • Teacher will explain that color-coding will again be used. • Student will color-code the problems by highlighting in green the first bottom number in the right column and the second bottom number in red. If there are three numbers, the middle number is highlighted in yellow. The concept of green = start, yellow = slow and red = stop is reinforced. • Teacher will write the example on graph paper so that there are additional squares on top of the columns to write the number being carried. • Teacher will use an example that multiplies a two digit number by a one digit number. • Teacher will ask how much is 2 x 4. Student will answer 8 and write 8 under the first column in green pen. • Teacher will ask how much is 2 x 5. Student will answer 10 and places the 10 in green under the second and third column so that each number has its own space. 54 x 2 108 • After the student understands the concept, the teacher will choose an example with carrying, such as: 66 x 7	• Teacher will ask the student how much is 7 x 6, and the student answers 42. • Student will be directed to place the 4 above the second column in green pen and the 2 under the first column in green pen. • Teacher will ask the student how much is 7 x 6. Student answers 42; however there is a number already placed above the second column. • Student will be directed to add this number to the 42 because that number has been waiting (or carried over) to be added to the next number. Student will say that the numbers written under the second and third column will be 46. The answer to the problem equals 462. (4) 66 x 7 462 • Teacher will continue to give the student these examples on graph paper until they become automatic. • Teacher will write a two-digit times two-digit example on the board within a graph paper illustration. • The problem is 28 x 24. Remember to write the first bottom number in green and the second bottom number in red. • Teacher will ask the student how much is 4 x 8. Student will answer 32 and then place the 3 in the graph square above the second column and the 2 under the first column in green.

Math: Operational Dyscalculia **Tier 3**

- Teacher will ask the student how much is 4 x 2. Student will answer 8; however, there is a number that has been waiting to be carried or added to the number 8. Student will add 8 + 3. The number is 11 and the student will place that number under the second and third columns in green.
- Student will be directed to use the red pencil because he will be multiplying by the second (red) number. Student will be directed to place a red 0, to be used as a spacer, to the right under the 2 of the first column.
- Teacher will ask the student how much is 2 X 8. The answer is 16 and the student now places the one above the second column in red. Student is told to only pay attention to the red number and ignore the green numbers. The red 6 is placed under the second column.
- Teacher will ask the student how much is 2 x 2. Student will answer 4 and is reminded that there is a 1 waiting to be added to the number 4. One (1) + 4 = 5 and the red 5 is placed under the third column.
- Student will be directed to draw a line under the entire example and place an addition symbol in the space to the left of the last number.
- Student will add the numbers starting with the right column. The answer = 672. The bottom numbers are not color coded but are written in black.

```
  (1)
  (3)  (crossed out)
   28
 x 24
  112
  560
  672
```

Math: Operational Dyscalculia **Tier 3**

- This procedure will be continued with three-digit times three-digit problems; four-digit times four-digit problems, etc.
- Remember, the answers to the multiplication example will be color-coded. The first row is in green, the second yellow and the third red. These colors correspond with the colors of the multipliers: first multiplier is green, the second multiplier is yellow and the third multiplier is in red.

Division Strategy for Division Facts:

- Teacher will illustrate and explain the different vocabulary and symbols used in division. Teacher will explain that to divide means to make numbers smaller by seeing how many of a smaller number is in the bigger number.
- Teacher will use the following materials to illustrate the division facts. The teacher will need 18 tokens.
- Teacher will put eighteen tokens in a box. Teacher will choose a number such as 6 and ask the student to see how many sets of 6 there are in the box with eighteen tokens.
- Student will retrieve three sets of 6 and respond with the number 3. There are three sets of 6. Teacher will write the division example on the board and explain the positioning of the numbers.
- The larger number 18 will be placed inside the division symbol. Outside of the division symbol, to the left is placed the number 6. The number 3 is placed on the top as that is the answer when 18 is divided by 6.

```
    3
6 / 18
```

Math: Operational Dyscalculia Tier 3	
• Teacher will use all the different kinds of phrases common in division such as: how many 6s are there in 18; 6 goes into 18 how many times? • Student will be asked to use a number line and see how many 9s are in 18. Student will find out that there are two 9s in 18. • Student will continue using the number line and will write the answer on graph paper and on the board using division symbols. • After this process, teacher will explain that division is the reverse operation of multiplication. If the student knows the multiplication facts, he will know the division facts. If he knows that 6 x 3 = 18, he knows that 18 divided by 3 = 6. If he knows that 3 x 6 =18, he knows that 18 divided by 6 =3. • Division facts will be taught by reversing the process of multiplication. • Each division fact will be written on 3 x 5 index cards. • Student will reinforce division facts by playing games such as Concentration or War.	

Programs & Products for Math (See Appendix C for web sites)

Product	Publisher	Tier	Type	Verbal Dysc.	Pract. Dysc.	Lexical Dysc.	Graphical Dysc.	Ideog. Dysc.	Oper. Dysc.	Concepts	Calcul.	Applied Problems
10th Planet:Numbers Bundle	Sunburst	3	Supplemental	X	X				X	X	X	
10th Planet:Fractions Collection	Sunburst	3	Supplemental	X	X				X		X	
10th Planet: Geometry Series	Sunburst	3	Supplemental	X	X				X		X	
A+ny Where Learning System	American Guidance	1	Supplemental	X	X	X	X	X	X	X	X	X
Accelerated Math	Renaissance Learning	2,3	Supplemental	X	X	X	X	X	X	X	X	X
ALEKS Online Math	Aleks Corp.	1	Software	X	X	X	X	X	X	X	X	
AlternativeMathTechniques	Riverdeep	1	Supplemental	X					X		X	
Awesome Animated Monster Maker Math	Sunburst	2	Supplemental	X	X				X		X	
Big Math for Little Kids	Pearson	1	Supplemental	X	X	X	X	X	X	X	X	X
Boosting Your Math Skills	Creative Pub.	2,3	Supplemental	X	X				X		X	
Boosting Your Math Skills	Creative Pub.	3	Supplemental	X					X		X	
Breakaway Math Intervention	Options Pub.	2,3	Supplemental	X	X	X	X	X	X	X	X	
Bridges	Sopris West	2,3	CORE			X		X	X	X	X	X
Building Blocks	SRA	2,3	Supplemental	X	X				X		X	
Combining Shapes	Sunburst	1,2,3	Software				X			X	X	
Compass Learning Math	Compass Learning Inc	2,3	Supplemental	X	X	X	X	X	X	X	X	X
Complete the Math Picture	Creative Thinking	2,3	Supplemental			X		X	X		X	
Connecting Math Concepts	SRA	2,3	Supplemental	X	X				X	X	X	
Connecting Math Concepts	SRA	2,3										
Corrective Math	SRA	3	Supplemental	X	X				X		X	
Corrective Math	SRA	2,3	CORE									

Programs & Products for Math (See Appendix C for web sites)

Product	Publisher	Tier	Type	Verbal Dysc.	Pract. Dysc.	Lexical Dysc.	Graphical Dysc.	Ideog. Dysc.	Oper. Dysc.	Concepts	Calcul.	Applied Problems
Count on It	Pearson	2,3	Supplemental	x	x	x			x		x	
Count On It	Peoples Education	2,3	Supplemental						x		x	
Creating Patterns from Shapes	Sunburst	1,2,3	Software				x			x	x	
Destination Math	Riverdeep	2,3	Supplemental	x	x	x	x	x	x	x	x	x
Developing Math Ideas	Pearson	2	Supplemental	x	x	x	x	x	x	x	x	x
Distar Math	SRA	3	Supplemental	x	x				x		x	
Do the Math	Scholastic	1	Supplemental	x					x		x	
Everyday Math	SRA-McGrawHill	1	CORE	x	x	x	x	x	x	x	x	x
Everyday Counts Partner Games	Great Source	2,3	Supplemental	x	x				x		x	
Everyday Counts Practice Counts	Great Source	2,3	Supplemental	x	x				x		x	
Everyday Math Games	Wright Group	2,3	Supplemental	x	x	x		x	x		x	
Everything You Need to Teach Money	Sunburst	3	Supplemental	x	x				x		x	
Exploring Math	Teacher Created Mats.	2,3	Supplemental			x		x	x		x	
Eye-hand puzzles	Sunburst	1,2,3	Software				x			x	x	
Fact Fluency	Sopris West	3	Supplemental	x	x				x		x	
FASTT Math	Scholastic	2,3	Supplemental									
First Steps in Math	First Steps	2,3	Supplemental									
Focused Instruction Education	Peoples	2	Supplemental	x	x				x		x	
Fundamentals	Funmath	2,3	Supplemental	x	x	x		x	x		x	

Programs & Products for Math (See Appendix C for web sites)

Product	Publisher	Tier	Type	Verbal Dysc.	Pract. Dysc.	Lexical Dysc.	Graphical Dysc.	Ideog. Dysc.	Oper. Dysc.	Concepts	Calcul.	Applied Problems
Get Ahead in Math	Get Ahead Learning	2,3	Supplemental									
Graph Club	Sunburst	3	Supplemental	X	X				X		X	
Harcourt Mathematics	Harcourt School Pub.	1	CORE	X	X	X	X	X	X	X	X	X
Head for Success	Pearson	2	Supplemental	X	X				X		X	
How the West Was Won	Sunburst	2,3	Software			X		X	X		X	
Ice Cream Truck	Sunburst	2,3	Supplemental	X	X	X		X	X		X	
Investigations in Number, Data,Space	Scott Foresman	2,3	CORE	X	X	X	X	X	X	X	X	X
It's Elementary	EPS	2,3	Supplemental			X		X	X		X	
Key Math Teach & Practice	American Guidance	2	Supplemental	X	X	X	X	X	X	X	X	X
Key Skills for math for Multiplication and Division	Sunburst	2,3	Supplemental	X	X				X		X	
Key Skills Math	Sunburst	3	Supplemental	X	X				X		X	
Knowing Math	Houghton Mifflin	1,2,3	Supplemental	X	X	X		X	X		X	
Landmark Method for Teaching Arithmetic	Landmark Foundation	3	Supplemental	X	X				X		X	
Larson Learning Math Courseware	Great Source	2,3	CORE	X	X	X	X	X	X	X	X	X
Math Intervention Packages	Continental Press	1	Supplemental	X					X		X	
Math Arena	Sunburst	2	Supplemental	X	X				X		X	
Math Detective	Creative Thinking	2,3	Software			X		X	X		X	

Programs & Products for Math (See Appendix C for web sites)

Product	Publisher	Tier	Type	Verbal Dysc.	Pract. Dysc.	Lexical Dysc.	Graphical Dysc.	Ideog. Dysc.	Oper. Dysc.	Concepts	Calcul.	Applied Problems
Math Diagnosis and Intervention System	Pearson	3	Supplemental	x	x	x	x	x	x	x	x	x
Math Essentials	Sunburst	2	Supplemental	x	x				x		x	
Math Essentials	Sunburst	3	Supplemental	x	x				x		x	
Math Facts in a Flash	SRA	2,3	Supplemental	x	x				x		x	
Math for the Real World	Sunburst	2,3	Software			x		x	x	x	x	x
Math Games	SRA	2,3	Supplemental	x	x				x		x	
Math Go Figure	Sopris West	1,2,3	Supplemental	x		x		x	x		x	
Math Intervention	Teacher Creative Mats.	2	Supplemental	x	x				x		x	
Math Intervention Package	Options Pub.	2,3	Supplemental									
Math Intervention Tool Kit	Peoples Education	2,3	Supplemental	x	x	x		x	x		x	
Math Munches Deluxe	Riverdeep	2,3	Software	x	x	x		x	x		x	
Math Pathways	Sunburst	3	Supplemental	x	x				x		x	
Math Pathways	Sunburst	2,3	Software			x		x	x		x	
Math Readers	Sopris West	1,2,3	Supplemental	x		x		x	x		x	x
Math Steps	Houghton Mifflin	2,3	Supplemental	x	x	x		x	x		x	
Math Wings	Success for All	2,3	Supplemental	x	x	x		x	x		x	
Math Word Problems	Creative Thinking	2,3	Software			x		x	x			x
MCP Math	Pearson	2	Supplemental	x	x				x		x	
MeasuringUp	Peoples Education	1	Supplemental	x					x		x	
Memory Fun	Sunburst	1,2,3	Software				x			x	x	
Mighty Math Calculating Crew	Riverdeep	2,3	Supplemental	x	x				x		x	

Programs & Products for Math (See Appendix C for web sites)

Product	Publisher	Tier	Type	Verbal Dysc.	Pract. Dysc.	Lexical Dysc.	Graphical Dysc.	Ideog. Dysc.	Oper. Dysc.	Concepts	Calcul.	Applied Problems
Mighty Math Number Heroes	Riverdeep	2,3	Supplemental	X	X				X		X	
Mighty Math Zoo Zillions	Riverdeep	2,3	Supplemental			X		X	X		X	
Mighty Workshop Deluxe	Riverdeep	2,3	Supplemental	X	X				X		X	
Northstar Math	Harcourt Achieve	1	Supplemental									
Number Power	Glencoe	1	Supplemental									
Number Words	SRA	3	Supplemental	X	X				X	X	X	X
Number Worlds	SRA	2,3	Supplemental									
Compass Learning Math	Compass Learning	2,3	Supplemental	X	X	X	X	X	X	X	X	X
On Cloud Nine	Gander Publishing	3	Supplemental	X	X				X		X	
Passkey: Prescriptive Learning System	Glencoe	2,3	Supplemental									
Pinpoint Math	Wright Group	2,3	Supplemental	X	X				X		X	
Pinpoint Math	Wright Group	3	Supplemental	X					X		X	
Plato Software	Plato Learning	2,3	Software	X	X	X		X	X		X	
Plato Math Expeditions	Inspired Teaching	3	Supplemental	X					X		X	
Problem Solving Step-by-Step	Sopris West	1,2,3	Supplemental	X	X	X		X				X
Read It;Draw It; Solve It	Pearson	2,3	Supplemental	X	X				X		X	
Real Math	SRA	2,3	Supplemental			X			X		X	
Real Math Technology	SRA	3	Supplemental	X	X				X		X	
Scratch Your Brain	Creative Thinking	2,3	Supplemental			X		X	X		X	
Sequencing Fun	Sunburst	1,2,3	Software				X			X	X	

Programs & Products for Math (See Appendix C for web sites)

Product	Publisher	Tier	Type	Verbal Dysc.	Pract. Dysc.	Lexical Dysc.	Graphical Dysc.	Ideog. Dysc.	Oper. Dysc.	Concepts	Calcul.	Applied Problems
Side Streets Math	Princeton Review	1,2,3	Supplemental									
Spatial Relationships	Sunburst	1,2,3	Software				X		X	X	X	
Steps to Math	Sopris West	2,3	Supplemental			X		X	X	X	X	
Succeed Math	Great Source	2,3	Supplemental	X	X				X		X	
Success Maker	Pearson	3	Supplemental	X	X	X	X	X	X	X	X	X
Targeted Math Intervention	Teacher Created Mats.	2,3	Supplemental			X		X	X		X	
Teaching Math Kit	SoprisWest	1	Supplemental	X					X		X	
Ten Tricky Tiles	Sunburst	3	Supplemental	X	X				X		X	
Ten Tricky Tiles	Sunburst	1,2,3	Software				X			X	X	
Tenth Planet Geometry Series	Sunburst	1,2,3	Software				X			X	X	
The Math Rescue	Sopris West	1,2,3	Supplemental	X	X				X		X	
TOPS	Pearson	2	Supplemental	X	X							X
Touchdown Math	Sunburst	3	Supplemental	X	X				X		X	
Touchmath	Innovative Learning	2,3	Supplemental		X				X		X	
Transitional Math	Sopris Math	1,2,3	CORE									
Turbo Math	Peoples	2	Supplemental	X	X				X		X	
Turnaround	Success for All	2,3	Supplemental	X	X				X		X	
Visual Mathematics Dictionary	Sunburst	1,2,3	Software				X			X	X	
Voyages	Sopris West	1,2,3	CORE	X	X	X	X	X	X	X	X	X
Waterford Early Learn. Math	Pearson	2,3	Supplemental	X	X	X	X	X	X	X	X	X

Chapter 6

Behavior

RTI is for behavior too! It offers a systematic process of intensifying, evidence-based interventions and supports matched to the student's behavior needs. Just as in other areas such as reading and math, RTI for behavior relies on the repeated collection of objective data (progress monitoring) to make decisions about whether the student is responder or a non-responder to the support being provided. The same essential components of RTI—universal screening, progress monitoring, data and intervention fidelity—are equally applicable to behavior issues.

Due in large measure to the passage of IDEIA, as described in the Introduction, there has been a paradigm shift for behavior which focuses on making interventions proactive. RTI does not "wait for a student to fail;" it addresses the behavior problem immediately. This includes behavior support that:

- Facilitates improving the educational environment, teaching new strategies and new behaviors, and using positive reinforcement strategies;
- Implies that by understanding the behavior and teaching alternatives or changing the environmental conditions, student needs are met;
- Implies that antecedent-based plans can result in changing environmental conditions and student skills so that lasting change is possible;
- Demonstrates that teaching positive behavior has the potential to create behavioral change.

The above is a welcome departure from past practice that was reactive and includes:

- Behavior management that focused on consequences, whether positive or negative;
- Only rare and infrequent attempts to understand the reasons a maladaptive behavior occurred;
- Consequence-based plans for students that had neither a strong enough punishment, nor a strong enough reinforcer to affect a change in behavior;
- The espousal of a model that waited for a student to fail in their behavior before anything was done.

Behaviors that most directly affect student achievement are:

- Inattention
- Impulsivity
- Hyperactivity
- Oppositional/Defiant
- Anxiety

Behavior: Inattention

<table>
<tr><th>Inattention</th><th>Behavior: Inattention Tier 1</th></tr>
<tr><td>

Inattention—difficulty focusing on one thing at a time; typically becoming bored with a task after a short period of time. This difficulty is particularly evident when attempting to consciously attend to organizing and completing a task or learning something new.

Key characteristics of difficulty with inattention in classroom:

- Becoming distracted by irrelevant sights and sounds as well as people and activities
- Failing to pay attention to details and making careless mistakes
- Difficulty following instructions carefully
- Losing or forgetting things needed for a task
- Skipping from one incomplete activity to another
- Difficulty in concentrating
- Difficulty listening or paying attention

Modifications/Accommodations:

- Plan ahead for problem situations
- Strive for consistency
- Use incentives before punishment
- Frequent and immediate feedback
- Practice forgiveness
- Maintain a neutral, non-personalized attitude towards a problem

</td><td>

Interventionist: General Education Teacher with consultation from the Psychologist, Social Worker, Guidance Counselor

Session: Individual or Small group, explicit behavior instruction within the classroom

Strategies/Activities for Inattention:

- Student is frequently distracted by other activities in the classroom:
  - —Teacher will establish a quiet area in the room where distracting stimuli is minimized.
  - —Teacher will gradually increase the required length of time for attending, and reinforce upon task achievement.
  - —Teacher will identify a peer who will help model appropriate on-task behavior.
  - —Teacher will frequently interact with the student to make certain that he is actively involved.
  - —Teacher will evaluate the required task and determine if the work is appropriate for the student based on his individual learning needs.
- Student demonstrates difficulty concentrating:
  - —Teacher will strategically situate the student's desk near the teacher or the source of information.
  - —Teacher will strategically place the student's desk away from possible distractions in the classroom.
  - —Teacher will break tasks down into smaller chunks.
  - —Teacher will establish an appropriate prompt with the student and provide it when necessary.
  - —Teacher will present material in the student's identified learning style (VAKT).

</td></tr>
</table>

Behavior: Inattention Tier 1	Behavior: Inattention Tier 2
• Student is unable to follow directions: —Teacher will frequently interact with the student to make certain that he understands teacher directives. —Teacher will attempt to reduce stimuli that may distract the student and inhibit his ability to follow directions. —Teacher will identify a peer who will assist the student in effectively following along with directives/activities. —Teacher will attempt to present one direction at a time to the student. Upon successful completion, teacher will present the next directive in the sequence. —Teacher will establish class rules and place the rules on piece of paper. Teacher will place these rules on the student's desk. —Teacher will have the student repeat or rephrase the direction back to the teacher to ensure understanding. —Student will look at the teacher when the teacher starts giving directions.	**Suggested Interventionist: Psychologist, Social Worker, Guidance Counselor** **Suggested Session: 30 minutes 2 to 3x a week in a small group or individual basis inside the classroom** **Strategies/Activities for Inattention:** • Teacher will provide the student with a carrel (divider) at his desk to reduce the stimuli in the classroom. • Teacher will provide the student with earphones or ear muffs to reduce the auditory stimuli within the classroom. • Teacher will reinforce the student for staying on task with a tangible reward. • Teacher will write a contract with the student specifying the behavior that is targeted. Teacher will establish the reinforcer for the targeted behavior within the contract. • Teacher will contract with the student's parents to follow the same targeted goals at home. • Teacher will encourage the student to question any explanations, directions or instructions he does not understand. • Teacher will allow the student to remove himself from the center of the classroom to a quiet place to finish work.

Behavior: Inattention Tier 2	Behavior: Inattention Tier 3
• Teacher will provide the student with shorter tasks than the other students. • Teacher will give the first part of an academic task in the morning and the second part of the academic task at a later time. • Teacher will try to present activities with physical movement in order to keep the student's interest. • Teacher will interact with the student often while the student is completing the assigned task. • Teacher will stay in close proximity to the targeted student. • Teacher will structure the environment to eliminate as much distraction as possible. • Teacher will assign a peer to work with the student in order to keep the student on task. • Teacher will stand near the student while giving instructions or directions. • Teacher will deliver instructions or directions one item at a time and check that the student understands and has heard what is expected of him. • Teacher will use visual cues when delivering directions, such as writing on the board, writing on an overhead, using pictures and diagrams. • Teacher will use activities with one-, two- and three-step directions. Teacher will teach strategies on listening to directions. • Teacher will present one task at a time and wait for the student to complete it.	**Suggested Interventionist: Psychologist, Social Worker, Guidance Counselor** **Suggested Session: 30 minutes 2x a week in a small group or individual basis outside the classroom or recommendation for services outside of the school.** **Strategies/Activities for Inattention:** • Teacher will refer the student to the psychologist for an observation within the classroom. • Psychologist will refer the student to a neurologist for an evaluation concerning the inattention. • Psychologist will perform the following: —Function-based behavior planning process • Functional Behavioral Assessment (FBA) • Behavioral Intervention Plan (BIP) developed from the FBA • Psychologist will review above and consider next steps, including recommendations for: —Family therapy —Multi-systemic community services —Cognitive Behavioral Therapy

Behavior: Impulsivity

Impulsivity	Behavior: Impulsivity Tier 1
Impulsivity—difficulty thinking before acting; difficulty curbing his immediate reactions. **Key characteristics that suggest difficulty with Impulsivity in the classroom:** • Difficulty waiting in line or taking turns • Grabbing things away from peers • Blurting out answers without being called on by teacher/adult • Interrupting or intruding on others • Difficulty focusing on one activity at a time • Difficulty remaining quiet • Rushing through assignments **Accommodations/Modifications:** • Plan ahead for problem situations • Strive for consistency • Use incentives before punishment • Frequent and immediate feedback • Practice forgiveness • Maintain a neutral, non-personalized attitude towards a problem.	**Interventionist: General Education Teacher with consultation from the Psychologist, Social Worker , Guidance Counselor** **Session: Individual or Small group, explicit behavior instruction within the classroom** **Strategies/Activities for Impulsivity:** • Teacher will ignore minor infractions. • Teacher will utilize rewards or consequences under the direction of a behavior specialist. • Teacher will use time-out procedure for misbehaviors. • Teacher will supervise closely during transition times. • Teacher will use "prudent" reprimands for misbehavior. • Teacher will respond to positive behavior with praise. • Teacher will set up behavior contract under the direction of the school behaviorist. • Teacher will instruct student in self-monitoring behavior. • Teacher will ignore calling out when hand is not raised. • Teacher will implement home-school behavior plan under the direction of the behavior specialist.

Behavior: Impulsivity **Tier 2**

Suggested Interventionist: Psychologist, Social Worker, Guidance Counselor

Suggested Session: 30 minutes 2 to 3x a week in a small group or individual basis inside the classroom

Strategies/Activities for Impulsivity:

- Student evidences difficulty waiting for his turn:
  - —Teacher will explain the importance of waiting for his turn during activity.
  - —Teacher will reinforce student for demonstrating appropriate turn-taking during game or activity.
  - —Teacher will encourage peers to take turns with the student and model appropriate turn-taking behavior.
  - —Teacher will recommend to student that objects in school are communal and not personal possessions.
  - —Teacher will closely supervise activities to help facilitate the turn-taking process and make certain that peers do not stimulate inappropriate conduct.
- Student grabs things away from peers:
  - —Teacher will educate the student on the importance of personal property and boundaries.
  - —Teacher will educate the student on the concept of loaning/borrowing and encourage the return of items previously taken.
  - —Based on the particular items the student had been grabbing, teacher will reinforce appropriate behavior using the items the student had grabbed.

Behavior: Impulsivity **Tier 2**

  - —Teacher will encourage peers to take turns with the student and model appropriate sharing behavior.
  - —Teacher will explain to the student the importance of waiting for one's own turn during an activity.
- Student blurts out answers without being called on by teacher/adult:
  - —Teacher will educate the student on the importance of being called on prior to providing a response.
  - —Teacher will reinforce student for demonstrating the ability to raise his/her hand and wait to be called on (privilege or tangible reward).
  - —Teacher will consistently reinforce other students in the room that demonstrate appropriate behavior.
  - —Teacher will provide the student with frequent opportunities to respond or contribute during activities.

Behavior: Impulsivity Tier 3	
Suggested Interventionist: Psychologist, Social Worker, Guidance Counselor **Suggested Session: 30 minutes 2x a week in a small group or individual basis outside the classroom or recommend services outside of the school environment.** **Strategies/Activities for Impulsivity:** • Teacher will refer the student to the psychologist for observation within the classroom. • Psychologist will refer the student to a neurologist for evaluation concerning the impulsivity. • Psychologist will perform the following: —Function-based behavior planning process • Functional Behavioral Assessment (FBA) • Behavioral Intervention Plan (BIP) developed from the FBA • Psychologist will review above and consider next steps, including recommendations for: —Family therapy —Multi-systemic community services —Cognitive Behavioral Therapy	

Behavior: Hyperactivity

Hyperactivity	Behavior: Hyperactivity Tier 1
Hyperactivity—characterized by excessive muscular activity and restlessness, giving the impression of constantly being "on the go" or in constant motion. **Key Characteristics of students with hyperactivity in the classroom:** • Feeling restless, often fidgeting with hands or feet, or squirming while seated • Running, climbing, or leaving a seat in situations where sitting or quiet behavior is expected • Making excessive noise • Becoming overexcited • Touching or playing with whatever is in sight • Talking incessantly **Accommodations/Modifications:** • Plan ahead for problem situations • Strive for consistency • Use incentives before punishment • Frequent and immediate feedback • Practice forgiveness • Maintain a neutral, non-personalized attitude towards a problem • Develop a sense of humor	**Interventionist: General Education Teacher with consultation from the Psychologist, Social Worker, Guidance Counselor** **Session: Individual or Small group, explicit behavior instruction within the classroom** **Strategies/Activities for Hyperactivity:** • Teacher will allow student to stand at times while working. • Teacher will provide opportunity for "seat breaks." • Teacher will provide short breaks between assignments. • Teacher will supervise during transition time. • Teacher will give extra time to complete tasks. • Teacher will allow student the opportunity to leave the classroom on errands or for a drink of water. • Teacher will allow the student the opportunity for physical activity such as distributing materials, getting materials for teacher, or taking part in demonstration activities. • Teacher will provide objects for the student to handle during lecture time. • Teacher will allow the student to have a walk pass. • Teacher will provide a consistent routine in order to enhance stability. • Teacher will provide the student with shorter tasks that do not require extended attention. • Teacher will make necessary modifications to the environment in order to prevent the student from getting over excited.

Behavior: Hyperactivity Tier 1	Behavior: Hyperactivity Tier 2
• Teacher will teach the student to think before acting. • Teacher and student will decide on a predetermined signal to be used when the student becomes too hyperactive and displays inappropriate behavior. • Teacher will teach the student to use problem-solving techniques that address his hyperactivity. • Teacher will encourage on-task behavior by providing a full schedule of daily tasks, including the ability to move around. • Teacher will give the student additional physical chores within the classroom.	**Suggested Interventionist: Psychologist, Social Worker, Guidance Counselor** **Suggested Session: 30 minutes 2 to 3x a week in a small group or individual basis inside the classroom** **Strategies/Activities for Hyperactivity:** • Student makes excessive noise: —Teacher will reinforce classmates who demonstrate appropriate noise level during instruction. —Teacher will reinforce the student for limiting his noise level. Reinforcement may include a specific privilege or tangible reward. —Teacher will frequently interact with the student to make certain that he is actively engaged in the activity. —Teacher will provide the student with an opportunity to make noise during appropriate moments of the school day. —Teacher will clearly define the rules and expectations of the classroom, and reiterate the importance of keeping one's voice at an appropriate level. • Student frequently moves around while seated and appears restless: —Teacher will clearly define what appropriate in-seat behavior entails. —Teacher will remain consistent with regard to the predetermined expectations of appropriate in-seat behavior and reinforce when necessary.

Behavior: Hyperactivity Tier 2	Behavior: Hyperactivity Tier 3
—Prior to lesson, teacher will establish appropriate prompt with the student and use it when he begins to act inappropriately. —Teacher will identify a peer who will sit next to the student and help model appropriate in-seat behavior. —Teacher will strategically situate the student's desk near the teacher. • Student becomes overexcited: —Teacher will create a classroom environment that will limit the frequency of distracting stimuli. —Teacher will educate the student on how to effectively cope with stimuli in the classroom. —Teacher will establish a routine to help the student experience a sense of stability in the classroom. —Teacher will reinforce the student for effectively demonstrating restraint in the presence of distracting stimuli. —Prior to the lesson, teacher will establish an appropriate prompt with the student and provide it when necessary.	**Suggested Interventionist: Psychologist, Social Worker, Guidance Counselor** **Suggested Session: 30 minutes 2x a week in a small group or individual basis outside the classroom or recommend services outside of the school environment.** **Strategies/Activities for Hyperactivity:** • Teacher will refer the student to the psychologist for observation within the classroom. • Psychologist will refer the student to a neurologist for evaluation concerning the inactivity. • Psychologist will perform the following: —Function-based behavior planning process • Functional Behavioral Assessment (FBA) • Behavioral Intervention Plan (BIP) developed from the FBA • Psychologist will review above and consider next steps, including recommendations for: —Family therapy —Multi-systemic community services —Cognitive Behavioral Therapy

Behavior: Oppositional/Defiant

Oppositional/Defiant	Behavior: Oppositional/Defiant Tier 1
Opposition/Defiant Behavior—typically presents in children and adolescents as uncooperative, defiant, and hostile behavior that contributes to academic and social difficulty in school. **Key characteristics of oppositional/defiant behavior in the classroom:** • Frequent temper tantrums • Excessive arguing with adults • Active defiance and refusal to comply with adult requests and classroom rules • Deliberate attempts to annoy or upset people • Blaming others for one's own mistakes • Ignoring consequences of behavior • General misbehavior **Accommodations/Modifications:** • Plan ahead for problem situations • Strive for consistency • Use incentives before punishment • Frequent and immediate feedback • Practice forgiveness • Maintain a neutral, non-personalized attitude towards a problem	**Interventionist: General Education Teacher with consultation from the Psychologist, Social Worker, Guidance Counselor** **Session: Individual or Small group, explicit behavior instruction within the classroom** **Strategies/Activities for Oppositional/Defiant:** • Teacher will praise compliant behavior. • Teacher will post class rules in conspicuous place. • Teacher will provide immediate feedback about behavior. • Teacher will ignore minor inappropriate behavior. • Teacher will use "prudent" reprimands for misbehavior. • Teacher will supervise closely during transition times. • Teacher will seat the student near positive role models or teacher. • Teacher will set up a behavior contract. • Teacher will instruct student in self-monitoring skills. • Teacher will establish rules for the classroom and post the rules on the board in front of the room. • Teacher will make sure the classroom environment is organized, predictable and structured. • Teacher will plan activities to produce a sense of community within the classroom. • Teacher will teach social skills (anger management). • Teacher will provide structured choices. • Teacher will learn to anticipate and de-escalate problem situations. • Teacher will provide instruction at student's academic level.

Behavior: Oppositional/Defiant Tier 2	Behavior: Oppositional/Defiant Tier 2
Suggested Interventionist: Psychologist, Social Worker, Guidance Counselor **Suggested Session: 30 minutes 2x a week in a small group or individual basis inside the classroom** **Ignores consequences of behavior:** • Teacher will establish rules that clearly identify acceptable/ unacceptable behavior in the classroom. • Teacher will individually speak with the student and explain what needs to be improved and explore strategies to assist compliance on a consistent basis. • Teacher will consistently reinforce peers for demonstrating appropriate behavior. • Teacher will create a behavior contract with the student indicating what is expected of him during class. • Teacher will determine whether the classroom work is too difficult for the student and modify if necessary. • Teacher will teach the student to utilize pro-social problem-solving strategies to effectively manage problems that may arise in the classroom. • Teacher will enforce school/classroom rules. • Teacher will establish rules that clearly identify acceptable/ unacceptable behavior. • Teacher will individually speak with the student, explain what needs to be improved and explore strategies to assist compliance on a consistent basis.	• Teacher will catch the student behaving well and provide positive feedback. • Teacher will make certain that school/classroom rules are posted and visible to the student. • Teacher will provide student with appropriate options. • Teacher will establish rules that clearly identify acceptable/ unacceptable behavior. • Teacher will individually speak with the student and explain what needs to be improved and explore strategies to assist him in complying on a consistent basis. • Teacher will provide student with the option to have specific class-room/school-wide responsibilities. • Teacher will present required/directed material in a manner that appears interesting and attractive. • Teacher will attempt to maintain a positive and respectful relation-ship with the student.

Behavior: Oppositional/Defiant Tier 3	
Suggested Interventionist: Psychologist, Social Worker, Guidance Counselor **Suggested Session: 30 minutes 2x a week in a small group or individual basis outside the classroom or for services outside of the school environment.** **Strategies/Activities for Oppositional/Defiant:** • Teacher will refer the student to the psychologist for observation within the classroom. • Psychologist will refer the student to a neurologist for evaluation. • Psychologist will perform the following: —Function-based behavior planning process • Functional Behavioral Assessment (FBA) • Behavioral Intervention Plan (BIP) developed from the FBA • Psychologist will consider next steps, including recommendations for: —Family therapy —Multi-systemic community services —Cognitive Behavioral Therapy	

Behavior: Anxiety

<table>
<tr><th>Anxiety</th><th>Behavior: Anxiety Tier 1</th></tr>
<tr><td>

Anxiety—a feeling of uneasiness, tension, and sense of imminent danger that can interfere with one's ability to adequately function; often associated with major events such as an examination or a significant family issue, or when having to make an important decision.

Key characteristics of an individual experiencing anxiety in the classroom:

- Racing heart
- Feeling weak, faint, or dizzy
- Tingling or numbness in the hands and fingers
- Feeling sweaty or having chills
- Breathing difficulties
- Feeling a loss of control
- Obsessions
- Compulsions
- Ritualistic behavior
- Fearfulness
- Nervous habits
- Phobic-type behavior
- Difficulty coming to school on a consistent basis

Modification/Accommodations:

- Plan ahead for problem situations
- Strive for consistency
- Use incentives before punishment
- Frequent and immediate feedback
- Create a nurturing and safe environment

</td><td>

Interventionist: General Education Teacher with consultation from the Psychologist, Social Worker, Guidance Counselor

Session: Individual or Small group, explicit behavior instruction within the classroom

Strategies/Activities for Anxiety:

- Teacher will provide reassurance and encouragement.
- Teacher will compliment positive behavior and work.
- Teacher will speak softly in non-threatening manner if student shows nervousness.
- Teacher will review instructions when giving new assignments to make sure student comprehends.
- Teacher will look for opportunities for student to display leadership role in class.
- Teacher will focus on student's talents and accomplishments.
- Teacher will conference frequently with parents to learn about student's interests and achievements.
- Teacher will send positive notes home.
- Teacher will make time to talk to the student privately to establish a safe environment.
- Teacher will encourage social interactions with classmates.
- Teacher will reinforce frequently when signs of frustration are noticed.
- Teacher will look for signs of stress and provide encouragement or reduced workload.
- Teacher will learn how to use calming techniques to encourage student.

</td></tr>
</table>

Behavior: Anxiety Tier 2	Behavior: Anxiety Tier 2
Suggested Interventionist: Psychologist, Social Worker, Guidance Counselor **Suggested Session: 30 minutes 2x a week in a small group or individual basis inside the classroom** **Strategies/Activities for Anxiety:** • Student demonstrates nervous habits: —Teacher will establish a nurturing and relaxed environment. —Teacher will determine what is creating stress for the student and attempt to reduce or modify the situation/activity. —Teacher will provide the student with additional time to complete the task/assignment. —Teacher will remove objects or instruments from the environment that may be contributing to the student's nervous behaviors. —Teacher will discuss and work with student on self-monitoring strategies to help control nervous tendencies. —Teacher will provide student with appropriate options that allow him to complete the task/assignment. • Student evidences phobic-type behavior: —Teacher will establish a nurturing and relaxed environment. —Teacher will determine what is creating stress for the student and attempt to reduce or modify the situation. —Teacher will provide student with appropriate options that allow him to complete the task/assignment.	—Teacher will have the student participate in the required activity that is making him/her nervous. —Teacher will enable the student to initially observe the activity without requiring him to participate. —After validating student's feelings/emotions, teacher will request that the student identify certain aspects of the activity or task he would be willing to partake in. —Teacher will gradually involve student in task/activity that creates stress for the student, immediately following the task with a reinforcement. • Student reacts physically: —Teacher will provide the student with a quiet place to work when involuntary physical reactions occur. —Teacher will teach self-control techniques designed to help the student regain control. —Teacher will provide an environment which is calm, consistent, structured and supportive. —Teacher will structure the environment so that the student has minimal opportunity to dwell on problems. —Teacher will minimize frustrating and anxiety producing situations from occurring.

Behavior: Anxiety Tier 3	
Suggested Interventionist: Psychologist, Social Worker, Guidance Counselor **Suggested Session: 30 minutes 2x a week in a small group or individual basis outside the classroom or for services outside of the school environment.** **Strategies/Activities for Anxiety:** • Teacher will refer the student to the psychologist for observation within the classroom • Psychologist will refer the student to a neurologist/psychiatrist for evaluation. • Psychologist will perform the following: —Function-based behavior planning process • Functional Behavioral Assessment (FBA) • Behavioral Intervention Plan (BIP) developed from the FBA • Psychologist will review above and consider next steps, including recommendations for: —Family therapy —Multi-systemic community services —Cognitive Behavioral Therapy	

Programs & Products for Behavior (See Appendix C for web sites)

Product	Publisher
Caring School Community	Child Development Project
Community of Caring	CommunityofCaring.org
Drug Abuse Resistance Education	DARE America
Emotional Literacy in Upper Elementary School	National Professional Resources, Inc.
Emotional Literacy in the Middle School	National Professional Resources, Inc.
High School Educational Approach	HighScope.org
I Can Problem Solve	Research Press
Learning for Life	LearningforLife.org
Lions Quest	LionsQuest.org
No Putdowns	NoPutdowns.org
PATHS: Promoting Alternative Thinking Strategies	Prevention Science
Peace Works	Peach Education foundation
Project ACHIEVE	ProjectAchieve.org
Resolving Conflict Creatively Program (RCCP)	ESRNational.org
Review 360	Psychological Software Solutions,Inc
Second Step	cfchildren.org
Social Decision Making and Problem Solving Curriculum	Research Press
Tribes TLC: New Way of Learning and Being Together	Tribes.com

APPENDIX A

FORMS

(Refer to end of Introduction for a listing and description of each form)

Form #1: Checklist for RTI Teams

Classroom Going to Tier 1

- ✓ Classroom Teacher report
- ✓ Data Sheet from teacher documenting Universal Screening scores
- ✓ RTI Team Initial Meeting Minutes for Tier 1, including RTI Action Plan (Form #2)
- ✓ RTI Strategies Tier 1 Form filled out during the RTI Meeting after 5 weeks of intervention implementation (Form #3)
- ✓ RTI Tier 1 Documentation Form, set to reconvene at most, 10 weeks later or halfway through Tier (Form #4)

Tier 1 Student transitioning to Tier 2

- ✓ RTI Team Initial Meeting Minutes for Tier 2, including change documented in Tier 1 Action Plan (Form #5)
- ✓ RTI Strategies Tier 2 Form, including Progress Monitoring results (Form #6)
- ✓ RTI Tier 2 Documentation Form: Student Interventions/Strategies (Form #7)
- ✓ Set up a time to reconvene 10 weeks later or halfway through Tier 2 to review progress in Tier 2

Tier 2 transitioning to Tier 3

- ✓ RTI Team Initial Meeting Minutes for Tier 3, including change documented in Tier 2 Action Plan (Form #8)
- ✓ RTI Strategies Tier 3, including Progress Monitoring results (Form #9)
- ✓ RTI Tier 3 Documentation Form: Student Interventions/Strategies (Form #10)
- ✓ Set up a time to reconvene, 10 weeks later or halfway through Tier 3
- ✓ RTI Team Report-to be used at the end of Tier 3 after determining that the student is a non-responder (Form #11)

Tier 3 transitioning to Evaluation for Special Education or Eligibility

- ✓ RTI Team Report (Form # 11)
- ✓ RTI Strategies Tier 3, Form including Progress Monitoring results (Form #9)
- ✓ RTI Tier 3 Documentation Form: Student Interventions/Strategies (Form # 10)

- ✓ Documentation Form: Student Interventions/Strategies Tier 1, Tier 2 (Forms # 4 and # 7)
- ✓ Complete results for Tier 3 on RTI Action Plan with input from case manager
- ✓ Indicate "Designate formal referral" by checking the appropriate box
- ✓ IDEIA Rights Booklet provided to parent
- ✓ Permission to evaluate is obtained by school psychologist
- ✓ Psychologist has:
    - Obtained parent input form
    - Has observed student in class and
    - Has interviewed teacher prior to meeting
    - Special Education Evaluation is requested
- ✓ All RTI Team forms, minutes and teacher documentation are given to special education eligibility team chair

Form # 2: RTI Team Initial Meeting Minutes for Tier 1

Student: ______________________________ **Grade :** ____________ **Teacher:** ______________________

Last **First** **MI**

Meeting Date: ______________________ **School :** ______________________________________

RTI Team Member Signatures:

__________________ __________________ __________________ __________________

__________________ __________________ __________________ __________________

Case Notes/Concerns: ____

____

____

____

____

Intervention Action Plan: ____

____

____

____

Resources/ materials necessary for special instructional or behavioral program implementation of suggested interventions :

____

____

____

____

Start date for Tier 1 intervention ______________ **Date of the follow-up RTI meeting** ______________

Location of the intervention implementation ______________ **Interventionist responsible** ______________

Intervention Integrity: How will the implementation and progress of this intervention be monitored?

Person monitoring progress ______________ **Method of measurement for the monitoring** ______________

Dates of data monitoring __________ __________ __________ __________

Assigned Case Manager from the RTI Team ______________

Form # 3: RTI Strategies Tier 1

Student: ______________________________ Birth Date : ______________

Last First MI

School: ____________ Grade: ________ Teacher: ________ Date of RTI Meeting: ________

Signatures of Team Members

____________ ____________ ____________ ____________

____________ ____________ ____________ ____________

TIER I INTERVENTIONS: (must be minimum of 10 weeks)

First Intervention:

Target Skill: ______________ Level of Performance Prior to Tier I Intervention (Universal Screening) (Baseline data) ______________________

Intervention Goal: ____

Intervention Implemented: ____

Beginning Date of # 1 Intervention Implementation ____________ Ending Date: ____________

Frequency ______ Beginning Score and date (Universal Screening) ________ ________

Ending Score and date of (Progress Monitoring) ________ ________

Second Intervention:

Target Skill: ______________________________

Intervention Goal: ____

Intervention Implemented: ____

Beginning Date of # 2 Intervention Implementation ________________________ **Ending Date:** _____________________

Frequency __________ **Beginning Score and date (Progress Monitoring)** _______________ _________________

Ending Score and date of (Progress Monitoring) ________________ _________________

Intervention Status: (Check one)

___**Exit Tier I**

___**Redesign or modify intervention at Tier I**

___**Initiate Tier II Intervention.**

Form # 4: RTI Tier 1 Documentation Form: Student Interventions/Strategies

Student: ______________________________ **Grade :** ______________ **Teacher:** ______________________________

Last **First** **MI**

Subject Area: ____________________ **Grade:** __________ **Date of RTI Meeting:** ____________________

The following strategies and interventions for improvement of the student's specific areas of weaknesses have been implemented:

Strategies / Intervention	Progress Monitoring Results	Dates To/From	Interventionist/s

__________________________________ **Date:** ____________________

Signature of Interventionist Implementing Tier 1

Form # 5: RTI Team Initial Meeting Minutes for Tier 2

Meeting Information:

Student: ______________________________ **Grade :** ____________ **Teacher:** ________________________

Last **First** **MI**

Meeting Date: ______________________ **School :** ____

RTI Team Member Signatures:

__________________ __________________ __________________ __________________

__________________ __________________ __________________ __________________

Case Notes/Concerns: ____

____

____

____

____

Intervention Action Plan Revised (Tier 2): ____

____

____

____

Resources/ materials necessary for special instructional or behavioral program implementation of suggested interventions :

____

____

____

____

Start date for Tier 2 Intervention ______________________ **Date of the follow-up RTI meeting** ______________________

Location of the intervention implementation ______________________ **Interventionist responsible** ______________________

Intervention Integrity: How will the implementation and progress of this intervention be monitored?

Professional monitoring progress ______________________ **Method of measurement for the monitoring** ______________________

Dates of data monitoring ______________ ______________ ______________ ______________

Assigned Case Manager for Tier 2 Action Plan from the RTI Team ______________________________

Form # 6: RTI Strategies Tier 2

Student:______________________________ **DOB:**__________ **Date of RTI Meeting:**_______________ **School/Grade:**___________________

Signatures of RTI Team Members :

__________________________ __________________________ __________________________ __________________________

__________________________ __________________________ __________________________ __________________________

TIER 2 INTERVENTIONS: (must be minimum of 10 weeks)

Target Skill:_____________________________ **Level of Performance Prior to Tier 2 Intervention (progress Monitoring data)**
(Baseline) ____

Interventions Implemented at Tier 1: **Beginning/Ending Dates**

☐ _____________________ **Date:**_______________ **Frequency:** _______________ **Progress Monitoring data:** _____________________

☐ _____________________ **Date:**_______________ **Frequency:** _______________ **Progress Monitoring data:** _____________________

☐ _____________________ **Date:**_______________ **Frequency:** _______________ **Progress Monitoring data:** _____________________

New Interventions Implemented at Tier 2:

☐ _____________________ **Date:**_______________ **Frequency:** _______________ **Progress Monitoring data:** _____________________

☐ _____________________ **Date:**_______________ **Frequency:** _______________ **Progress Monitoring data:** _____________________

Intervention Status (Check one):

_____ **Exit Tier 2 return to Tier 1**

_____ **Remain at Tier 2 level with no changes to Action Plan**

_____ **Redesign or modify intervention at Tier 2 level**

_____ **Initiate Tier 3 status**

Form # 7: RTI Tier 2 Documentation Form: Student Interventions/Strategies

Student:____

Last First MI

Subject Area:____________________ Grade:__________ Date of RTI Meeting:____________________

The following strategies and interventions for improvement of the student's specific areas of weaknesses have been implemented:

Strategies / Intervention	Progress Monitoring Results	Dates To/From	Interventionist/s

__________________________________ Date: ________________

__________________________________ Date: ________________

Signature of Interventionists Implementing Tier 2

Form # 8: RTI Team Initial Meeting Minutes for Tier 3

Student: ______________________________ **Grade :** ______________ **Teacher:** ________________________

Last **First** **MI**

Meeting Date: ______________________ **School :** ______________________________________

RTI Team Member Signatures:

__________________ __________________ __________________ __________________

__________________ __________________ __________________ __________________

Case Notes/Concerns:

____

____

____

____

____

Intervention Action Plan Revised (Tier 3):

____

____

____

____

Resources/ materials necessary for special instructional or behavioral program implementation of suggested interventions :

____

____

____

____

Start date for Tier 3 Intervention ____________________ **Date of the follow-up RTI meeting** ____________________

Location of the intervention implementation ____________________ **Interventionist responsible** ____________________

Intervention Integrity: How will the implementation and progress of this intervention be monitored?

Professional monitoring progress ____________________ **Method of measurement for the monitoring** ____________________

Dates of data monitoring ____________ ____________ ____________ ____________

Assigned Case Manager for Tier 3 Action Plan from the RTI Team ______________________________

Form # 9: RTI Strategies Tier 3

Student:____________________ **DOB:**________ **Date of RTI Meeting:**__________ **School/Grade:**____________

Signatures of RTI Team Members :

________________ ________________ ________________ ________________

________________ ________________ ________________ ________________

TIER 3 INTERVENTIONS: (must be minimum of 10 weeks)

Target Skill:____________________ **Level of Performance Prior to Tier 2 Intervention (progress Monitoring data) (Baseline)** ______________________________

Interventions Implemented : **Beginning/Ending Dates**

☐ ______________ **Date:**__________ **Frequency:** __________ **Progress Monitoring data:** ______________

☐ ______________ **Date:**__________ **Frequency:** __________ **Progress Monitoring data:** ______________

☐ ______________ **Date:**__________ **Frequency:** __________ **Progress Monitoring data:** ______________

☐ ______________ **Date:**__________ **Frequency:** __________ **Progress Monitoring data:** ______________

Intervention Status (Check one):

_____ **Exit/stay Tier 3**

_____ **Return to Tier 2**

_____ **Redesign or modify intervention at Tier 3**

_____ **Student does not make adequate progress; initiate formal referral for eligibility to Special Education**

Form # 10: RTI Tier 3 Documentation Form: Student Interventions/Strategies

Student:____

Last First MI

Subject Area:_______________________ Grade:___________ Date of RTI Meeting:_______________________

The following strategies and interventions for improvement of the student's specific areas of weaknesses have been implemented:

Strategies / Intervention	Progress Monitoring Results	Dates To/From	Interventionist/s

______________________________________ Date: ___________________

______________________________________ Date: ___________________

______________________________________ Date: ___________________

Signatures of Interventionists Implementing Tier 3

Form # 11: RTI Team Report

Student:____________________________ DOB:__________ Date of RTI Meeting:_______________ School/Grade:__________________

Signatures of RTI Team Members :

_________________________ _________________________ _________________________ _________________________

_________________________ _________________________ _________________________ _________________________

Form Completed by:

____ **Date:**_________________________

BEFORE OTHER TESTING IS REQUESTED THE RTI TEAM MUST REVIEW ALL INFORMATION ON THE Tier1, Tier2 and Tier 3 Documents

- -

Indicate the Problems in the classroom____

____

Explain how the student's performance is not commensurate with his/her grade level. ____

____

Date:________ **Tier 1 Intervention Forms; Universal Screening Score:** ____________ **Progress Monitoring Score:** _________________

Date:________ **Tier 2 Intervention Forms; Progress Monitoring Score:**____________ **Progress Monitoring Score:** _________________

Date:________ **Tier 3 Intervention Forms; Progress Monitoring Score:**____________ **Progress Monitoring Score:** _________________

Date:________ **Formal referral for eligibility determination for Special Education**

Completion of Team Report

Check:

______ Tier 1 ,2, and 3 Intervention Forms listed above include Action Plans and strategies that are appropriate

______ Tier 1, 2, and 3 Intervention Forms listed above include Action Plans and strategies have not resulted in expected growth rate

______ Complete Team Report and terminate process.

______ Formal referral to Special Education Committee

______________________________________ Date: ____________________

Signature of Interventionist

______________________________________ Date: ____________________

Signature of Interventionist

______________________________________ Date: ____________________

Signature of Principal / Assistant Principal

______________________________________ Date: ____________________

Signature of School Psychologist

Appendix B

Bibliography

Bibliography: RTI General

Danielson, L., Doolittle, J., & Bradley, R. (2007). Professional development, capacity building, and research needs: Critical issues for response to intervention implementation. *School Psychology Review*, 36(4), 632-637.

Fuchs, L.S. & Fuchs, D. (2006). Implementing responsiveness to intervention to identify learning disabilities. *Perspectives*, 32(1), 39-43.

Glover, T.A. & DiPerna, J.C., (2007). Service delivery for response to intervention: Core components and directions for future research. *School Psychology Review,* 36(4), 526-540.

Glover, T.A., DiPerna, J.C., & Vaughn, S. (2007). Introduction to the special series on service delivery systems for response to intervention: Considerations for research and practice. *School Psychology Review*, 36(4), 523-525.

Glover, T.A., & DiPerna, J.C. (2007). Service delivery for response to intervention: Core components and directions for future research. *School Psychology Review*, 36, 526-540.

Hoover, J.J., & Patton, J.R. (2008). The role of special educators in a multitiered instructional system. *Intervention in School and Clinic*, 43(4), 195-202.

IDEA Reauthorization Signed Into Law. (2005, Jan. 18). *The ASHA Leader,* pp. 1-22.

Johnson, E.S., & Smith, L. (2008). Implementation of response to intervention at middle school challenges and potential benefits. *Teaching Exceptional Children,* 40(3), 46-52.

Johnson, E., Mellard, D.F., Fuchs, D. & McKnight, M.A. (2006). *Responsiveness to intervention (RTI): How to do it.* Lawrence, KS: National Research Center.

Justice, L.M. (2006). Evidence-based practice, response to intervention, and the prevention of reading difficulties. *Language, Speech, and Hearing Services in Schools,* 37, 284-297.

Kovaleski, J.F. (2007). Response to intervention: considerations for research and systems change. *School Psychology Review*, 36(4), pp. 638-646.

Kratochwill, T.R., Volpiansky, P., Clements, M., & Ball, C. (2007). Professional development in implementing and sustaining multitier prevention models: Implications for response to intervention. *School Psychology Review*, 36(4), 618-631.

McMaster, K.L., Kung, S., & Cao, M. (2008). Peer-assisted learning strategies: A “tier 1” approach to promoting english learners’ response to intervention. *Exceptional Children*, 74(2), 194-214.

No Child Left Behind Act of 2001. PL 107-110, 115 Stat. 1425 (2002).

National Association of State Directors of Special Education, Inc. (2007). Reauthorization of the elementary and secondary education act (ESEA) NASDSE reauthorization priorities. *National Association of State Directors of Special Education, Inc. Reading First Guidance*, 1-2. .

Samuels, C.A. (2008). Response to intervention sparks interest, questions. *Education Week;* 27(20), 1-13.

Ukrainetz, T.A. (2006). The implications of RTI and EBP for SLPs: Commentary on l.m. justice. *Language, Speech, and Hearing Services in Schools,* 37, 298-303.

Web Sites

www.ed.gov/programs/readingfirst/guidance.pdf (2008).

Bibliography: Auditory Processing/Language

Atwell, N. (1987). *In the middle: Writing, reading, and learning with adolescents.* Upper Montclair, NJ: Boynton/Cook.

Atwell, N. (1998). *In the middle: New understandings about writing, reading, and learning*. Upper Montclair, NJ: Boyton/Cook.

Auan, M. (2008). *Step up to writing.* Boston: Sopris West.

Bellis, T. J.. (1996). *Assessment and management of central auditory processing disorders in the educational setting.* San Diego, CA: Singular Publishing Group, Inc.

Berninger, V.W. (1996). *Reading and writing acquisition: A developmental neuropsychological perspective (developmental psychology series).* Boulder, CO: Westview Press.

Black, H., and Black, S. (1990). *Organizing thinking: Graphic organizers (Vol. 2).* Pacific Grove: Critical Thinking Press and Software.

Brewster, C., and Klump, J. (2004). *Writing to learn, learning to write: Revisiting writing across the curriculum in northwest secondary schools.* Portland, OR: Northwest Regional Educational Laboratory.

Cairney, T. (1990). *Teaching reading comprehension.* Milton Keynes, UK: Open University Press.

Calkins, L. (1986). *The art of teaching writing.* Portsmouth, NH: Heinemann.

Chermak, G. & Musiek, F. (2007). *Handbook of (central) auditory processing disorder.* San Diego: Plural Publishing.

Chermak, G. D. and Musiek, F. E. (1997). *Central auditory processing disorders: New perspectives.* San Diego, CA: Singular Publishing Group, Inc.

Cudd, E., & Roberts, L. (1989). Using writing to enhance content area learning in the primary grades. *The Reading Teacher,* 42, 392-404.

Englert, C. S., and Mariage, T. (1991). Shared understandings: Structuring the writing experience through dialogue. *Journal of Learning Disabilities,* 24, 330-342.

Ferre, J. M. (1997). *Processing power: A guide to CAPD assessment and treatment.* San Antonio, TX: The Psychological Corporation.

Gersten, R., and Baker, S. (2001). Teaching expressive writing to students with learning disabilities: A meta-analysis. *The Elementary School Journal* 101, 3, 251-272.

Gibson, M. and McCloy, C. (2003). *Recipe for writing student cookbook.* Arlington, Virginia: Council for Exceptional Children.

Gillet, P. (1993). *Auditory processes.* Novato, CA: Academic Therapy Publications

Graham, S., Harris, K.R., MacArthur, C.A., and Schwarts, S. (1991). Writing and writing instruction for students with learning disabilities: Review of a research program. *Learning Disability Quarterly,* 14(2), 89-114.

Graham, S., and Perin, D. (2007). *Writing next: Effective strategies to improve writing of adolescents in middle and high schools—A report to Carnegie Corporation of New York.* Washington, DC: Alliance for Excellent Education.

Graves, D. H. (1983). *Writing: Teachers and children at work.* Exeter, NH: Heinemann Educational Books.

Hamaguchi, P.M. (1995). *It's time to listen: A program for children with listening problems.* San Antonio, TX: The Psychological Corporation.

Hanson, A. (2002). *Write brain write.* San Diego: The Brain Store.

Jeffries, J. & Jeffries, R. (1991). *Auditory processing activities.* Youngtown, Arizona: ECL Publications.

Kelly, D. (1995). *Central auditory processing disorder: Strategies for use with children and adolescents.* San Antonio, TX: The Psychological Corporation.

Levine, E. (1989). *I hate english!* New York: Scholastic, Inc.

Mokhemar, M. A. (1999). *The central auditory processing kit: Book 1.* East Moline, IL: Linguisystems.

Mokhemar, M. A. (1999). *The central auditory processing kit: Book* 2. East Moline, IL: Linguisystems.

Mokehemar, M. A. (1999). *The central auditory processing kit: Book 3.* East Moline, IL: Linguisystems.

Nichols, J. (1980). Using paragraph frames to help remedial high school students with written assignments. *Journal of Reading,* 24(3), 228-231.

Schumacher, J., Nolan, S., and Deshler, D. (1985). *The error monitoring strategy.* Lawrence: University of Kansas Center for Research on Learning.

Sebranek, P., Meyer, V., and Kemper, D. (1996). *Writers INC: A student handbook for writing and learning.* Lexington, KY: D. C. Heath and Co.

Tarricone, J. (1995). *The Landmark method for teaching writing.* Prides Crossing, MA.

Vellecorsa, A., Ledford, R. and Parnell, G. (1991). Strategies for teaching composition skills to students with learning disabilities. *Teaching Exceptional Children,* 23(2), 52-55.

Wallace, G., and Bott, D. (1989). Statement-PIE: A stragegy to improve the paragraph writring skills of adolescents with learning disabilities. *Journal of Learning Disabilities,* 22(9), 541-553.

Worsham, S. (1996). Five good writing ideas. *Teachers and Writers,* 27(5), 9-12.

Worsham, S. (2001). *Essential ingredients: Recipes for teaching writing.* Alexandria, VA: Association for Supervision and Curriculum Development.

Bibliography: Visual Processing

Breitmeyer, B.G., (1980). Unmasking visual masking: a look at the 'why' behind the veil of the 'how.' *Psychology Review,* 87, 52–69.

Chun, M. and Nakayama, K. (2000). On the Functional Role of Implicit Visual Memory for the Adaptive Deployment of Attention Across Scenes. *Visual Cognition,* 7(1-3), 65-81.

Eden, G.F., Stein, J.F., Wood, M.H., and Wood, F.B. (1995). Verbal and visual problems in reading disability. *Journal of Learning Disabilities,* 28, 272–290.

Evans, B.J., Drasdo, N., and Richards, I.L. (1994). An investigation of some sensory and refractive visual factors in dyslexia. *Vision Research,* 34, 1913–1926.

Fleishman, E., and Hempel Jr, W. (1995). The relation between abilities and improvement with practice in a visual discrimination reaction task. *Journal of Experimental Psychology,* 49(5), 301-312.

Evans, B.J., Drasdo, N., and Richards, I.L. (1994). Investigation of accommodative and binocular function in dyslexia. *Ophthalmic Physiology Options,* 14, 5–19.

Fleishman, E. A., Hempel Jr., W. E. (1977). The relation between abilities and improvement with practice in a visual discrimination reaction task. *Journal of Experimental Psychology,* 49(5), 301-312.

Galaburda, A.M., Sherman, G.F., Rosen, G.D., Aboitiz, F., and Geschwind, N. (1985). Developmental dyslexia: four consecutive patients with cortical anomalies. *Annals of Neurology*, 18, 222–233.

Galaburda, A.M., Menard, M.T., and Rosen, G.D. (1994). Evidence for aberrant auditory anatomy in developmental dyslexia. *Proceedings of the National Academy of Science U.S.A.,* 91, 8010–8013.

Goyen,T.A.,Woods R.,(1998). Visual-motor, visual-perceptual, and fine motor outcomes in very-low-birthweight children at 5 years. *Dev. Med Child Neurol,* 40(7), 500-502.

Gross-Glen, K., Skottun, B.C., Glenn, W., Kushch, A., Lingua, R., Dunbar, M., Jallad, B, Lubs, H.A., Levin, B., and Rabin, M. (1995). Contrast sensitivity in dyslexia. *Visual Neuroscience,* 12, 153–163.

Humphreys, P., Kaufmann, W.E., and Galaburda, A.M. (1990). Developmental dyslexia in women: neuropathological findings in three patients. *Annals of Neurology,* 28, 727–738.

Johannes, S., Münte, T.F., Heinze, H.J., and Mangun, G.R. (1995). Luminance and spatial attention effects on early visual processing. *Cognitive Brain Research,* 2, 189–205.

Lehmkuhle, S., Garzia, R.P, Turner, L., Hash, T., and Baro, J.A. (1993). A defective visual pathway in children with reading disability. *New England Journal of Medicine,* 328, 989–996.

Livingstone, M.S., Rosen, G.D., Drislane, F.W, and Galaburda, A.M. (1991). Physiological and anatomical evidence for a magnocellular defect in developmental dyslexia. *Proceedings of the National Academy of Science U.S.A.*, 88, 7943–7947.

Lovegrove, W. (1995). Weakness in the transient visual system: a causal factor in dyslexia?. *Annals of the NY Academy of Science,* 682, 57–69.

Mangun, G.R., Hillyard, S.A., and Luck, S.J. (1993). Electrocortical substrates of visual selective attention. In: D. Meyer and S. Kornblum, (Eds.) *Attention and Performance XIV* (pp. 219–243). Cambridge, MA: MIT Press.

Moran, J. (1985). Selective attention gates visual processing in the extrastriate cortex. *Science*, 229(4715), 782.

Neville, H.J., Coffey, S.A., Holcomb, P.J., and Tallal, P. (1993). The Neurobiology of sensory and language processing in language-impaired children. *Journal of Cognitive Neuroscience*, 5, 235–253.

Orton, S. (1937). *Reading, Writing and Speech Problems in Children.* New York: Norton.

Schafer, R.; Murphy, G. (1943). The role of autism in a visual figure-ground relationship. *Journal of Experimental Psychology,* 32(4), 335-343.

Shaywitz, S.E., Bennett, A., Fletcher, J.M. and Escobar, M.D. (1990). Prevalence of reading disability in boys and girls. *Journal of the American Medical Association,* 264, 998–1002.

Shiffrin, R.M., and Schneider, W. (1977). Controlled and automatic human information processing: Perceptual learning, automatic attending and a general theory. *Psychological Review,* 84(2), 127-190.

Thorpe, S., Fize, D., and Marlot, C. (1996). Speed of processing in the human visual system. *Nature*, 381.

Victor, J.D., Conte, M.M., Burton, L. and Nass, R.D. (1993). Visual evoked potentials in dyslexics and normals: failure to find a difference in transient or steady-state responses. *Visual Neuroscience*, 10, 939–946.

Watt , R.J. (1990). *Visual processing: computational, psychophysical, and cognitive research: Computational, Psychophysical, and Cognitive Research.* Psychology Press; New edition.

Witelson, S.F. (1977). Developmental dyslexia: two right hemispheres and none left. *Science*, 195(4275), 309 – 311.

Bibliography: Reading

Adam, M.J. (1990). *Beginning to read: Thinking and Learning about print.* Cambridge: MIT Press.

Aoki, C., & Siekevitz, P. (1988). Plasticity in brain development. *Scientific American,* 259(6), 56-64.

Ball, E., & Blachman, B., (1991). Does phoneme awareness training in kindergarten make a difference in early word recognition and developmental spelling? *Reading Research Quarterly,* 26(1), 49-66.

Bird, T., & Bishop, D.V.M. (1992). Perception and Awareness of phonemics in phonologically impaired children. *European Journal of Disorders of Communication,* 27, 289-311.

Blachman, B.,(1994). What we have learned from longitudinal studies of phonological processes and reading and one unanswered questions: A response to Torgesen, Wagner, and Rashorfe. *Journal of Learning Disabilities,* 27, 287-291.

Blachman, B.(1997). *Early Intervention and Phonological Awareness: A Cautionary Tale. Foundations for early reading acquisition an dyslexia: Implications for early Interventions.* Hillsdale, NJ: Erlbaum Associates.

Bowers, P.G. (1993). Text reading and rereading: predictors of fluency beyond word recognition. *Journal of Reading Behaviors,* 25,133-153.

Bradley, L. & Bryant, P. (1985). *Rhyme and Reason in reading and spelling.* Ann Arbor: University of Michigan Press

Cacace, A. T., & McFarland, D. J. (1998). Central auditory processing disorder in school aged. *Journal of Speech, Language & Hearing Research,* 41(2), 355-375.

Campbell, R. & Butterworth, B. (1985). Phonological dyslexia and dysgraphia in a highly literate subject: A developmental case with associated deficits of phonemic processing and awareness. *The Quarterly Journal of Experimental Psychology,* 37A, 435-475.

Cataldo, S., & Ellis, N. (1988). Interactions in the development of spelling,reading and phonological skills. *Journal of Research in Reading,* 11, 86-109.

Catts, H. W. (1993). The relationship between speech-language impairments and reading disabilities. *Journal of Speech and Hearing*, 36, 948-958.

Chall, J. (1983). *Learning to Read: The Great Debate.* New York: McGraw-Hill.

Chall, J. (1983). *Stages in Reading Development (2nd.Ed.)* New York: Harcourt Brace College Publishers.

Clark, D. B. (1988). *Dyslexia: Theory & Practice of Remedial Instruction.* Maryland: York Press.

Cox, A. R. (1985). Alphabetic Phonics: An organization and expansion of Orton-Gillingham. *Annals of Dyslexia,* 35, 187-198.

Denkler, M.B. (1993). A Neurologist's Overview of Developmental Dyslexia. In P. Tallal, A. M. Galaburda, R. Llinas & C. von Euler (Eds.), *Temporal Information Processing in the Nervous System: Special reference to dyslexia and dysphasia,* 23-26. New York Academy of Sciences.

Dickinson, D., & McCabe, A. (1987). The Acquisition and Development of Language: A Social Interactionist Account of Language and Literacy Dervelpment. In J. F.Kavanagh (Ed.), *The Language Continuum From Infancy to Literacy.* New York Press.

Dickinson, D. K., & Snow, C. E. (1987). Interrelationships among prereading and oral language skills in kindergarten from two social classes. *Early Childhood Research Quarterly,* 2, 1-25.

Freebody, P., & Byrne, B. (1988). Word-reading strategies in elementary school children: Relations to comprehension, reading time, & phonemic awareness. *Reading Research Quarterly*, 23, 441-53.

Fowler, A. E. (1991). How early phonological development might set the stage to phoneme awareness. In S. A. Brady & D. P.Shankweiler (Eds.), *Phonlogical Processes in Literacy: A Tribute to I.Y. Liberman,* Hillsdale, NJ: Erlbaum Associates.

Galaburda, A., & Livingstone, M. (1993). Evidence for a Magnocellular Defect in Developmental Dyslexia. In P.Tallal, A. Galaburda, R. Llinas, & C. von Euler (Eds.) Temporal Information Processing in the Nervous System, *Annals of New York Academy of Sciences*, Vol. 682.

Gough, P. B., & Tunmer, W. E. (1986). Decoding, Reading, and Reading Disability. *Remedial and Special Education,*7, 6-10.

Goswani, U. & Bryant, P. E. (1990). *Phonological Skills and Learning to Read.* Hillsdale, NJ: Erlbaum Associates.

Ingram, D. (1986). Phonological development: Productions. In P. Fletcher & M. Garman (Eds.), *Language acquisition (2nd ed.).* New York: Cambridge University Press.

Jerger, S., Martin, R. C., & Jerger, J. (1987). Specific auditory perceptual dysfunction in a leaning disabled child. *Ear & Hearing,* 8, 78-86.

Kamhi, P., Catts, H., Mauer, D., Apel, K., & Gentry, B. (1988). Phonological and spatial processing abilities in language and reading-impaired children. *Journal of Speech and Hearing Disorders*, 53, 316-327.

Liberman, I. Y., & Shankweiler, D. (1985). Phonology and the problems of learning to read and write. *Remedial and Special Education*, 6, 8-17.

Liberman, I.Y., & Shankweiler, D., (1991). Phonology and beginning reading: A tutorial. In L. Reuben & C.A. Perfetti. *Learning to Read: Basic Research and Its Implications,* Hillsdale, NJ: Erlbaum Associates.

Liberman, I.Y., Shankweiler, D., & Liberman, A.M. (1989). The alphabetic principle and learning to read. In D.Shankweiler & I.Y. Liberman (Eds.), *Phonology and reading disability: Solving the reading puzzle.* Ann Arbor: University of Michigan Press.

Mann, V., Shankweiler, D., & Smith, S. (1984). The association between comprehension of spoken sentences and early reading ability: The role of phonetic representation. *Journal of Child Language,* 11, 627-643.

Merzenich, M. M., Jenkins, W. M., Johnston, P., Schreiner, C., Miller, S. L., & Tallal, P. (1996). Temporal processing deficits of language-learning impaired children ameliorated by training. *Science*, 271, 77-80.

Merzenich, M. M., Schreiner, C., Jenkins, W., & Wang, X. (1993). Neural mechanisms underlying temporal integration segmentation and input sequence representations: Some implications for the origin of learning disabilities. *Annals of The New York Academy of Sciences,* Vol. 686.

Mody M., Studdert-Kennedy, M., & Brady, S. (1997). Speech perception deficits in poor readers: Auditory processing or phonological coding? *Journal of Experimental Child Psychology,* 64, 199-231.

Moore, D. R. (1993). Plasticity of binaural hearing and some possible mechanisms following late-onset deprivation. *Journal of the American Academy of Audiology,* 4(5), 227-283.

Morais, J. (1991). Constraints on the development of phonemic awareness. In D. Shankweiler & S.A. Brady (Eds.), *Phonological processes in literacy,* 5-27. Hillsdale, NJ: Erlbaum Associates.

Nicholson, T. (1997). Closing the gap on reading failure: Social background, phonemic awareness, and learning to read. In B. Blachman (Ed.), *Foundation of reading acquisition and dyslexia: Implications for early intervention* (305-325). Hillsdale, NJ: Erlbaum Associates.

Perfetti, C. A., & Roth, S. (1981). Some of the interactive processes in reading and their role in reading skill. In A. M. Lesgold, & C. A. Prfetti (Eds.), *Interactive Processes in Reading* (269-297). Hillsdale, NJ: Erlbaum Associates.

Snowling, M. (1983). The comparison of acquired and developmental disorders of reading: A discussion. *Cognition*, 14, 105-118.

Stanovich, K. (1980). Toward an interactive-compensatory model of individual differences in the development of reading fluency. *Reading Research Quarterly,* 16, 32-71.

Stanovich, K. (1990). Concepts in developmental theories of reading skill: Cognitive resources, automaticity, and modularity. *Developmental Review,* 10, 72-100.

Stanovich, K. E. (1986). Effects in reading: Some consequences of individual differences in the acquisition of literacy. *Reading Research Quarterly,* 21,360-407.

Stanovich, K. E., Cunningham, A. E., & Cramer, B. B. (1984). Assessing phonological awareness in kindergarten children: Issues of task comparability. *Journal of Experimental Child Psychology,* 38, 1-90.

Stark, R., & Tallal, P. (1988). *Language, speech, and reading disorders in children: Neuropsychological studies*. Boston: College Hill Press.

Stone, B., & Brady, S. (1995). Evidence for phonological processing deficits in less-skilled readers. *Annals of Dyslexia,* 45 , 51-78.

Traub, N., & Bloom, F. (1975). *Recipe For Reading*. Cambridge: Educators Publishing Services.

Van Kleek, A. (1990). Emergence literacy: Learning about print before learning to read. *Topics in Language Disorders*, 10, 25-45.

Wagner, R. K. & Torgesen, J. K. (1987). The nature of phonological processing and its causal role in the acquisition of reading skill. *Psychological Bulletin,* 101, 192-212.

Williams, J.P. (1987). Educational treatments for dyslexia at the elementary and secondary levels. In R.F. Bowler (Ed.), *Intimacy with language: a forgotten basic in teacher education.* Baltimore: Orton Dyslexia Society.

Bibliography: Dyscalculia

Ackerman,P.T., & Dykman, R.A. (1995) Reading disabled students with and without comorbid arithmetic disability. *Developmental Neuropsychology,* 11, 351- 371.

Adler, B. (2001) *What is Dyscalculia?*, www.dyscalculiainfo.org

Attwood, Tony. *Dyscalculia in Schools: What It Is and What You Can Do.* First and Best in Education Ltd. ISBN 1-86083-614-3, www.firstandbest.co.uk

Branch, W. B., Cohen, M. J., & Hynd, G. W. (1995). Academic achievement and attention deficit/hyperactivity disorder in children with left or right hemisphere dysfunction. *Journal of Learning Disabilities,* 28, 35- 43.

Bryant, D. P. (2005). Commentary on early identification and intervention for students with mathematics difficulties. *Journal of Learning Disabilities,* 38, 340-345.

Bryant, D. P., Bryant, B. R., & Hammill, D.D. (1990). Characteristic behaviors of students with LD who have teacher-identified math weaknesses. *Journal of Learning Disabilities,* 33, 168-177.

Bull, R., & Johnston, R. S. (1997). Children's Arithmetical Difficulties: Contributions from Processing Speed, Item Identification, and Short Term Memory. *Journal of Experimental Psychology,* 65, 1- 24.

D'Angiulli, A., Siegel, L.S. (2003). Cognitive functioning as measured by the WISC R: Do children with learning disabilities have distinctive patterns of performance? *Journal of Learning Disabilities,* 36, 1, 48- 58.

Davis, H., Bryson, S. & Hoy, C. (1992). Case study of language and numerical disability: A sequential processing deficit? *Annals of Dyslexia,* 42, 69- 89.

Ericsson, K. A. & Kintsch, W. (1995). Long-term working memory. *Psychological Review,* 102, 211-245.

Geary, D. C. (2000). Mathematical disorders: An overview for educators. *Perspectives*, 26, 6-9.

Geary, D.C. & Brown, S.C. (1991) Cognitive addition strategy choice and speed of processing differences in gifted, normal, and mathematically disabled children. *Developmental psychology,* 27, 398- 406.

Geary, D. C. (2004). Mathematics and learning disabilities. *Journal of Learning Disabilities,* 37, 4-15.

Geary, D. C. (1999). *Mathematical Disabilities: What We Know and Don't Know.* LD Online. http://www.ldonline.org/ld_indepth/math_skills/geary_math_dis.html

Gersten, R., Jordan, N., & Flojo, J. R. (2005). Early identification and interventions for students with mathematics difficulties. *Journal of Learning Disabilities,* 38, 293-304.

Gray, E. M. & Tall, D. O. (1994). Duality, ambiguity and flexibility: A "Proceptual" view of simple arithmetic. *Journal for Research in Mathematics Education,* 25(2), 116- 140.

Gordon, N. (1992). Children with developmental dyscalculia. *Developmental Medicine and Child Neurology,* 34(5), 459- 463.

Hallahan, D. P., Lloyd, J. W. Kauffman, J. M., Weiss, M. & Martinez, E. A. (2005). *Learning disabilities: Foundations, characteristics, and effective teaching.* Boston: Allyn and Bacon.

Hittmair D. M., Sailer, U. & Benke, T. (1995). Impaired arithmetic facts but intact conceptual knowledge: A single case study of dyscalculia. *Cortex*, 31(1), 139- 147.

Hughes, S., Kolstad, R. K. & Briggs, L. D. (1994). Dyscalculia and mathematics achievement *Journal of Instructional Psychology*, 21, 64-7.

Jordan, D. R. (1996). *Overcoming dyslexia in children, adolescents and adults: 2nd ed.* Austin, TX : Pro Ed, Inc.

Jordan, N., Hanich, L., & Kaplan, D. (2003). A longitudinal study of mathematical competencies in children with specific mathematics difficulties versus children with comorbid mathematics and reading difficulties. *Child Development,* 74(3), 834-850.

Kaufmann, L. (2002). More evidence for the role of the central executive in retrieving arithmetic facts: A case study of severe developmental dyscalculia. *Journal of Clinical and Experimental Neuropsychology*, 24(3), 302- 310.

Levin, H.S.; Goldstein, F.C.; Spiers, P.A.: "Acalculia," Heilmann, K.M.; Valenstein, E. (1993). *Clinical neurophysiology,* Oxford University Press, 91-122

Lindsay, R.L., Tomazic, T., Levine, M.D. & Accardo, P.J. (2001). Attentional function as measured by a continuous performance task in children with dyscalculia. *Journal of Developmental and Behavioral Pediatrics,* 22(5), 287- 292.

Mazzocco, M. (2005). Challenges in identifying target skills for math disability screening and intervention. *Journal of Learning Disabilities,* 38(4), 318-323.

McCloskey, M. (1992). Cognitive mechanisms in numerical processing: Evidence from acquired dyscalculia. *Cognition*, 44, 107- 157.

McCloskey, M., Aliminosa, D., Macaruso, P. (1991). Theory based assessment of acquired dyscalculia. *Brain and Cognition*, 17(2), 285- 308.

Montague, M., Applegate, B., & Marquard, K. (1993). Cognitive strategy instruction and mathematical problem-solving performance of students with learning disabilities. *Learning Disabilities Research and Practice,* 29, 251-261.

Ostad, S.A. (1999). Developmental progression of subtraction strategies: A comparison of mathematically disabled and mathematically normal children. *Mathematical Cognition,* 4, 1- 20.

Rivera, D. P. (1997). Mathematics education and students with learning disabilities: Introduction to the special series. *Journal of Learning Disabilities,* 30, 2-19, 68.

Robinson, C., Menchetti, B., and Torgesen, J. (2002). Toward a two-factor theory of one type of mathematics disabilities. *Learning Disabilities Research and Practice,* 17(2), 81-89.

Rourke, B. P. (1993). Arithmetic disabilities, specific and otherwise: A neuropsychological perspective. *Journal of Learning Disabilities,* 26, 214- 226.

Shalev, R.S., Manor, O. , Kerem, B. & Ayali, M. (2001). Developmental dyscalculia is a familial learning disability. *Journal of Learning Disabilities,* 34, 1, 59- 72.

Sharma, M. (1990). *NCTM math notes.* Reston, VA: National Council of Teachers of Mathematics.

Silver, C.H., Pennett, D. L., Black, J. L., Fair, G. W. & Balise, R. R. (1999). Stability of arithmetic disability subtypes. *Journal of Learning Disabilities,* 32(2), 108 - 119.

Whalen, J., McCloskey, M., Lindemann, M. & Bouton, G. (2002). Representing arithmetic table facts in memory: Evidence from acquired impairments. *Cognitive neuropsychology,* 19(6), 505.

Bibliography: Behavior

Adelman, H. S., and Taylor, L. (1998). Reframing mental health in schools and expanding school reform. *Educational Psychologist,* 33, 135-152.

Albin, R. W., Horner, R. H., Koegel, R. L., and Dunlap, G. (1987). *Extending competent performance: Applied research on generalization and maintenance in learners with developmental disabilities.* Eugene, Oregon: University of Oregon.

Algozzine, R., Horner, R., Sugai G., and Irvin, L., (in progress). *Developing a system of effectiveness indicators: Identifying, evaluating, and reporting outcomes of school-wide positive behavior support programs.*

Anderson, C. M., and Spaulding, S. A. (2007). Using positive behavior support to design effective classrooms. *Beyond Behavior,* 16(2), 27-31.

Bear, G. G. (1990). Best practices in school discipline. In A. Thomas and J. Grimes (Eds.), *Best practices in school psychology-II.* (pp. 649-663). Washington, DC: National Association of School Psychologists.

Beard, K. Y., and Sugai, G. (2004). First step to success: An early intervention for elementary children at risk for antisocial behavior. *Behavioral Disorders,* 29, 396-409.

Benazzi, L., Horner, R.H., and Good, R.H. (2006). Effects of behavior support team composition on the technical adequacy and contextual fit of behavior support plans. *Journal of Special Education,* 40(3), 160-170.

Bohanon, H., Fenning, P., Carney, K., Minnis, M., Anderson-Harriss, S., Moroz, K., Hicks, K., Kasper, B., Culos, C., Sailor, W., and Piggott, T. (2006). School-wide application of positive behavior support in an urban high school: A case study. *Journal of Positive Behavior Interventions,* 8(3), 131-145.

Brooks, A., Todd, A. W., Tofflemoyer, S., and Horner, R. H. (2003). Use of functional assessment and a self-management system to increase academic engagement and work completion. *Journal of Positive Behavior Intervention,* 5, 144-152.

Carnine, D. (1997). Bridging the research-to-practice gap. *Exceptional Children,* 63, 513-521.

Colvin, G., and Lazar, M. (1997). *The effective elementary classroom: Managing for success.* Longmont, CO: Sopris West.

Colvin, G., Kameenui, E. J., and Sugai, G. (1993). School-wide and classroom management: Reconceptualizing the integration and management of students with behavior problems in general education. *Education and Treatment of Children,* 16, 361-381.

Colvin, G., Sugai, G., and Kam'eenui, E. (1994). *Curriculum for establishing a proactive school-wide discipline plan: Project PREPARE.* Eugene, OR: Behavioral Research and Teaching, College of Education, University of Oregon.

Crone, D. A., and Horner, R. H. (2003). *Building positive behavior support systems in schools: Functional behavioral assessment.* New York: Guildford Press.

Crone, D. A., Horner, R. H., and Hawken, L. S. (2004). *Responding to problem behavior in schools: The behavior education program.* New York: Guilford Press.

Darch, C. B., and Kameenui, E. J. (2003). *Instructional classroom management: A proactive approach to behavior management. (2nd ed.).* White Plains, NY: Longman.

Doolittle, J.H., Horner, R.H., Bradley, R., Sugai, G., and Vincent, C.G. (2007). Importance of student social behavior in the mission statements, personnel preparation standards, and innovation efforts of state departments of education. *Journal of Special Education,* 40(4), 239-245.

Epstein, M. H., Kutash, K., and Duchnowski, A. (Eds.) (1998). *Outcomes for children and youth with emotional and behavioral disorders and their families: Programs and evaluation best practices.* Austin, TX: Pro-Ed.

Ervin, R.A., Kern, L., Clarke, S., DuPaul, G.J., Dunlap, G., and Friman, P.C. (2000). Evaluating assessment-based intervention strategies for students with ADHD and comorbid disorders within the natural classroom context. *Behavioral Disorders,* 25, 344-358.

Fox, L., Dunlap, G., and Powell, D. (2002). Young children and challenging behavior: Issues and considerations for behavior support. *Journal of Positive Behavior Interventions,* 4, 208-217.

Freeman, R. L., Smith, C., Britten, J., McCart, A. and Sailor, W. (Eds.) (2000). *Development and implementation of PBS plans [Online].* Lawrence, KS: Kansas University Affiliated Program, Center for Research on Learning. Available: Onlineacademy.org.

Gee, K., Graham, N., Sailor, W., and Goetz, L. (1995). Use of integrated, general education, and community settings as primary contexts for skill instruction of students with severe, multiple disabilities. *Behavior Modification*, 19(1), 33-58.

Handler, M., Rey, J., Connell, J., Their, T., Feinberg, A. and Putnam R. (2006). Practical considerations in creating school-wide positive behavior support in public schools. *Psychology in the Schools*, 44(1), 29-39.

Hieneman, M., Dunlap, G., and Kincaid, D. (2005). Positive support strategies for students with behavioral disorders in general education settings. *Psychology in the Schools,* 42, 779-794.

Kern, L., Childs, K. E., Dunlap, G., Clarke, S., and Falk, G. D. (1994). Using assessment-based curricular intervention to improve the classroom behavior of a student with emotional and behavioral challenges. *Journal of Applied Behavior Analysis,* 27, 7-19.

Lewis, T. J, Sugai, G., and Colvin, G. (1998). Reducing problem behavior through a school-side system of effective behavioral support: Investigation of a school-wide social skills training program and contextual interventions. School Psychology Review, 27, 446-459.

Martella, R. C., Nelson, J. R., and Marchand-Martella, N. E. (2003). *Managing disruptive behaviors in the schools: A schoolwide, classroom, and individualized social learning approach*. Boston, MA: Allyn and Bacon.

Powell, D., Fixsen, D., Dunlap, G., Smith, B., and Fox, L. (2007). A synthesis of knowledge relevant to pathways of service delivery for young children with or at risk of challenging behavior. *Journal of Early Intervention*, 29(2), 81-103.

Scott, T. M., and Caron, D. B. (2005). Conceptualizing functional behavior assessment as prevention practice within positive behavior support systems. *Preventing School Failure,* 50(1), 13.

Scott, T. M., McIntyre, J., Liaupsin, C., Nelson, C. M., Conroy, M., and Payne, L. (2005). An examination of the relation between functional behavior assessment and selected intervention strategies with school-based teams. *Journal of Positive Behavior Interventions,* 7(4), 205-215.

Warren, J. S., Edmonson, H.M., Griggs, P., Lassen, S., McCart, A., Turnbull, A., and Sailor, W. (2003). Urban applications of school-wide positive behavior support: Critical issues and lessons learned. *Journal of Positive Behavior Interventions,* 5(2), 80-91.

APPENDIX C

PUBLISHERS/WEB SITES

Publisher/Producer	Website Address	Publisher/Producer	Website Address
Academic Therapy	www.AcademicTherapy.com	Curriculum Associates	www.curriculumassociates.com
Achieve Publications	www.achievepublications.com	Dominie	www.dominie.com
Addison Wesley	www.pearsonhighered.com	Don Johnson	www.donjohnson.com
Adventure Learning	www.adventurelearningcenter.com	ECL	www.ecls.sourceforge.net
Anatex	www.anatex.com	Educational Insights	www.edin.com
Ann Arbor	www.annarbor.co.uk	Educational Publishers Svc.	www.epsbooks.com
Be Dazzle Inc.	www.b-dazzle.com	Edushape	www.edushape.com
Benchmark	www.benchmarkeducation.com	Exceptional Teaching Inc.	www.exceptionalteaching.net
Beyond Play	www.beyondplay.com	Failure Free Reading	www.failurefree.com
Brain Train	www.braintrain.com	Find It Games	www.finditgames.com
Briar Patch	www.briarpatch.com	First Steps	www.myread.org
Brighter Child Interactive	www.brightermindsmedia.com	Frank Schaffer Publications	www.frankschaffer.com
Cambria Learning	www.cambrialearningtechnologies.com	Gail Kushnir	www.gkushnir.com
Cambridge Development Lab.	www.edumatch.com	Game Development Group	www.parents-choice.org
		Gamewright	www.gamewright.com
Ceaco	www.ceaco.com	Gander	www.cdli.ca
Charlesbridge	www.charlesbridge.com	Get Ahead Learning	www.getaheadlearning.com
CLD	www.cldinternational.org	Glencoe	www.glencoe.com
Cognitive Concepts	www.earobics.com	Great Source	www.greatsource.com
Compass Learning	www.compasslearning.com	Hape International	www.hape-international.com
Continental Press	www.continentalpress.com	Harcourt Achieve	www.harcourtachieve.com
Creative Publications	www.wrightgroup.com	Harcourt Brace	www.harcourt.com
Critical Thinking Co.	www.CriticalThinking.com	Harcourt School Pubs.	www.harcourtschool.com

Publisher/Producer	Website Address
Hasbro	www.hasbro.com
HEC Software	www.readinghorizons.com
Highlights for Children	www.highlights.com
Houghton Mifflin	www.hmco.com
Imagability	www.wedgits.com
Innovative Learning Concepts	www.touchmath.com
Inspired Teaching	www.inspiredteaching.org
Kay Pictures	www.kpictures.co.uk
KLIK Enterprises	www.klikbooks.com
Klutz	www.klutz.com
Kumon	www.kumon.com
Landmark Foundations	www.landmarkeducation.com
Laura Sena	www.asha.org
Laureate	www.laureatelearning.com
Learning Resources	www.learningresources.com
LEGO	www.LEGO.com
Leisure Learning Products	www.mightymind.com
Lexia Learning	www.lexialearning.com
Lingui Ssytems	www.linguisystems.com
Locutour Multimedia	www.learningfundamentals.com
MacMillan/McGraw Hill	www.macmillanmh.com
Media Materials	www.m-mc.org

Publisher/Producer	Website Address
Mindplay	www.mindplay.com
Mindware	www.mindwareonline.com
National Professional Resources, Inc.	www.nprinc.com
Options Publications	www.optionsmadison.com
Pacific Learning	www.pacificlearning.com
Paul Brooks Publishing	www.brookespublishing.com
PCI	www.pcieducation.com
Pearson	www.pearson.com
Peoples Education	www.peopleseducation.com
Phonics Q	www.phonicsq.com
Plato	www.phx.corporate-ir.net
Playmore	www.playmorebooks.com
Playroom Entertainment	www.playrooment.com
Princeton Review	www.princetonreview.com
ProLexia	www.prolexia.com
Ravenburger	www.americanpuzzles.com
Read AmericaWright/ McGrawHill	www.mde.k12.ms.us
Read Naturally	www.readnaturally.com
Reading Recovery	www.readingrecovery.org
Remedia	www.rempub.com
REX Games	www.rexgames.com

Publisher/Producer	Website Address
Rigby	www.rigby.com
Riverdeep	www.riverdeep.net
Sammons Preston	www.sammonspreston.com
Scholastic	www.scholastic.com
School Specialty	www.schoolspecialty.com
Schoolhouse	www.schoolhousetech.com
Scientific Learning Corp.	www.scilearn.com
Scott Foresman	www.sfreading.com
SET Enterprises	www.setgame.com
Smethport	www.smethporttoy.com
Sopris West	www.sopriswest.com
SRA	www.sraonline.com
Steck-Vaughn	www.steck-vaughn.com
Success for All	www.successforall.net
Sunburst	www.sunburst.com
SWEPS Educational	www.sweps.co.uk
TAG Toys	www.tagtoys.com
Teacher Creative Materials	www.teachercreativematerials.com
Teacher Support Inc.	www.teacherssupportnetwork.com
ThinkFun	www.thinkfun.com
Voyager	www.voyagerlearning.com
Voyager Learning	www.voyagerlearning.com
Wilson Learning	www.wilsonlearning.com
World Class Learning Materials	www.wclm.com
Wright Group	www.wrightgroup.com
Your Therapy Source Inc.	www.yourtherapysource.com
Yriondo Educational	www.myokapi.com
Zaner-Bloser	www.zaner-bloser.com

APPENDIX D

ASSESSMENT/PROGRESS MONITORING PRODUCTS

Progress Monitoring	Areas of Academics	Publisher	Web Site
Accelerated Math	Math	Renaissance Learning	Renlearn.com
Accelerated Reading	Reading	Renaissance Learning	Renlearn.com
AIM Sweb	Early Literacy	Pearson	Aimsweb.com
	Early Numeracy		
	Math		
	Maze		
	Reading		
	Spelling		
	Written Expression		
DIBELS	Initial Sound Fluency	Sopris West	dibels.uoregon.edu
	Nonsense Word Fluency		
	Oral Reading Fluency		
	Phonic Sound Fluency		
	Retell Fluency		
	Word Use Fluency		
Ed Checkup	Maze	EdCheckup	Edcheckup.com
	Reading		
iSTEEP	Reading Fluency	STEEP	iSTEEP.com
MBSP	Basic Skills	ProEd	Proedinc.com
	Math		
	Reading		

Progress Monitoring	Areas of Academics	Publisher	Web Site
PASeries	Math	Pearson	Edpearsonassessments.com
	Reading		
STAR	Early Literacy	California state	http://star.cde.ca.gov/
	Math		
	Reading		
TOWRE	Phonemic Decoding	Pearson	Edpearsonassessments.com
	Sight Word Efficiency		
Vital Indicators of Progress	Initial Sound Fluency	Voyager Expanded Learning	
	LNF		
	NWF		
	PS		
Yearly Progress Pro	Math	Yearly Progress Pro	Yearlyprogresspro.com
	Reading		

Appendix E

Resources:

Print and Video Materials

Available from National Professional Resources, Inc.

1-800 453-7461 • www.NPRinc.com

Aldrich, Seth. (2009). *RTI for English Language Learners: Understanding, Differentiation and Support.* Port Chester, NY: Dude Publishing.

Allington, Richard L. & Sean A. Walmsley. (2007) *No Quick Fix.* New York, NY: Teachers College Press.

Allington, Richard L. & Patricia M. Cunningham. (1996). *Schools That Work: Where all Children Read and Write.* New York, NY: Harper Collins.

Allington, Richard L. (2009). *What Really Matters in Response to Intervention: Researched-Based Designs*. Atlanta, GA: Prentice Hall.

Andrini, Beth. (1993). *Cooperative Learning & Mathematics.* Grade K-8. San Clemente, CA: Kagan Publishing.

Appelbaum, Maryln. (2008). *The One-Stop Guide to Implementing RTI(K-12).* Thousand Oaks, CA: Corwin Press.

ASCD. (2006). *Teaching Students with Learning Disabilities in the Regular Classroom* (Video). Baltimore, MD: ASDC.

Beecher, Margaret. (1995). *Developing the Gifts & Talents of All Students in the Regular Classroom.* Mansfield Center, CT: Creative Learning Press, Inc.

Bender, William. (2002). *Differentiating Instruction for Students with Learning Disabilities.* Thousand Oaks, CA: Corwin Press.

Bender, William. (2005). *Differentiating Math Instruction: Strategies That Work for K-8 Classrooms!* Thousand Oaks, CA: Corwin Press.

Bender, William & Martha Larkin. (2008). *Reading Strategies for Elementary Students with Learning Difficulties, 2nd ed.* Thousand Oaks, CA: Corwin Press.

Bender, William. (2007). *Response to Intervention: A Practical Guide for Every Teacher.* Thousand Oaks, CA: Corwin Press.

Bray, Marty & Abbie Brown, et al. (2004). *Technology and the Diverse Learner.* Thousand Oaks, CA: Corwin Press.

Brown-Chidsey, Rachel & Mark W. Steege. (2005). *Response to Intervention.* New York, NY: Guilford Press.

Buffum, Austin, Mike Mattos & Chris Weber. (2009). *Pyramid Response to Intervention.* Bloomington, IN: Solution Tree.

Casbarro, Joseph. (2008). *RTI Classroom Reference Guide.* Port Chester, NY: Dude Publishing.

Casbarro, Joseph. (2005). *Test Anxiety & What You Can Do About It: A Practical Guide for Teachers, Parents, & Kids.* Port Chester, NY: Dude Publishing.

Chapman, Carolyn & Rita King. (2003). *Differentiated Instructional Strategies for Reading in the Content Areas.* Thousand Oaks, CA: Corwin Press.

Coggins, Debra, et al. (1999). *A Mathematics Source Book for Elementary and Middle School Teachers: Key Concepts, Teaching Tips, and Learning Pitfalls.* Novato, CA: Arena Press.

Council for Exceptional Children and Merrill Education. (2005). *Universal Design for Learning.* Atlanta, GA.

Crone, Deanne A. & Robert H. Horner. (2003). *Building Positive Behavior Support Systems in Schools: Functional Behavioral Assessment.* New York, NY: Guilford Press.

Dieker, Lisa. (2006). *Co-Teaching Lesson Plan Book* (Third Edition). Whitefish Bay, WI: Knowledge By Design Inc.

Dodge, Judith. (2005). *Differentiation in Action*. Jefferson City, MO: Scholastic Inc.

Elias, Maurice, Brian Friedlander & Steven Tobias. (2001). *Engaging the Resistant Child Through Computers: A Manual to Facilitate Social & Emotional Learning*. Port Chester, NY: Dude Publishing.

Elias, Maurice & Harriett Arnold. (2006). *The Educator's Guide to Emotional Intelligence and Academic Achievement.* Thousand Oaks, CA: Corwin Press.

Flockhart, Dan. (2007). *Fantasy Football and Mathematics/Fantasy Basketball and Mathematics/Fantasy Soccer and Mathematics/Fantasy Baseball and Mathematics.* Thousand Oaks, CA: Corwin Press.

Friedlander, Brian S. (2005). *Assistive Technology: A Way to Differentiate Instruction for Students with Disabilities.* (Video) Port Chester, NY: National Professional Resources, Inc.

Fuchs, D., Mock, D., Morgan, P., & Young, C. (2003). *Responsiveness-to-intervention: Definitions, evidence, and implications for learning disabilities construct.* Learning Disabilities: Research and Practice, 18(3), 157-171.

Fuchs, L. (2003). *Assessing intervention responsiveness: conceptual and technical issues.* Learning Disabilities: Research and Practice, 18(3), 172-186.

Fuchs, L.S., & Fuchs, D. (2006). *A framework for building capacity for responsiveness to intervention.* School Psychology Review, 35, 621-626.

Gardner, Howard. (1996). *How Are Kids Smart?* (Video) Port Chester, NY: National Professional Resources, Inc.

Goleman, Daniel. (1996). *Emotional Intelligence: A New Vision for Educators* (Video). Port Chester, NY: National Professional Resources, Inc.

Good, R.H. & Kaminski, R.A. (2001). *Dynamic indicators of basic early literacy skills* (6th ed.). Eugene, OR: Institute for the Development of Educational Achievement.

Gregory, Gale & Carolyn Chapman. (2002). *Differentiated Instructional Strategies: One Size Doesn't Fit All.* Thousand Oaks, CA: Corwin Press.

Gusman, Jo. (2004). *Differentiated Instruction & the English Language Learner: Best Practices to Use With Your Students (K-12)* (Video). Port Chester, NY: National Professional Resources, Inc.

Haager, Diane, Janette Klingner & Sharon Vaughn. (2007). *Evidence-Based Reading Practices for Response to Intervention.* Baltimore, Maryland: Paul H. Brookes Publishing Co.

Hall, Susan L. (2008). *Implementing Response to Intervention: A Principal's Guide.* Thousand Oaks, CA: Corwin Press.

Hanson, Helene. (2009) *RTI & DI: Optimizing Teaching & Learning.* Port Chester, NY. Dude Publishing.

Heacox, Diane. (2002). *Differentiated Instruction: How to Reach and Teach All Learners (Grades 3-12)*. Minneapolis, MN: Free Spirit Press.

Heintzman, Lynn & Helene Hanson. (2009). *RTI & DI: The Dynamic Duo* (Video). Port Chester, NY. National Professional Resources, Inc.

Hoover, John J. (2009). *RTI Assessment Essentials for Struggling Learners.* Thousand Oaks, CA: Corwin Press.

Hosp, Michelle K., John L. Hosp & Kenneth W. Howell. (2007). *The ABCs of CBM: A Practical Guide to Curriculum-Based Measurement.* New York, NY: The Guilford Press.

Howell, Robert, Sandra Patton & Margaret Deiotte. (2008). *Understanding Response to Intervention.* Bloomington, IN: Solution Tree.

Jensen, Eric. (2000). *Successful Applications of Brain-Based Learning* (Video). Port Chester, NY: National Professional Resources, Inc.

Jennings, Matthew. (2008). *Before the Special Education Referral.* Thousand Oaks, CA: Corwin Press.

Kagan, Spencer & Laurie Kagan. (1999). *Reaching Standards Through Cooperative Learning: Providing for ALL Learners in General Education Classrooms (Tape 2: Mathematics)*. Port Chester, NY: National Professional Resources, Inc.

Kagan, Spencer & Miguel Kagan. (1998). *Multiple Intelligences: The Complete MI Book.* San Clemente, CA: Kagan Publishing.

Kame'enui, Edward J. & Deborah C. Simmons. (1999). *Adapting Curricular Materials, Volume 1: An Overview of Materials Adaptations—Toward Successful Inclusion of Students with Disabilities: The Architecture of Instruction*. Reston, VA: Council for Exceptional Children.

Kemp, Karen. (2007). *RTI Tackles Reading* (Video). Port Chester, NY: National Professional Resources, Inc.

Kemp, Karen. (2007). *RTI: The Classroom Connection for Literacy.* Port Chester, NY: Dude Publishing.

Kemp, Karen. (2009). *RTI & Math: The Classroom Connection.* Port Chester, NY: Dude Publishing.

Kennedy, Eugene. (2003). *Raising Test Scores for All Students: An Administrator's Guide to Improving Standardized Test Performance.* Thousand Oaks, CA: Corwin Press.

Lasater, Mary. (2009). *RTI and the Paraeducator's Roles: Effective Teaming.* Port Chester, NY: Dude Publishing.

Little, Mary E. (2008). *Response To Intervention for Teachers Classroom Instructional Problem-Solving.* Denver, CO: Love Publishing Company

MacDonald, Sharon. (2007). *Math in Minutes: Easy Activities for Children 4 –8.* Beltsville, MD: Gryphon House Inc.

Matricardi, Joanne & Jeanne McLarty. (2005). *Math Activities A to Z.* Clifton Park, NY: Delmar Cengage Learning.

McCarney, Stephen B. (1993). *The Pre-Referral Intervention Manual.* Columbia, MO: Hawthorne Educational Services.

Mellard, Daryl E. & Evelyn Johnson. (2008). *RTI: A Practitioner's Guide to Implementing Response to Intervention.* Thousand Oaks, CA: Corwin Press.

Minton, Leslie (2007). *What if Your ABCs Were Your 123s? Building Connections Between Literacy and Numeracy.* Thousand Oaks, CA: Corwin Press.

Moll, Anne M. (2003). *Differentiated Instruction Guide for Inclusive Teaching.* Port Chester, NY: Dude Publishing.

Munk, Dennis D. (2003). *Solving the Grading Puzzle for Students with Disabilities.* Whitefish Bay, WI: Knowledge by Design, Inc.

Muschla, Judith A. & Gary Robert Muschla. (2008). *The Math Teacher's Problem-a-Day: Over 180 Reproducible Pages of Quick Skill Builders, Grades 4-8.* San Francisco, CA: Jossey-Bass.

National Association of State Directors of Special Education (NASDSE). (2005). *Response to Intervention: Policy, Considerations, and Implementation.* Alexandria, VA: NASDSE.

Norlander, Karen. (2006). *RTI Tackles the LD Explosion: A Good IDEA Becomes Law* (Video). Port Chester, NY: National Professional Resources, Inc.

Overholt, James L., James Lindsey & Nancy H. Aaberg. (2008) *Math Stories for Problem Solving Success Ready-to-Use Activities Based on Real-Life Situations.* San Francisco, CA: Jossey-Bass.

Purcell, Sherry & Debbie Grant. (2004). *Using Assistive Technology to Meet Literacy Standards.* Verona, WI: IEP Resources.

Rief, Sandra F. (1998). *The ADD/ADHD Checklist.* Paramus, NJ: Prentice Hall.

Rief, Sandra F. (2004). *ADHD & LD: Powerful Teaching Strategies & Accommodations* (Video). Port Chester, NY: National Professional Resources, Inc.

Ronis, Diane. (2007). *Brain-Compatible Mathematics.* Thousand Oaks, CA: Corwin Press.

Rose, D. & A. Meyer (Editors). (2002). T*eaching Every Student in the Digital Age.* Alexandria, VA: ASCD.

Rose, D. & A. Meyer (Editors). (2005). *The Universally Designed Classroom: Accessible Curriculum and Digital Technologies.* Cambridge, MA: Harvard University Press.

Salovey, Peter. (1998). *Optimizing Intelligences: Thinking, Emotion, and Creativity* (Video). Port Chester, NY: National Professional Resources, Inc.

Shinn, M. (1989). *Curriculum-Based Measurement: Assessing Special Children.* New York: Guilford Press.

Shores, Cara & Kim Chester. (2009). *Using RTI for School Improvement.* Thousand Oaks, CA: Corwin Press.

Shumm, Jeanne Shay. (1999). *Adapting Curricular Materials, Volume 2: Kindergarten Through Grade Five—Adapting Reading & Math Materials for the Inclusive Classroom*. Reston, VA: Council for Exceptional Children.

Solomon, Pearl Gold. (2006). *The Math We Need to Know and Do in Grade PreK-5: Concepts, Skills, Standards, and Assessments.* Thousand Oaks, CA: Corwin Press.

Sousa, David A. (2008). *Brain-Compatible Activities (Grade K-2) (Grades 3-5).* Thousand Oaks, CA: Corwin Press.

Stone, Randi. (2007). *Best Practices for Teaching Mathematics: What Award-Winning Classroom Teachers Do.* Thousand Oaks, CA: Corwin Press.

Tate, Marcia L. (2008). *Graphic Organizers and Other Visual Strategies (Grade 1) (Grade 2) (Grade 3) (Grade 4) (Grade 5).* Thousand Oaks, CA: Corwin Press.

Tate, Marcia L. (2008). *Math Worksheets Don't Grow Dendrites: 20 Numeracy Strategies That Engage the Brain, PreK-8.* Thousand Oaks, CA: Corwin Press.

Thompson, Sandra, Rachel Quenemeen, Martha Thurlow, & James Ysseldyke. (2001). *Alternate Assessments for Students with Disabilities.* Thousand Oaks, CA: Corwin Press.

Thurlow, Martha L., Judy L. Elliott & James E. Ysseldyke. (1998). *Testing Students with Disabilities: Practical Strategies for Complying With District and State Requirements.* Thousand Oaks, CA: Corwin Press.

Tilton, Linda. (2003). *Teacher's Toolbox for Differentiating Instruction: 700 Strategies, Tips, Tools, & Techniques.* Shorewood, MN: Covington Cove Publications.

Tomlinson, Carol Ann. (2001). *How to Differentiate Instruction in Mixed-Ability Classrooms, 2nd Edition.* Alexandria, VA: ASCD.

Wall, Edward S. & Alfred S. Posamentier. (2007). *What Successful Math Teachers Do, Grades PreK-5.* Thousand Oaks, CA: Corwin Press.

Wormel, Rick. (2006). *Fair Isn't Always Equal.* Portland, ME: Stenhouse Publishers.

Wright, J. (2009). *The Power of RTI: Classroom Management Strategies K-6* (Video). Port Chester, NY: National Professional Resources, Inc.

Wright, J. (2009). *RTI & Classroom Behaviors.* Port Chester, NY: Dude Publishing.

Wright, J. (2007). *RTI Toolkit: A Practical Guide for Schools.* Port Chester, NY: Dude Publishing.

Wright, J. (2009). *Success with Secondary RTI: A Toolkit for Middle and High School.* Port Chester, NY: Dude Publishing.

About the Authors

Dr. Concetta (Connie) Russo is currently a full-time assistant professor at Seton Hall University, having previously held the position of Director of Special Education for the Massapequa Public Schools for 18 years. Her research, teaching and clinical practices are in the nature and treatment of reading disorders, specializing in the remediation of dyslexia and phonological processing and the implementation of the "Response to Intervention" process. Dr. Russo has had a private practice as a learning specialist for 29 years and currently consults with public and private schools in establishing "Response to Intervention" and "Alternative Reading Programs." Dr. Russo has presented her expertise at many conferences and seminars throughout the Northeast.

She has published *Recipe for Reading Workbooks* for Educational Publishing Services as well as her own Orton-Gillingham based reading program, *Bridging the Gap*. Her consulting firm is known as "Crossroads for Educational Services, Inc."

Dr. Ellenmorris Tiegerman is Founder/Executive Director of the School for Language and Communication Development (SLCD) which serves children with language and autism spectrum disorders in New York City and on Long Island. She has served as an academic faculty member of several universities and as a full professor at Adelphi University. She earned her Doctoral degree from the Graduate Center at City University in 1979, having also received Masters degrees in Speech Pathology, Philosophy, Special Education, and Social Work.

She has written/published extensively in the areas of autism, child language disorders, inclusion, collaboration and parent education including *Language Disorders in Children, Real Families, Real Issues and Real Interventions*, Merrill Prentice Hall, 2008; *Language and Communication Disorders in Children*, Allyn & Bacon, 2008; *Collaborative Decision Making, The Pathway to Inclusion*, Merrill Prentice Hall, 1998; *Language and Communication Intervention in Preschool Children*, Allyn & Bacon, 1995; *Baby Signals*, 1987, as well as articles which have appeared in the New York Times, Newsday and Empire State Report concerning the plight of children with disabilities in special education. Dr. Tiegerman has served on several State commissions including the New York State Commission on 21st Century Schools, the New York State Early Intervention Coordinating Council and Governor Pataki's Transition Team on Educational Policy.

Dr. Christine Radziewicz attended Gallaudet University and subsequently received her doctoral degree in speech/language pathology from Adelphi University where she became a professor and clinical director of the Hy Weinberg Center for Communication Disorders. Her more recent research has concentrated on the realities of inclusion for children with and without special needs, and the role of central auditory processing in language and learning development. Presently she is Director at the School for Language and Communication Development, where she has developed an inclusion program for special-needs pre-school-age students. In addition, Dr. Radziewicz oversees the educational programming for students at this school, focusing on a differentiated instructional approach to meet the individualized needs of students.

Dr. Radziewicz has co-authored two books with her friend and colleague Dr. Ellenmorris Tiegerman, *Collaborative Decision Making, The Pathway to Inclusion* (1998) Prentice-Hall, Inc., and *Language Disorders in Children Real Families, Real Issues, and Real Interventions* (2008) Pearson Education, Inc., and has also authored several chapters in *Language and Communication Intervention* (1994, 1995) Allyn and Bacon, and *Language and Communication Disorders in Children* (1993) Macmillan Publishing Co.